Claims Adjuster Exam

D1558061

SECRETS

Study Guide
Your Key to Exam Success

DEAR FUTURE EXAM SUCCESS STORY

First of all, **THANK YOU** for purchasing Mometrix study materials!

Second, congratulations! You are one of the few determined test-takers who are committed to doing whatever it takes to excel on your exam. **You have come to the right place.** We developed these study materials with one goal in mind: to deliver you the information you need in a format that's concise and easy to use.

In addition to optimizing your guide for the content of the test, we've outlined our recommended steps for breaking down the preparation process into small, attainable goals so you can make sure you stay on track.

We've also analyzed the entire test-taking process, identifying the most common pitfalls and showing how you can overcome them and be ready for any curveball the test throws you.

Standardized testing is one of the biggest obstacles on your road to success, which only increases the importance of doing well in the high-pressure, high-stakes environment of test day. Your results on this test could have a significant impact on your future, and this guide provides the information and practical advice to help you achieve your full potential on test day.

Your success is our success

We would love to hear from you! If you would like to share the story of your exam success or if you have any questions or comments in regard to our products, please contact us at **800-673-8175** or **support@mometrix.com**.

Thanks again for your business and we wish you continued success!

Sincerely,
The Mometrix Test Preparation Team

> **Need more help? Check out our flashcards at:**
> **http://MometrixFlashcards.com/ClaimsAdjuster**

TABLE OF CONTENTS

Introduction

Thank you for purchasing this resource! You have made the choice to prepare yourself for a test that could have a huge impact on your future, and this guide is designed to help you be fully ready for test day. Obviously, it's important to have a solid understanding of the test material, but you also need to be prepared for the unique environment and stressors of the test, so that you can perform to the best of your abilities.

For this purpose, the first section that appears in this guide is the **Secret Keys**. We've devoted countless hours to meticulously researching what works and what doesn't, and we've boiled down our findings to the five most impactful steps you can take to improve your performance on the test. We start at the beginning with study planning and move through the preparation process, all the way to the testing strategies that will help you get the most out of what you know when you're finally sitting in front of the test.

We recommend that you start preparing for your test as far in advance as possible. However, if you've bought this guide as a last-minute study resource and only have a few days before your test, we recommend that you skip over the first two Secret Keys since they address a long-term study plan.

If you struggle with **test anxiety**, we strongly encourage you to check out our recommendations for how you can overcome it. Test anxiety is a formidable foe, but it can be beaten, and we want to make sure you have the tools you need to defeat it.

1

Secret Key #1 – Plan Big, Study Small

There's a lot riding on your performance. If you want to ace this test, you're going to need to keep your skills sharp and the material fresh in your mind. You need a plan that lets you review everything you need to know while still fitting in your schedule. We'll break this strategy down into three categories.

Information Organization

Start with the information you already have: the official test outline. From this, you can make a complete list of all the concepts you need to cover before the test. Organize these concepts into groups that can be studied together, and create a list of any related vocabulary you need to learn so you can brush up on any difficult terms. You'll want to keep this vocabulary list handy once you actually start studying since you may need to add to it along the way.

Time Management

Once you have your set of study concepts, decide how to spread them out over the time you have left before the test. Break your study plan into small, clear goals so you have a manageable task for each day and know exactly what you're doing. Then just focus on one small step at a time. When you manage your time this way, you don't need to spend hours at a time studying. Studying a small block of content for a short period each day helps you retain information better and avoid stressing over how much you have left to do. You can relax knowing that you have a plan to cover everything in time. In order for this strategy to be effective though, you have to start studying early and stick to your schedule. Avoid the exhaustion and futility that comes from last-minute cramming!

Study Environment

The environment you study in has a big impact on your learning. Studying in a coffee shop, while probably more enjoyable, is not likely to be as fruitful as studying in a quiet room. It's important to keep distractions to a minimum. You're only planning to study for a short block of time, so make the most of it. Don't pause to check your phone or get up to find a snack. It's also important to **avoid multitasking**. Research has consistently shown that multitasking will make your studying dramatically less effective. Your study area should also be comfortable and well-lit so you don't have the distraction of straining your eyes or sitting on an uncomfortable chair.

The time of day you study is also important. You want to be rested and alert. Don't wait until just before bedtime. Study when you'll be most likely to comprehend and remember. Even better, if you know what time of day your test will be, set that time aside for study. That way your brain will be used to working on that subject at that specific time and you'll have a better chance of recalling information.

Finally, it can be helpful to team up with others who are studying for the same test. Your actual studying should be done in as isolated an environment as possible, but the work of organizing the information and setting up the study plan can be divided up. In between study sessions, you can discuss with your teammates the concepts that you're all studying and quiz each other on the details. Just be sure that your teammates are as serious about the test as you are. If you find that your study time is being replaced with social time, you might need to find a new team.

Secret Key #2 – Make Your Studying Count

You're devoting a lot of time and effort to preparing for this test, so you want to be absolutely certain it will pay off. This means doing more than just reading the content and hoping you can remember it on test day. It's important to make every minute of study count. There are two main areas you can focus on to make your studying count:

Retention

It doesn't matter how much time you study if you can't remember the material. You need to make sure you are retaining the concepts. To check your retention of the information you're learning, try recalling it at later times with minimal prompting. Try carrying around flashcards and glance at one or two from time to time or ask a friend who's also studying for the test to quiz you.

To enhance your retention, look for ways to put the information into practice so that you can apply it rather than simply recalling it. If you're using the information in practical ways, it will be much easier to remember. Similarly, it helps to solidify a concept in your mind if you're not only reading it to yourself but also explaining it to someone else. Ask a friend to let you teach them about a concept you're a little shaky on (or speak aloud to an imaginary audience if necessary). As you try to summarize, define, give examples, and answer your friend's questions, you'll understand the concepts better and they will stay with you longer. Finally, step back for a big picture view and ask yourself how each piece of information fits with the whole subject. When you link the different concepts together and see them working together as a whole, it's easier to remember the individual components.

Finally, practice showing your work on any multi-step problems, even if you're just studying. Writing out each step you take to solve a problem will help solidify the process in your mind, and you'll be more likely to remember it during the test.

Modality

Modality simply refers to the means or method by which you study. Choosing a study modality that fits your own individual learning style is crucial. No two people learn best in exactly the same way, so it's important to know your strengths and use them to your advantage.

For example, if you learn best by visualization, focus on visualizing a concept in your mind and draw an image or a diagram. Try color-coding your notes, illustrating them, or creating symbols that will trigger your mind to recall a learned concept. If you learn best by hearing or discussing information, find a study partner who learns the same way or read aloud to yourself. Think about how to put the information in your own words. Imagine that you are giving a lecture on the topic and record yourself so you can listen to it later.

For any learning style, flashcards can be helpful. Organize the information so you can take advantage of spare moments to review. Underline key words or phrases. Use different colors for different categories. Mnemonic devices (such as creating a short list in which every item starts with the same letter) can also help with retention. Find what works best for you and use it to store the information in your mind most effectively and easily.

3

Secret Key #3 – Practice the Right Way

Your success on test day depends not only on how many hours you put into preparing, but also on whether you prepared the right way. It's good to check along the way to see if your studying is paying off. One of the most effective ways to do this is by taking practice tests to evaluate your progress. Practice tests are useful because they show exactly where you need to improve. Every time you take a practice test, pay special attention to these three groups of questions:

- The questions you got wrong
- The questions you had to guess on, even if you guessed right
- The questions you found difficult or slow to work through

This will show you exactly what your weak areas are, and where you need to devote more study time. Ask yourself why each of these questions gave you trouble. Was it because you didn't understand the material? Was it because you didn't remember the vocabulary? Do you need more repetitions on this type of question to build speed and confidence? Dig into those questions and figure out how you can strengthen your weak areas as you go back to review the material.

Additionally, many practice tests have a section explaining the answer choices. It can be tempting to read the explanation and think that you now have a good understanding of the concept. However, an explanation likely only covers part of the question's broader context. Even if the explanation makes sense, **go back and investigate** every concept related to the question until you're positive you have a thorough understanding.

As you go along, keep in mind that the practice test is just that: practice. Memorizing these questions and answers will not be very helpful on the actual test because it is unlikely to have any of the same exact questions. If you only know the right answers to the sample questions, you won't be prepared for the real thing. **Study the concepts** until you understand them fully, and then you'll be able to answer any question that shows up on the test.

It's important to wait on the practice tests until you're ready. If you take a test on your first day of study, you may be overwhelmed by the amount of material covered and how much you need to learn. Work up to it gradually.

On test day, you'll need to be prepared for answering questions, managing your time, and using the test-taking strategies you've learned. It's a lot to balance, like a mental marathon that will have a big impact on your future. Like training for a marathon, you'll need to start slowly and work your way up. When test day arrives, you'll be ready.

Start with the strategies you've read in the first two Secret Keys—plan your course and study in the way that works best for you. If you have time, consider using multiple study resources to get different approaches to the same concepts. It can be helpful to see difficult concepts from more than one angle. Then find a good source for practice tests. Many times, the test website will suggest potential study resources or provide sample tests.

Practice Test Strategy

If you're able to find at least three practice tests, we recommend this strategy:

1. Take the first test with no time constraints and with your notes and study guide handy. Take your time and focus on applying the strategies you've learned.
2. Take the second practice test open-book as well, but set a timer and practice pacing yourself to finish in time.
3. Take any other practice tests as if it were test day. Set a timer and put away your study materials. Sit at a table or desk in a quiet room, imagine yourself at the testing center, and answer questions as quickly and accurately as possible.
4. Keep repeating step 3 on a regular basis until you run out of practice tests or it's time for the actual test. Your mind will be ready for the schedule and stress of test day, and you'll be able to focus on recalling the material you've learned.

Secret Key #4 – Pace Yourself

Once you're fully prepared for the material on the test, your biggest challenge on test day will be managing your time. Just knowing that the clock is ticking can make you panic even if you have plenty of time left. Work on pacing yourself so you can build confidence against the time constraints of the exam. Pacing is a difficult skill to master, especially in a high-pressure environment, so **practice is vital**.

Set time expectations for your pace based on how much time is available. For example, if a section has 60 questions and the time limit is 30 minutes, you know you have to average 30 seconds or less per question in order to answer them all. Although 30 seconds is the hard limit, set 25 seconds per question as your goal, so you reserve extra time to spend on harder questions. When you budget extra time for the harder questions, you no longer have any reason to stress when those questions take longer to answer.

Don't let this time expectation distract you from working through the test at a calm, steady pace, but keep it in mind so you don't spend too much time on any one question. Recognize that taking extra time on one question you don't understand may keep you from answering two that you do understand later in the test. If your time limit for a question is up and you're still not sure of the answer, mark it and move on, and come back to it later if the time and the test format allow. If the testing format doesn't allow you to return to earlier questions, just make an educated guess; then put it out of your mind and move on.

On the easier questions, be careful not to rush. It may seem wise to hurry through them so you have more time for the challenging ones, but it's not worth missing one if you know the concept and just didn't take the time to read the question fully. Work efficiently but make sure you understand the question and have looked at all of the answer choices, since more than one may seem right at first.

Even if you're paying attention to the time, you may find yourself a little behind at some point. You should speed up to get back on track, but do so wisely. Don't panic; just take a few seconds less on each question until you're caught up. Don't guess without thinking, but do look through the answer choices and eliminate any you know are wrong. If you can get down to two choices, it is often worthwhile to guess from those. Once you've chosen an answer, move on and don't dwell on any that you skipped or had to hurry through. If a question was taking too long, chances are it was one of the harder ones, so you weren't as likely to get it right anyway.

On the other hand, if you find yourself getting ahead of schedule, it may be beneficial to slow down a little. The more quickly you work, the more likely you are to make a careless mistake that will affect your score. You've budgeted time for each question, so don't be afraid to spend that time. Practice an efficient but careful pace to get the most out of the time you have.

6

Secret Key #5 – Have a Plan for Guessing

When you're taking the test, you may find yourself stuck on a question. Some of the answer choices seem better than others, but you don't see the one answer choice that is obviously correct. What do you do?

The scenario described above is very common, yet most test takers have not effectively prepared for it. Developing and practicing a plan for guessing may be one of the single most effective uses of your time as you get ready for the exam.

In developing your plan for guessing, there are three questions to address:

- When should you start the guessing process?
- How should you narrow down the choices?
- Which answer should you choose?

When to Start the Guessing Process

Unless your plan for guessing is to select C every time (which, despite its merits, is not what we recommend), you need to leave yourself enough time to apply your answer elimination strategies. Since you have a limited amount of time for each question, that means that if you're going to give yourself the best shot at guessing correctly, you have to decide quickly whether or not you will guess.

Of course, the best-case scenario is that you don't have to guess at all, so first, see if you can answer the question based on your knowledge of the subject and basic reasoning skills. Focus on the key words in the question and try to jog your memory of related topics. Give yourself a chance to bring the knowledge to mind, but once you realize that you don't have (or you can't access) the knowledge you need to answer the question, it's time to start the guessing process.

It's almost always better to start the guessing process too early than too late. It only takes a few seconds to remember something and answer the question from knowledge. Carefully eliminating wrong answer choices takes longer. Plus, going through the process of eliminating answer choices can actually help jog your memory.

Summary: Start the guessing process as soon as you decide that you can't answer the question based on your knowledge.

How to Narrow Down the Choices

The next chapter in this book (**Test-Taking Strategies**) includes a wide range of strategies for how to approach questions and how to look for answer choices to eliminate. You will definitely want to read those carefully, practice them, and figure out which ones work best for you. Here though, we're going to address a mindset rather than a particular strategy.

Your chances of guessing an answer correctly depend on how many options you are choosing from.

How many choices you have	How likely you are to guess correctly
5	20%
4	25%
3	33%
2	50%
1	100%

You can see from this chart just how valuable it is to be able to eliminate incorrect answers and make an educated guess, but there are two things that many test takers do that cause them to miss out on the benefits of guessing:

- Accidentally eliminating the correct answer
- Selecting an answer based on an impression

We'll look at the first one here, and the second one in the next section.

To avoid accidentally eliminating the correct answer, we recommend a thought exercise called **the $5 challenge**. In this challenge, you only eliminate an answer choice from contention if you are willing to bet $5 on it being wrong. Why $5? Five dollars is a small but not insignificant amount of money. It's an amount you could afford to lose but wouldn't want to throw away. And while losing $5 once might not hurt too much, doing it twenty times will set you back $100. In the same way, each small decision you make—eliminating a choice here, guessing on a question there—won't by itself impact your score very much, but when you put them all together, they can make a big difference. By holding each answer choice elimination decision to a higher standard, you can reduce the risk of accidentally eliminating the correct answer.

The $5 challenge can also be applied in a positive sense: If you are willing to bet $5 that an answer choice *is* correct, go ahead and mark it as correct.

Summary: Only eliminate an answer choice if you are willing to bet $5 that it is wrong.

Which Answer to Choose

You're taking the test. You've run into a hard question and decided you'll have to guess. You've eliminated all the answer choices you're willing to bet $5 on. Now you have to pick an answer. Why do we even need to talk about this? Why can't you just pick whichever one you feel like when the time comes?

The answer to these questions is that if you don't come into the test with a plan, you'll rely on your impression to select an answer choice, and if you do that, you risk falling into a trap. The test writers know that everyone who takes their test will be guessing on some of the questions, so they intentionally write wrong answer choices to seem plausible. You still have to pick an answer though, and if the wrong answer choices are designed to look right, how can you ever be sure that you're not falling for their trap? The best solution we've found to this dilemma is to take the decision out of your hands entirely. Here is the process we recommend:

Once you've eliminated any choices that you are confident (willing to bet $5) are wrong, select the first remaining choice as your answer.

Whether you choose to select the first remaining choice, the second, or the last, the important thing is that you use some preselected standard. Using this approach guarantees that you will not be enticed into selecting an answer choice that looks right, because you are not basing your decision on how the answer choices look.

This is not meant to make you question your knowledge. Instead, it is to help you recognize the difference between your knowledge and your impressions. There's a huge difference between thinking an answer is right because of what you know, and thinking an answer is right because it looks or sounds like it should be right.

Summary: To ensure that your selection is appropriately random, make a predetermined selection from among all answer choices you have not eliminated.

Test-Taking Strategies

This section contains a list of test-taking strategies that you may find helpful as you work through the test. By taking what you know and applying logical thought, you can maximize your chances of answering any question correctly!

It is very important to realize that every question is different and every person is different: no single strategy will work on every question, and no single strategy will work for every person. That's why we've included all of them here, so you can try them out and determine which ones work best for different types of questions and which ones work best for you.

Question Strategies

READ CAREFULLY

Read the question and answer choices carefully. Don't miss the question because you misread the terms. You have plenty of time to read each question thoroughly and make sure you understand what is being asked. Yet a happy medium must be attained, so don't waste too much time. You must read carefully, but efficiently.

CONTEXTUAL CLUES

Look for contextual clues. If the question includes a word you are not familiar with, look at the immediate context for some indication of what the word might mean. Contextual clues can often give you all the information you need to decipher the meaning of an unfamiliar word. Even if you can't determine the meaning, you may be able to narrow down the possibilities enough to make a solid guess at the answer to the question.

PREFIXES

If you're having trouble with a word in the question or answer choices, try dissecting it. Take advantage of every clue that the word might include. Prefixes and suffixes can be a huge help. Usually they allow you to determine a basic meaning. Pre- means before, post- means after, pro - is positive, de- is negative. From prefixes and suffixes, you can get an idea of the general meaning of the word and try to put it into context.

HEDGE WORDS

Watch out for critical hedge words, such as *likely, may, can, sometimes, often, almost, mostly, usually, generally, rarely*, and *sometimes*. Question writers insert these hedge phrases to cover every possibility. Often an answer choice will be wrong simply because it leaves no room for exception. Be on guard for answer choices that have definitive words such as *exactly* and *always*.

SWITCHBACK WORDS

Stay alert for *switchbacks*. These are the words and phrases frequently used to alert you to shifts in thought. The most common switchback words are *but, although*, and *however*. Others include *nevertheless, on the other hand, even though, while, in spite of, despite, regardless of*. Switchback words are important to catch because they can change the direction of the question or an answer choice.

FACE VALUE

When in doubt, use common sense. Accept the situation in the problem at face value. Don't read too much into it. These problems will not require you to make wild assumptions. If you have to go beyond creativity and warp time or space in order to have an answer choice fit the question, then you should move on and consider the other answer choices. These are normal problems rooted in reality. The applicable relationship or explanation may not be readily apparent, but it is there for you to figure out. Use your common sense to interpret anything that isn't clear.

Answer Choice Strategies

ANSWER SELECTION

The most thorough way to pick an answer choice is to identify and eliminate wrong answers until only one is left, then confirm it is the correct answer. Sometimes an answer choice may immediately seem right, but be careful. The test writers will usually put more than one reasonable answer choice on each question, so take a second to read all of them and make sure that the other choices are not equally obvious. As long as you have time left, it is better to read every answer choice than to pick the first one that looks right without checking the others.

ANSWER CHOICE FAMILIES

An answer choice family consists of two (in rare cases, three) answer choices that are very similar in construction and cannot all be true at the same time. If you see two answer choices that are direct opposites or parallels, one of them is usually the correct answer. For instance, if one answer choice says that quantity x increases and another either says that quantity x decreases (opposite) or says that quantity y increases (parallel), then those answer choices would fall into the same family. An answer choice that doesn't match the construction of the answer choice family is more likely to be incorrect. Most questions will not have answer choice families, but when they do appear, you should be prepared to recognize them.

ELIMINATE ANSWERS

Eliminate answer choices as soon as you realize they are wrong, but make sure you consider all possibilities. If you are eliminating answer choices and realize that the last one you are left with is also wrong, don't panic. Start over and consider each choice again. There may be something you missed the first time that you will realize on the second pass.

AVOID FACT TRAPS

Don't be distracted by an answer choice that is factually true but doesn't answer the question. You are looking for the choice that answers the question. Stay focused on what the question is asking for so you don't accidentally pick an answer that is true but incorrect. Always go back to the question and make sure the answer choice you've selected actually answers the question and is not merely a true statement.

EXTREME STATEMENTS

In general, you should avoid answers that put forth extreme actions as standard practice or proclaim controversial ideas as established fact. An answer choice that states the "process should be used in certain situations, if..." is much more likely to be correct than one that states the "process should be discontinued completely." The first is a calm rational statement and doesn't even make a definitive, uncompromising stance, using a hedge word *if* to provide wiggle room, whereas the second choice is a radical idea and far more extreme.

BENCHMARK

As you read through the answer choices and you come across one that seems to answer the question well, mentally select that answer choice. This is not your final answer, but it's the one that will help you evaluate the other answer choices. The one that you selected is your benchmark or standard for judging each of the other answer choices. Every other answer choice must be compared to your benchmark. That choice is correct until proven otherwise by another answer choice beating it. If you find a better answer, then that one becomes your new benchmark. Once you've decided that no other choice answers the question as well as your benchmark, you have your final answer.

PREDICT THE ANSWER

Before you even start looking at the answer choices, it is often best to try to predict the answer. When you come up with the answer on your own, it is easier to avoid distractions and traps because you will know exactly what to look for. The right answer choice is unlikely to be word-for-word what you came up with, but it should be a close match. Even if you are confident that you have the right answer, you should still take the time to read each option before moving on.

General Strategies

TOUGH QUESTIONS

If you are stumped on a problem or it appears too hard or too difficult, don't waste time. Move on! Remember though, if you can quickly check for obviously incorrect answer choices, your chances of guessing correctly are greatly improved. Before you completely give up, at least try to knock out a couple of possible answers. Eliminate what you can and then guess at the remaining answer choices before moving on.

CHECK YOUR WORK

Since you will probably not know every term listed and the answer to every question, it is important that you get credit for the ones that you do know. Don't miss any questions through careless mistakes. If at all possible, try to take a second to look back over your answer selection and make sure you've selected the correct answer choice and haven't made a costly careless mistake (such as marking an answer choice that you didn't mean to mark). This quick double check should more than pay for itself in caught mistakes for the time it costs.

PACE YOURSELF

It's easy to be overwhelmed when you're looking at a page full of questions; your mind is confused and full of random thoughts, and the clock is ticking down faster than you would like. Calm down and maintain the pace that you have set for yourself. Especially as you get down to the last few minutes of the test, don't let the small numbers on the clock make you panic. As long as you are on track by monitoring your pace, you are guaranteed to have time for each question.

DON'T RUSH

It is very easy to make errors when you are in a hurry. Maintaining a fast pace in answering questions is pointless if it makes you miss questions that you would have gotten right otherwise. Test writers like to include distracting information and wrong answers that seem right. Taking a little extra time to avoid careless mistakes can make all the difference in your test score. Find a pace that allows you to be confident in the answers that you select.

12

KEEP MOVING

Panicking will not help you pass the test, so do your best to stay calm and keep moving. Taking deep breaths and going through the answer elimination steps you practiced can help to break through a stress barrier and keep your pace.

Final Notes

The combination of a solid foundation of content knowledge and the confidence that comes from practicing your plan for applying that knowledge is the key to maximizing your performance on test day. As your foundation of content knowledge is built up and strengthened, you'll find that the strategies included in this chapter become more and more effective in helping you quickly sift through the distractions and traps of the test to isolate the correct answer.

Now it's time to move on to the test content chapters of this book, but be sure to keep your goal in mind. As you read, think about how you will be able to apply this information on the test. If you've already seen sample questions for the test and you have an idea of the question format and style, try to come up with questions of your own that you can answer based on what you're reading. This will give you valuable practice applying your knowledge in the same ways you can expect to on test day.

Good luck and good studying!

Insurance Regulation

PRODUCER'S INSURANCE LICENSE, RESIDENT AND NONRESIDENT

There are various types of licenses available for individuals. Within the insurance industry, a **producer's license** indicates that the individual, partnership, or corporation is permitted to transact business and enter into contracts on behalf of an insurer in a particular state. A **resident producer license** will be issued to any producer who resides within the given state, or who retains a principal place of business in that state. In order to acquire a resident producer license, an individual must complete a pre-licensing education program, pass an examination, and complete a battery of forms. There is also a substantial fee for a producer's license. **Nonresident licenses**, which are issued to the parties looking to transact insurance business in states in which they do not reside, are only available to professionals who are already licensed as producers in their home state. Nonresident licenses are typically only issued on a temporary basis, with an expiration date of 180 days. These licenses are often issued to estate administrators and members of the military.

SURPLUS LINES BROKERS, RESIDENT AND NONRESIDENT REQUIREMENTS

A surplus lines broker is a person or business that obtains or negotiates insurance coverage with insurance companies. In order to serve as a **surplus lines broker**, it is not necessary to obtain a license. However, surplus lines brokers must receive **approval** in order to conduct business in a particular state. As with producers, there are resident and nonresident surplus lines broker standards. An applicant for a **resident surplus lines broker** must have held a property and casualty license for at least two years, or must have two years of professional experience working on behalf of a property and casualty insurer. These two years of experience must also be acquired during the past three years. **Nonresident applicants** must submit a letter of certification to the state department of insurance, indicating that the applicant is approved to serve as a surplus lines broker in his or her home state. There is also a standard fee for the nonresident surplus lines broker approval.

INSURANCE PRODUCER LICENSE REQUIREMENTS

The standards for obtaining and maintaining an **insurance producer's license** vary by state. Typically, however, licenses are issued for two years at a time. The standard renewal fee is $50. In the event that the state denies licensure to a person or business, notification must be provided in writing. Applicants may submit written demands for a hearing when licensure is denied. So long as the producer meets the continuing education requirements and submits the appropriate fees, he or she should be allowed to have the license reinstated within five years of its lapse. Some requirements related to the obtaining and maintenance of a producer's license may be waived for disabled applicants or veterans.

INSURANCE PRODUCER LICENSE APPLICATION STANDARDS

In order to obtain licensure as an insurance producer, a person must apply with the **state insurance licensing authority**. The applicant must indicate whether he or she holds a license in another state. A license that is suspended, revoked, or denied renewal must also be indicated on the producer's license application. The applicant must indicate if he or she owes money to a general producer or insurer. Applicants who are only planning to work part-time as insurance producers must describe their other occupations and outline the amount of time that will be devoted to insurance. The applicant will typically be required to complete an **approved course** administered by the licensing authority and lasting 32 hours. Most applicants will need to pass a written examination, though those who have passed such an exam in their home state may be exempt from

15

this requirement. The applicant must be at least 18 years old, and must attest that the license will not be used to obtain more than a quarter of the applicant's income through the placement of controlled business.

INSURANCE PRODUCER CONTINUING EDUCATION REQUIREMENTS

Although the continuing education requirements for maintaining an insurance producer's license vary by state, there are some typical characteristics. People who hold only a **property and casualty producer license** usually need to take 24 hours of continuing education courses in a two-year period. Those who hold the **property and casualty and life and health licenses** must complete 20 hours of continuing education in order to retain the property and casualty license. Those who seek only to retain licensure for **life and health insurance** are required to take 16 hours of continuing education courses. Life insurance producers with both **life and health and property and casualty insurance** are usually required to complete the sum of their constituent parts' hours of continuing education courses. Any licensed producers who are older than 65 or who have at least 15 years of experience are not required to meet the continuing education requirements. At least half of the continuing education requirements must be fulfilled in a classroom. License holders may carry over up to 10 excess hours from one period to the next.

REPORTABLE EXAMPLES OF PRODUCER MISCONDUCT

There are certain examples of producer misconduct that are immediately reportable to the licensing authority. If an insurance agent is subject to **disciplinary action** in another jurisdiction, this must be reported within 30 days. If the insurance agent is convicted of a **felony**, the licensing authority must be notified within 30 days, and must be provided with copies of the bill of information and the indictment. Any **pertinent changes** must be submitted to the licensing authority at once, or the insurance producer will be subject to fines or other penalties. When an insurance producer **leaves a state**, he or she must surrender his or her license within 30 days. Insurance producers may lose their licenses by **hiring a convicted felon** without receiving the approval of the licensing authority. Finally, insurance producers who conduct business under **another name** must give notification to the licensing authority before using this name. If an insurance producer does business under an unapproved trade name, he or she may be fined up to $250, and may be subject to a fine of $5000 if he or she continues to use the unapproved name.

STANDARD DISCIPLINARY ACTIONS FOR PRODUCER MISCONDUCT

If an insurance producer is found to have behaved **unethically**, the licensing authority may suspend, revoke, or deny the renewal of his or her license. When an insurance producer has his or her license revoked, suspended, or denied renewal, he or she may not **reapply** for one year after the first offense, and five years after any subsequent offenses. The licensing authority may punish insurance producers for any **intentional misstatements or misrepresentations of facts** relative to the terms and conditions of an insurance contract. A failure to notify policyholders about **relevant exclusions** may be cause for penalty. Any insurance producer who obtains his or her license through **fraud or misrepresentation** may lose that license. There is also a set of actions that may result in a license holder being put on **probation**. For instance, failing to pay child support may result in probation. Professionals may also be put on probation for failing to serve the interest of the insurance company or the client, violating insurance laws, or intentionally misstating or misrepresenting the characteristics of an insurance contract.

LICENSING AUTHORITY HEARINGS FOR THE VIOLATION OF INSURANCE LAWS AND RULES

Before a **cease and desist order** will be issued after a customer complaint, the insurance licensing authority must hold a **hearing**. A cease and desist order is typically issued after a producer has been engaged in an unfair or deceptive practice. The order asserts that the producer must immediately cease this method of competition. A hearing is also necessary when a company or producer becomes **bankrupt**. It is standard for this insolvency hearing to occur within five days of the bankruptcy filing. Insurance producers may also be required to appear at a hearing at the request of the **licensing authority**. Typically, the licensing authority will request this sort of hearing when it believes that a company or producer has engaged in unfair trade practices. A hearing on demand typically must be held within 30 days of the original notification. Following a hearing, the licensing authority is required to issue a **ruling** within 30 days. This ruling should include the action taken, the effective date of action, the evidence, and the findings supporting the action.

STANDARD FINES, PENALTIES, AND APPEALS PROCESS FOR AN INSURANCE LICENSING AUTHORITY

Accidental or unintentional violations of insurance regulations typically result in a fine of $1000. The **standard maximum fine** for intentional violations is $25,000. If a license is suspended or revoked, the producer may not reapply for one year following the first offense, and for five years following the second offense. However, a producer or company may **appeal** to the appropriate judicial district within 30 days of the suspension or revocation. Insurance producers who violate a **cease-and-desist order** may be penalized $25,000, or may have their license suspended or revoked. The general penalty for **violations by corporations** is $50,000, and the maximum general penalty for **violations by individuals** is a $10,000 fine accompanied by a five-year prison term. According to the Violent Crime Control and Law Enforcement Act of 1994, any individual who has been convicted of a felony must obtain the explicit consent of the licensing authority in order to participate in the insurance business.

STATE AND FEDERAL INSURANCE REGULATIONS, AND AUDITING REGULATIONS FOR PRODUCERS

In order to be licensed in a particular state, an insurance company must be **formed or domiciled** there. In an insurance company, the principal agent responsible for dealing with third parties and their clients is known as the **law of agency insurer**. This agent is given power of attorney on behalf of the insurance company. It is standard for the state insurance licensing authority to retain the right to examine the books and records of all insurance companies, producers, and surplus lines brokers who are issued licensure by the state. New companies must submit to **auditing** every six months for their first three years of operation, and then once a year for the subsequent two years. However, the state licensing authority retains the right to audit all insurance companies whenever it deems necessary. Once established, an insurance company will be audited at least once every five years.

MISREPRESENTATION; FALSE ADVERTISING; DEFAMATION; BOYCOTT, COERCION, AND INTIMIDATION; FALSE FINANCIAL STATEMENTS; UNFAIR DISCRIMINATION; REBATING; AND CONTROLLED BUSINESS

In the insurance industry, a **misrepresentation** is an intentionally false presentation of facts that are pertinent to the policy. **False advertising charges** may be applied to any form of communication to consumers. **Defamation** is the dissemination of false or malicious information about another insurance professional. **Boycott, coercion, and intimidation** are all illegal behaviors that unreasonably restrain competition and promote monopoly. It is also illegal for insurance professionals to create **false financial statements**, which are defined as any financial records that intend to deceive users. It is illegal for insurance providers to unfairly **discriminate** against certain clients. **Rebating**, or offering inducements for the purchase of insurance, is generally illegal, although policyholders may be granted dividends. Finally, it is typically illegal for insurance providers to participate in **controlled business**, which is when personal income is greater than 25 percent of gross commission from insurance.

UNFAIR CLAIM SETTLEMENT PRACTICES AND INSURANCE FRAUD

In the insurance industry, certain claim settlement practices are defined as **unfair**. For instance, it is unfair to settle a claim based on a **misrepresentation** of the pertinent facts about the policy. It is also unfair to fail to acknowledge, settle, or deny a claim **promptly**. It is considered unfair to **delay** the investigation or the payment of a claim without sufficient reason. Finally, it is unfair to settle a claim for **less** than the amount originally stated in the insurance policy. **False advertisements** about insurance products and false statements about competitors are also considered to be unfair practices. **Insurance fraud**, meanwhile, is any intentional misrepresentation or concealment of important information that causes damage or loss to another party. Intentionally presenting several claims related to the same loss with a **fraudulent intent** is considered fraud. **Selling** the policies or **diverting** the funds of an insolvent insurer is also defined as fraud.

COMMISSION, DISTRIBUTION, AND THE TERMINATION OF APPOINTMENTS

State insurance licensing authorities typically allow producers to share a **commission** with other licensed producers, including nonresident producers, so long as the primary producer retains at least half of the commission. Failure to do so may result in a fine of $2000 or a prison term of six months. The state authorities do not allow any producer to pay money, commissions, or other items of value to individuals or businesses without licensure for that type of insurance. When an insurance company or producer wishes to **terminate** the relationship, 30 days of notice must be provided to the other party. Also, the insurance company must let the licensing authority know about the termination within 30 days. In situations where the producer has intentionally violated fair trade practices, the producer is responsible for notifying the licensing authority within 15 days, although this interval is decreased to five days in cases of fraud.

Contracts

CONCEPT OF MUTUAL ASSENT IN A CONTRACT OFFER

A **contract** is an agreement between two or more parties, both of which are competent to represent themselves, to exchange things of value or refrain from doing a particular thing. A contract is not considered valid if it requires one of the parties to do something that is either impossible or illegal. In order for a contract to be **valid**, there must be **mutual assent**: that is, all involved parties must agree to all the terms of the contract. Mutual assent can only exist when both parties understand all the terms of the contract and willingly agree to abide by them. It is the product of an open offer that is authentically accepted by the offeree.

REQUIREMENTS OF A CONTRACT OFFER

In order for a contract offer to be considered **valid**, it must meet three requirements: It must have serious intent, it must be expressed clearly and in reasonably definite terms, and it must be communicated to the offeree. To say that a contract offer has **serious intent** means that it assures the offeree that the offeror is intending to enter into a binding agreement. The offer must be stated **clearly** enough to eliminate any doubt regarding the intentions of the offeror, though most courts do not demand absolute definition in a contract offer. Finally, the offer must be **communicated** through whatever means are desirable and convenient. The communication of a contract offer may be expressed or implied. A public offer may be made through the media if the offer is being extended to one party whose identity or address is unknown.

ACCEPTANCE OF A CONTRACT OFFER

When the offeree **accepts** a contract offer, he or she is agreeing to be bound by the terms established by the offeror. No one other than the offeree may accept the offer. By accepting the offer, the offeree is indicating that he or she accepts all of the terms stated in the offer. This is known as the **mirror image rule**, meaning that the terms expressed in the acceptance are an exact duplicate of the terms expressed in the offer. In some cases, the offeree does not need to make a verbal or written acceptance in order for his or her agreement to be established. **Implied acceptance** is especially common in unilateral contracts, where the offeror is expecting a particular action rather than a promise in return for the offer. In such a case, performance of the desired action implies acceptance of the offer.

METHODS OF ACCEPTING A CONTRACT OFFER

There are various methods of accepting a contract offer, and the contract becomes **official** at a different time depending on which of these methods is used. For instance, when the contract offer is accepted **in person**, the acceptance becomes complete and effective when the offeror hears the verbal acceptance. The same rules apply to acceptance made over the **telephone**: acceptance is considered complete and effective when the offeror hears the words of acceptance. If the acceptance is **mailed** or sent by another authorized means of communication, it is considered complete and effective when its transit is initiated. So, for instance, a mailed acceptance is considered to be complete and effective when the offeree places it in the mail. In the event that an acceptance is improperly dispatched, it is not considered valid until the offeror receives it.

CONSIDERATION A NECESSARY PART OF A VALID CONTRACT

For a contract to be valid, it must entail an exchange of either **benefits** or **sacrifices** by the parties. The exchange of things of value is known as **consideration**. When one of the parties to a contract does not receive consideration, the contract cannot be considered binding. Moreover, consideration must entail a **mutual exchange** of gains and losses by the parties to the contract. In legal terms, the sacrifice made by each party is a **legal detriment**. This means that the party is doing something he or she does not have the legal right to do, not doing something he or she has a legal right to do, or giving up something he or she has a legal right to keep. Refraining from doing something which one has a legal right to do is known as **forbearance**.

CHARACTERISTICS OF LEGAL CONSIDERATION

There are three basic criteria for legal consideration in a contract: it must be bargained for, it must be adequate, and it must be legal. Consideration is **bargained for** when one promise is made in exchange for another promise, act, or forbearance. The underlying point of specifying that consideration must be bargained for is to ensure that each party has the potential to suffer a loss if the terms of the contract are not fulfilled. In order to be **adequate**, consideration must represent something of value. The precise value of consideration is not important, only that all parties agree to the existence of value. Finally, consideration may not involve **illegal goods**, and may not require one party to perform an **illegal act** or refrain from performing an act which he or she is legally obliged to perform.

BASIC TYPES OF CONSIDERATION

In most contracts, consideration is property, money, or services. There are also contracts in which charitable pledges or the promise not to sue is treated as consideration. A promise not to sue is considered **forbearance**. Contracts in which one party promises not to sue are often used to settle pending lawsuits. There are a few types of agreement that may be enforceable even without consideration. For instance, a **promise under seal** (a rather antiquated method of authenticating a contract) may be enforced without consideration if it does not involve goods. Promises to pay debts that have been barred by a **statute of limitations** may also be enforceable. However, promises of a **gift** are unenforceable because a gift implies that the receiving party will not be offering anything in exchange.

CAPACITY AS A REQUIREMENT FOR LEGAL CONTRACTS

In order for a contract to be considered valid, all parties must have **capacity**. That means they must have the legal ability to enter a contract. A person is considered to have such ability if he or she is **well-informed** about the contract and possesses **free will**. A person's capacity may be challenged if he or she is a minor. The age of majority varies from state to state, but in most places and with regard to most types of contracts it is 18 years. There are a few exceptions in which a minor may not rescind his or her participation in a contract. For instance, emancipated minors may have their contractual agreements enforced. The agreements entered into by a mentally impaired person may also be voidable if the degree of disability is severe, or if the individual was severely intoxicated at the time.

LEGALITY AS A REQUIREMENT FOR CONTRACTS

A contract will not be considered valid if it requires one or more parties to perform **illegal acts**, whether these are crimes or torts. The court system will not enforce any contract that requires the performance of an unlawful act. For instance, agreements related to illegal gambling are invalid and unenforceable. Even in locations where gambling is legal, it is often illegal to borrow money for the purpose of gambling. Furthermore, agreements that run contrary to **public policy** are unenforceable. For example, agreements to obstruct justice, interfere with public service, or defraud creditors will all be rendered invalid.

20

UNILATERAL AND BILATERAL CONTRACTS

Contracts are typically described as either unilateral or bilateral. In a **unilateral contract**, one party promises to do something in return for the performance of a particular act, and the contract is considered accepted when the action is performed. A unilateral contract offer is often made without regards to the identity of the accepting party. For instance, a person creates a unilateral contract by offering to give $100 to whomever returns his lost dog. The return of the dog constitutes an acceptance of the offer of $100. In a **bilateral contract**, on the other hand, both parties make promises. If one of the parties to a bilateral contract fails to keep his or her promise, a breach is said to have occurred. A bilateral contract offer requires an explicit acceptance from the offeree.

ALEATORY CONTRACTS AND CONDITIONAL CONTRACTS

In an aleatory contract, the performance of one or both parties depends on whether a named event occurs. Insurance policies are generally defined as **aleatory contracts** because the insurance company only becomes obliged to make payments when an insurable event occurs. A **conditional contract** is similar to an aleatory contract, in that it is an agreement that only becomes enforceable if another action is performed. The difference between an aleatory and a conditional contract is that, in the latter, the action must be performed or the condition must be satisfied by one of the parties to the contract. In other words, the contractual obligations of one party do not begin to exist until the other party has performed a certain action or satisfied a certain condition.

WAIVER AND ESTOPPEL

In legal terms, a **waiver** is the intentional abandonment or delegation of a right. For instance, an insurance producer may waive some of the conditions of a policy in order to secure the agreement of the customer. The waived terms are no longer active in the policy. On the other hand, a customer may implicitly waive his or her rights by violating the terms of the insurance policy in some way. An **estoppel**, meanwhile, is a restraint. With regard to contracts, estoppel generally applies by preventing one party from denying the existence of an agreement. Estoppel is applied to prevent unjust actions from taking place.

Insurance Basics

RISK, HAZARD, AND PERIL

The intention of insurance is to provide a protection against the harm that would be caused by a specific **risk**. A **hazard** is a factor that increases the chance of loss. Hazards may be physical, moral, political, or legal. A *physical hazard* derives from the use, conditions, or occupancy of a property. A *moral hazard* is caused by the negligence or irresponsible behavior of the insured party. A *political hazard* is related to the passage of a law or ordinance. *Legal hazard*, finally, is the regulatory environment within which the insured party is operating. With regard to insurance policies, **peril** is defined as the specific cause of loss or damage. The loss may be considered from the perspective of economics or indemnity. An *economic loss* is the total estimated cost of repairing or replacing the property that has been damaged or lost. *Indemnity*, meanwhile, is the compensation for loss provided by a property and casualty liability insurance policy. In an indemnity situation, the insurance company will seek to restore the position of the insured to where it was before the loss.

INSURABLE INTEREST, DEDUCTIBLE, LOSS, AND NAMED PERIL

A party is said to have **insurable interest** when damage or loss to a specific property would cause a financial loss for that party. In order to receive insurance coverage, the insured party must have an interest in the property at the time of loss. A **deductible** is the amount of a loss above which the insurance company will make payment. In other words, any damages below the value of the deductible must be borne by the insured party. A **direct loss** is defined as a financial loss caused by the damage or destruction of a covered property by a covered peril. A **consequential or indirect loss** is a financial loss that is caused by direct loss. Consequential and indirect losses are only covered by some policies. In order to be covered, a **specific peril** must be explicitly covered by the policy: that is, it must be a named peril. Some policies do offer special or open peril coverage, in which any peril not specifically excluded by the insurance policy is covered.

COVERAGE, VALUATION, AND REPLACEMENT COST

Insurance policies provide different degrees of **coverage**. For instance, an insurance policy may offer *specific coverage single insurance*, in which a single type of property is covered at one location. A policy may offer *blanket coverage*, which extends to more than one type of property in the same location, the same type of property in multiple locations, or multiple types of property in multiple locations. The **valuation** of a property loss is the basis on which the cost of loss is paid. A common method of valuation is *actual cash value*, in which the value of the loss is the cost of replacing the damaged or destroyed property with new property of similar value, taking account of depreciation and obsolescence. If the deductions for depreciation or obsolescence are eliminated, the valuation is said to be at **replacement cost**. The *functional replacement cost* is the expense that would be incurred in the process of restoring a commercial building to a functional condition.

SALVAGE VALUE, MARKET VALUE, STATED VALUE, AGREED VALUE, AND VALUE POLICY

The **salvage value** of a property is the amount that the insurer could expect to receive for property it takes possession of after providing replacement or restoration payment to the policyholder. The **market value**, or actual cash value, of a piece of property is the amount that the property could be bought or sold for at the present time (in claims context, consider the state of the property prior to the loss). The **stated value** is a value, often supplied by the property owner, that establishes the maximum amount that the insurance company is required to pay out in the event of a loss. It does not typically impact the minimum payout. The **agreed value** is a value specified in the insurance contract for how much will be paid out in the event of a loss. It may exceed or be less than the

22

market value. A **value policy** is a policy that requires an agreed value payout. Value policies are typically used to insure items whose market value does not accurately reflect their value to the owner or items for which a sufficient market does not exist.

Loss Payee, Misrepresentation, Breach of Warranty Statement, Concealment, and Negligence

In an insurance policy, the **loss payee** is the party to whom insurance payments are made in the event of a loss. The loss payee may or may not be the owner of the property. For instance, a loss payee may be a mortgage holder or lien holder. Insurance contracts are rendered void when the policyholder misrepresents pertinent facts on the application. A **breach of warranty** occurs when the policyholder violates a provision that was extremely significant with respect to the policy. A breach of warranty will typically result in the voiding of the insurance policy. In the context of insurance, **concealment** is the intentional hiding of a relevant factor by the policyholder. **Negligence**, finally, is the failure to exercise the amount of care that would be necessary to protect covered property or individuals from reasonably predictable sources of harm.

Adjusting Losses

GOOD FAITH AND THE IMMEDIATE CONTACT RULE

Claims adjusters are required to act in **good faith** at all times. This is particularly important for claims adjusters because they so often are employed by one of the sides involved in an insurance dispute. The claims adjuster has the obligation to produce an accurate and comprehensive report without showing **favoritism** to either side. The claims adjuster should ignore any undue influence from either of the conflicting parties. As for the **immediate contact rule** in claims adjusting, it asserts that the claims adjuster should contact the insured and the insurance company as soon as possible after an investigation. The investigation cannot be complete and effective if it does not begin as soon as possible. Therefore, the claims adjuster should contact all involved parties immediately.

MULTILINE, ALL-LINES, PUBLIC, AND INDEPENDENT INSURANCE ADJUSTERS

There are various specializations within claims adjusting. Adjusters who handle property claims and liability claims are called **multiline adjusters**. **All-lines adjusters** handle property and liability claims, as well as professional liability, excess liability, bond losses, boiler and machinery damage, and other claims. Claims adjusters are also distinguished as either public or independent. A **public adjuster** only works for the policyholder, and is therefore an advocate for the interests of the policyholder as a liaison with the insurance company. **Independent adjusters**, on the other hand, work for insurance companies or self-insured entities. No matter who employs an insurance adjuster, he or she is responsible for completing his or her reports as accurately and comprehensively as possible.

CLAIMS REPORTS

When a claims adjuster takes on a project, he or she will be required to submit three different reports. The first report, known as the **initial or first field report**, is a preliminary summation of all the evidence related to the claim. In this document, the claims adjuster should include any potentially pertinent information he or she discovers during the first assessment of the claim. While the claim is being processed, the claims adjuster will issue an **interim or status report**, indicating a range of possible outcomes for the claim. This enables both the insurance company and the insured individual to prepare their finances. The final report issued by the claims adjuster is known as the **full formal report**: it contains the claims adjuster's final verdict with respect to the claim.

DEALING WITH COVERAGE DISPUTES

In the insurance industry, a **reservation of rights letter** is a formal warning to other parties that the letter writer plans to maintain his or her full rights with respect to a property, and therefore that these rights should be respected. In situations where an insurance company decides to investigate a claim, it may issue a reservation of rights letter so that the insured party will be alerted to the possibility of claim disputation. A **non-waiver agreement**, on the other hand, is a formal statement that both parties agree not to waive certain rights with respect to their contract. In an insurance contract, either the insurance company or the insured may suggest a non-waiver agreement to formalize certain aspects of the policy. Finally, a **declaratory judgment action** indicates whether potential litigants have the legal standing to bring the charges planned. Parties will often ask for a declaratory judgment in advance of a more formal trial.

ARBITRATION, MEDIATION, AND NEGOTIATION

Arbitration, mediation, and negotiation are three alternative dispute resolution techniques: that is, they are protocols for resolving disputes outside of court. In **arbitration**, the parties refer their dispute to a neutral third party or group of third parties. The disputing parties agree to be bound by the decision of the arbitrators. In **mediation**, a third party is called in to help the disputing parties come to an agreement. The decision or advice of the third party is not binding to the disputing parties in mediation. A **negotiation** is the least formal of the three varieties of alternative dispute resolution. Negotiation is simply the creation of a dialogue between the disputing parties with the aim of reaching a compromise or agreement.

Dwelling Policy

Standard Dwelling Insurance Policy

COVERAGE A: DWELLING

Coverage A of the standard dwelling insurance policy relates to **dwellings**. Specifically, the insurance company will promise to cover all dwellings on the location described on the declarations page, so long as these structures are used principally for **residence purposes**. Coverage A applies as well to **structures** attached to the dwelling. Coverage A also applies to **materials and supplies** found on or next to the described location, provided that these are used to construct or repair the dwelling or related structures. Also, Coverage A applies to any building and outdoor **equipment** used to service the dwelling, assuming this equipment is not covered elsewhere in the policy. Coverage A does not apply to land, even the land on which the dwelling is found.

COVERAGE B: OTHER STRUCTURES

Coverage B of the standard dwelling insurance policy applies to **other structures** found on the described location, specifically structures that are set apart from the described location by a defined space. Coverage B applies to structures that are connected to the dwelling merely by a **utility line or fence**. However, Coverage B does not apply to any land, including the land on which the other structures are built. Coverage B does not apply to other structures either rented or held for rental to anyone who is not a tenant of the dwelling. Coverage B also does not apply to any structures that are used entirely or partly for farming, commercial operations, or manufacturing. This coverage may apply to structures that house commercial, farming, or manufacturing property, so long as the property does not also include fuel tanks outside of the equipment. Finally, Coverage B does not apply to gravesites or mausoleums.

COVERAGE C: PERSONAL PROPERTY

Coverage C of the standard dwelling insurance policy relates to **personal property**. This part of the policy covers the property of the insured that is typically **within** the dwelling or that is **used** by the insured or members of the insured's family while residing in the dwelling. Some property owned by guests or servants may be covered while they are on the described location. Coverage C of the standard dwelling insurance policy does not cover any animals, including birds and fish. It does not cover any motor vehicles, including watercraft, aircraft, or hovercraft. It does not cover any accounts, letters of credit, manuscripts, bank notes, bills, deeds, or currency. It does not cover gold other than goldware, silver other than silverware, or platinum other than platinumware. It does not cover any data or records, regardless of whether they are stored in computers or on paper. It does not cover credit cards or electronic funds transfer cards. Finally, it does not cover water or steam.

COVERAGE D: FAIR RENTAL VALUE

Coverage D of the standard dwelling insurance policy relates to the **fair rental value**. In the typical formulation, the policy states that when losses to property described in Coverages A, B, or C make that location **unfit for its normal use**, the fair rental value of the rentable portion of the dwelling will be covered by the insurance company. However, the insurance company will not pay any expenses that do not continue while the property is not being rented. Also, payments under Coverage D will only be made for the smallest amount of time required to repair or replace the damaged or destroyed part of the rental property. Coverage D only applies for a maximum of two weeks if a civil authority forbids occupancy of the described location because of a covered incident at an adjoining property. Losses or expenses caused by the cancellation of a lease or agreement are not covered here.

MISCELLANEOUS COVERAGES

OTHER STRUCTURES; DEBRIS REMOVAL; AND IMPROVEMENTS, ALTERATIONS, AND ADDITIONS

There are a few **miscellaneous coverages** included in the standard dwelling insurance policy. To begin with, the insured party is typically entitled to use up to 10 percent of the limit of liability under Coverage A to pay for damages to **other structures** described in Coverage B. This payment will reduce the Coverage A limit of liability by the amount paid for the same loss. The standard dwelling insurance policy will also pay any reasonable expense for the **removal of debris** left over from a covered loss. The insurance company will also pay for any ash, dust, or particles resulting from a volcanic eruption. If the insured party is a tenant of the location described on the declarations page, he or she may use up to 10 percent of the Coverage C limit of liability for covered losses to **improvements, alterations, and additions**. However, payments made for damage or destruction of improvements, alterations, and additions reduce the limit of liability under Coverage C for the same loss.

WORLDWIDE COVERAGE, RENTAL VALUE, AND REASONABLE REPAIRS

In the standard dwelling insurance policy, the insurance company will allow the insured party to use up to 10 percent of the limit of liability under Coverage C for covered property **anywhere in the world**. However, this coverage will not apply to the property of servants or guests. If payments are made under this policy, the Coverage C limit of liability is reduced by an equivalent amount. Similarly, the standard dwelling insurance policy gives the insured party the option to use up to 20 percent of the limit of liability under Coverage A for losses of **fair rental value**. Each month in which the rentable part of the described location and is unfit for use, the insurance company will pay a maximum of one-twelfth of the 20 percent. Finally, when covered property is damaged, the insurance company will pay for any **reasonable cost** incurred as part of necessary measures to prevent further damage.

PROPERTY REMOVED, AND FIRE DEPARTMENT SERVICE CHARGE

The standard dwelling insurance policy provides coverage for covered property that is damaged while being **removed** from the premises because of an impending peril. This coverage will apply for a maximum of five days. The overall limit of liability that applies to the property being removed is not changed by this coverage. The standard dwelling insurance policy will also pay up to $500 of the liability incurred when the fire department must come to protect or save covered property. The **fire department service charge** is considered additional insurance, and is not subject to a deductible. However, fire department service charges are not covered when the property is within the city or district limits of the fire department.

PERILS INSURED AGAINST

FIRE OR LIGHTNING, INTERNAL EXPLOSION, AND WINDSTORM OR HAIL

The standard dwelling policy provides insurance coverage for physical losses that are directly caused by one of the indicated perils. To begin with, the standard dwelling policy will cover any loss caused by **fire or lightning**. The policy will also cover loss due to **internal explosion**, which does not include broken water pipes, broken pressure relief devices, or electric arcing. Also, the internal explosion coverage does not apply to any losses related to the explosion of steam pipes or steam boilers when these devices are owned or operated by the tenant. The remaining perils insured against are only included as part of this policy when a premium for extended coverage is indicated on the declarations page. The first of these additional perils is **windstorm or hail**, though this does not include damage to the inside of the property when it is caused by these environmental factors unless the inside of the dwelling is exposed by windstorm or hail.

RIOT OR CIVIL COMMOTION, AIRCRAFT, VEHICLES, SMOKE, VOLCANIC ERUPTION, AND VANDALISM OR MALICIOUS MISCHIEF

If the premium for extended coverage is included on the declarations page, then the standard dwelling policy will cover loss due to **riot or civil commotion**. The standard dwelling policy will also cover losses caused by **aircraft**, including spacecraft and self-propelled missiles. Some losses caused by **vehicles** are covered, but not losses caused by vehicles to driveways or fences. Also, if the vehicle is owned or operated by the insured or a resident of the insured dwelling, the loss is not covered. The standard dwelling policy will also cover damage caused by **smoke**, including damage related to boilers or furnaces. The smoke damage caused by fireplaces or agricultural or industrial operations is not covered by the standard dwelling policy. The standard dwelling policy covers loss due to **volcanic eruption**, though this does not include losses caused by tremors or earthquakes. Finally, if the insured is paying a special premium for **vandalism or malicious mischief**, he or she will be covered against these perils. However, this will not include damage to glass or safety glazing material.

EXCLUSIONS

ORDINANCE OR LAW

The standard dwelling policy contains a few general exclusions. These exclusions are events that are not covered by the policy. The exclusions apply even when the event causes significant damage over a large area. To begin with, the standard dwelling policy has exclusions for losses related to **ordinance or law**. Specifically, the standard dwelling policy excludes losses related to ordinances or laws that mandate or govern the **construction, repair, or removal of property**. The policy also excludes losses sustained when the requirements of an ordinance or law causes a **decrease in the value** of the property. The standard dwelling policy also excludes any losses related to ordinances or laws that require the insured to monitor, test, treat, or neutralize **pollutants**.

EARTH MOVEMENT AND WATER DAMAGE

The standard dwelling policy includes exclusion for losses caused by **earth movement**. For this policy, earth movement means earthquake, landslide, mudslide, sinkholes, and other instances of subsidence. The exclusion obtains regardless of whether the earth movement is caused by human, animal, or natural forces. The only exception to this exclusion is when the earth movement causes a fire or explosion, in which case all of the loss that is the direct result of the fire or explosion will be covered by insurance policy. The standard dwelling policy also includes an exclusion for **water damage**: that is, property loss caused by flood, waves, tidal water, or wind-driven spray. This exclusion also applies to any water that backs up or overflows from sewers or drains, or that leaks through a driveway, building, sidewalk, or other structure. As with the earth movement exclusion, however, any loss that is sustained from an ensuing fire or explosion caused by said water damage is still covered.

POWER FAILURE, NEGLECT, AND WAR

The standard dwelling policy contains exclusion for losses caused by **power failure** when the failure takes place off of the premises. However, if the failure of power or some other utility service causes a loss from a covered peril on the insured location, all of the damages caused by that peril will be insured against. The standard dwelling policy also has exclusion for losses related to **neglect**, meaning that the policy will not cover losses when the insured party has not used all reasonable means to preserve property before, during, and after loss. The standard dwelling policy also includes an exclusion for **war**, which includes any military action. The accidental discharge of military weapons may be considered a warlike act.

Nuclear Hazard, Intentional Loss, and Governmental Action

The standard dwelling policy contains exclusion for losses caused by **nuclear hazard**, whether related to radiation or contamination. The policy also contains exclusion for **intentional loss**, which means any loss that is caused by an action taken by the named insured or an additional insured on purpose and with the intention of causing a loss. When loss is caused intentionally, even those insured parties who were not responsible for or associated with the loss are not entitled to coverage. The final exclusion in the standard dwelling policy is for losses caused by **governmental action**. In the context of this insurance policy, governmental action is the destruction or confiscation of covered property by a governmental agency or public authority. There is an exception to this exclusion for actions taken by a government during a fire to prevent greater damage. The standard dwelling insurance policy will not cover any loss to plants, trees, shrubs, or lawns that is the result of governmental action.

Conditions

Policy Period, Insurable Interest and Limit of Liability, and Concealment or Fraud

The first condition of the standard dwelling policy states that the policy only applies to losses that occur during the **policy period**. The second condition states that the limits of liability for any one loss will not exceed the applicable **limit of liability** or the **interest** of a person insured under this policy at the time of loss. These restrictions hold true even when more than one person has an insurable interest in the property covered. The standard dwelling policy also states that the insurance company will not provide any coverage to parties who intentionally **conceal or misrepresent** material facts, engage in **fraudulent conduct**, or make **false statements** related to the insurance policy.

Duties After Loss

The standard dwelling policy states that the insured party has certain **duties** immediately after a loss. To begin with, the insured party must provide **prompt notice** either to the insurance company or to an agent of the insurance company. The insured party is also responsible for avoiding any **further damage**, specifically by making any reasonable and required repairs. The insured party is responsible for maintaining an accurate set of **records** for these repair expenses. If the insurance company decides to investigate a claim, the insured party is responsible for **cooperating** with this investigation. The insured party should also compile an **inventory** of all the property that has been damaged. This inventory should include information about quantity, amount of loss, and actual cash value. Upon the request of the insurance company, the insured party should be prepared to display the damaged property, provide any relevant records, and submit to an examination under oath. Finally, the insured party is obliged to send a signed, sworn **proof of loss** to the insurance company within 60 days of a request for such documentation. This document should include information about the event, about any other insurance that may cover the loss, and any other relevant information

Loss Settlement, Loss to a Pair or Set, and Glass Replacement

The standard dwelling policy outlines the conditions for the **settlement of losses**. Any losses to covered property will be settled at the **actual cash value** at the time of the loss, and no more value will be supplied than the amount that is required to repair or replace the damaged property. If the property loss is a **pair or set**, the insurance company may decide whether to repair or replace the necessary part to restore the pair or set to its pre-loss value, or simply to pay the difference between the actual cash value of the property both pre-loss and post-loss. With regard to **glass**

replacement, the insurance company will promise to render sufficient coverage so that glass may be replaced with safety glazing materials when these are required by ordinance or law, so long as the original glass breakage was caused by a covered peril.

APPRAISAL

The standard dwelling policy outlines the conditions for **appraisal**, which occurs when the insurance company and the insured party disagree about the amount of loss. Either side is entitled to request an appraisal. First, each side will select an **impartial and qualified appraiser** within 20 days of the appraisal request. However, the two chosen appraisers will cooperate to select an **umpire**. If the appraisers cannot agree on an umpire within 15 days, the insurance company or the insured party may request that the umpire be selected by a judge whose jurisdiction includes the described location. Once an umpire has been selected, the appraisers will independently submit their **estimates** of the loss. If these estimates agree, then this will be the amount of the loss. If the appraisers disagree, however, the differences will be submitted to the umpire. The umpire will then make an estimate and, if this estimate agrees with either of the appraiser's estimates, this will be the final valuation of the loss. In appraisal, each party is responsible for paying its own appraiser. All other costs, including the cost of the umpire, are divided equally.

OTHER INSURANCE AND SERVICE AGREEMENT, AND SUBROGATION

The standard dwelling insurance policy outlines the conditions for property that is covered by **other insurance policies**. For instance, when the property covered by the standard dwelling policy is also covered by other fire insurance, the insurance company issuing the standard dwelling policy will only pay the proportion of a loss that is the result of a peril covered under the dwelling policy to the limit of liability applying under the dwelling policy, while also taking into consideration the total amount of covering fire insurance. If property covered by dwelling insurance is also covered by a **service agreement**, the dwelling insurance is considered to be excess to any amounts that are payable under the service agreement. Examples of service agreements are property restoration plans and home warranties. According to the principle of **subrogation**, the insured party retains the right to submit a written waiver of all rights of recovery against any person before a loss. When many rights of recovery are not waived, the insurance company is allowed to require the assignments of rights of recovery for the loss in amounts equal to whatever payment is made by the insurance company. When an assignment is sought, the insured party is required to sign and deliver any related paperwork.

SUITS BROUGHT AGAINST THE INSURANCE COMPANY, LOSS PAYMENT, AND ABANDONMENT OF PROPERTY

According to the conditions of the standard dwelling policy, no action can be brought **against the insurance company** unless there has already been full compliance with all of the terms of the policy and the legal action is initiated in the two years following the date of the loss. The insurance company reserves the right to **repair or replace** any part of damaged property with material or property of a similar kind or quality; so long as written notice of this action is given to the insured party in the 30 days after the insurance company receives the signed and sworn proof of loss. With regard to losses, all **payments** will be made by the insurance company to the named insured. Payment is typically rendered 60 days after the proof of loss is received and the insurance company has reached an agreement with the insured party. In the event that the insured party **abandons** his or her property, the insurance company is under no obligation to accept it.

MORTGAGE CLAUSE

The standard dwelling policy includes a condition that outlines the protocol for handling **mortgaged properties**. If there is a mortgagee named in the policy, then any loss payable under

30

Coverages A and B will be apportioned to the named insured and the mortgagee as is deemed appropriate. In the case of **multiple mortgagees**, the order of payments will be the same as the order of precedence for the mortgages. The denial of a claim by the named insured does not necessarily indicate the denial of the mortgagee's claim, so long as the mortgagee has met certain conditions: namely, the mortgagee must have notified the insurance company of any changes in ownership, occupancy, or risk; must have paid any outstanding premiums; and must have submitted a signed, sworn statement of loss within 60 days of receiving a demand for this statement. The insurance company is obliged to give the mortgagee at least 10 days of notice before declining to cancel or fail to renew the policy. Finally, **subrogation** will not prevent the mortgagee from recovering the full amount of his or her claim.

NO BENEFITS TO BAILEES, AND CANCELLATION

In the standard dwelling policy, the insurance company will not provide any coverage or acknowledge any assignment that provides benefit to a party that **stores or transports** property for a fee. If the insured party wishes to **cancel** the policy, this may be done by returning it to the insurance company or notifying the insurance company of the effective date of cancellation. If the insurance company wishes to cancel the policy, it must notify the insured party in writing of the effective date of cancellation. The cancellation notice needs only to be mailed to be considered as delivered. In order for the policy to be canceled by the insurance company, however, certain criteria must be met. First, if the insured party does not pay the premium, the insurance company may cancel the policy with 10 days of notice.

CANCELLATION (PART TWO)

In the **first 60 days** of a new policy, the insurance company may cancel for any reason, but must give 10 days of notice. Policies that extend for more than one year may be canceled upon their **anniversary** for any reason, but the insurance company must give at least 30 days of notice. Once any policy has been in effect for at least 60 days, it may be canceled if there is a **substantial change in risk**, or if a **material misrepresentation of fact** is discovered. If the policy is canceled, any premium remaining until the expiration date of the policy will be prorated and refunded. This refund will be provided by the insurance company within a reasonable time after the effective date of cancellation.

NONRENEWAL AND LIBERALIZATION

The standard dwelling policy contains a **nonrenewal clause**, which asserts the right of the insurance company to decide not to renew the policy. Nonrenewal may be indicated by providing written notice to the insured party at least 30 days before the policy's expiration. When the insurance company makes a change to the policy that broadens coverage without increasing the premium, in what is known as **policy liberalization**, the change applies to the existing policy as soon as it becomes law in the state of jurisdiction. The liberalization clause does not obtain in situations where the policy revision includes both restrictions and expansions of coverage.

WAIVER OR CHANGE OF POLICY PROVISIONS, ASSIGNMENT, AND DEATH

In the standard dwelling policy, any **waivers or provision changes** must be presented in writing in order to be considered valid. Any request by the insurance company for examination, inspection, or appraisal does not constitute a waiver of the insurance company's rights. Any **assignments** of the insurance policy will not be considered valid unless they come with the written consent of the insurance company. Upon the **death** of the insured party, the insurance company will provide coverage to the legal representatives of the insured, though only insofar as it relates to the covered property of the deceased. Any party with temporary custody of the deceased's property will be covered until a legal representative can be appointed.

NUCLEAR HAZARD CLAUSE, RECOVERED PROPERTY, VOLCANIC ERUPTION PERIOD, AND LOSS PAYABLE CLAUSE

The standard dwelling policy defines **nuclear hazard** as any controlled or uncontrolled nuclear reaction, radioactive contamination, or radiation. Any loss related to nuclear hazard will not be defined as loss from smoke, fire, or explosion, even if one of these perils is involved in the event. The standard dwelling policy does not apply to losses resulting from nuclear hazard. In the event that either the insurance company or the insured party **recovers property** for which payment has already been made under the policy, the other party should be notified as soon as possible. The insured party will have the option of either receiving the property or retaining the loss payment and seating the property to the insurance company. In the standard dwelling policy, any **volcanic eruptions** that occur within a three-day period are considered to be a single eruption. The final condition of the standard dwelling policy is that any person listed as a **loss payee** for certain property on the declarations page is defined as an insured with respect to the property, and is therefore entitled to notification of policy cancellation or nonrenewal.

Homeowners Policy

Standard Homeowners' Policy

SECTION I (PROPERTY COVERAGES)
COVERAGE A (DWELLING) AND COVERAGE B (OTHER STRUCTURES)

Section I of the standard homeowners' policy describes the various property coverages. **Coverage A** is for **dwellings**. The insurance company promises to provide insurance coverage for the dwelling found on the residence premises listed on the declarations page. Dwelling coverage applies as well to any structures attached to the dwelling. Coverage A also applies to any materials and supplies on or adjacent to the residence premises which are used to create, adjust, or repair the dwelling or other structures on the residence premises. It should be noted that Coverage A does not apply to land. **Coverage B** is for **other structures**. These include any structures located on the residence premises and separated from the dwelling by a clear space. Structures that are connected to the dwelling by a fence or utility line are considered to be other structures. Coverage B does not apply to other structures that are used for business, or which are rented to a person who is not a tenant of the dwelling. The limit of liability for Coverage B will not be greater than 10 percent of the limit of liability for Coverage A. However, the use of Coverage B does not reduce the limits of liability under Coverage A.

COVERAGE C (PERSONAL PROPERTY)

Coverage C of the standard homeowners' policy applies to **personal property**. The insurance company promises to cover any personal property that is used or owned by the insured party regardless of where it is located. Moreover, the insurance company will cover, at the request of the insured, any personal property owned by others while it is on the residence premises of the insured, or any personal property owned by a guest of the residence owned by the insured. Any personal property that is usually located at an insured's residence but not the residence premises is subject to a smaller limit of liability: 10 percent of the limit of liability for Coverage C, or $1000, whichever is greater. If the insured party acquires a new residence, personal property is not subject to this limitation for the first 30 days after property is moved into the house.

SPECIAL LIMITS OF LIABILITY FOR COVERAGE C (PERSONAL PROPERTY)

An insurance company typically will outline some **special limits of liability to Coverage C**. These limits do not increase the overall Coverage C limit of liability. To begin with, there is a $200 limit of liability on money, bank notes, gold other than goldware, silver other than silverware, platinum, coins, and medals. There is a $1000 limit of liability on securities, accounts, deeds, letters of credit, notes other than banknotes, personal records, manuscripts, passports, stamps, and tickets. This limited liability applies regardless of whether the documents reside on paper or computer software. There is a $1000 limit of liability on watercraft, including related outboard engines, equipment, furnishings, motors, and trailers. There is a $1000 limit of liability on trailers not used with watercraft. There is also a $1000 limit of liability on loss related to the theft of jewelry, furs, watches, and precious and semiprecious stones.

The list of special limits of liability for Coverage C continues by declaring that there is a $2000 limit of liability for the loss of firearms by theft. There is also a $2500 limit of liability for loss by theft of silverware, pewterware, and any silver-plated or gold-plated ware. There is also a $2500 limit of liability on property located on the residence premises but used for business purposes. There is a $250 limit of liability on property located away from the residence premises and used for business.

33

There is a $1000 limit of liability for losses to electronic apparatus, like antennas, tapes, or discs, while in or on a motor vehicle. Finally, there is a $1000 limit of liability for loss to other electronic apparatus on the residence premises if it is to be used for business purposes.

Property Not Covered Under Coverage C

The standard homeowners' policy will include a brief list of the property that is **not covered under Coverage C**. To begin with, the insurance company typically will not cover any articles that are separately described and subject to specific coverage in this policy or any other insurance policy. Coverage C does not apply to animals, fish, or birds. Coverage C does not apply to motor vehicles, vehicle equipment, or vehicle accessories. It does not apply to any electrical apparatus that is designed to be powered by the electrical system of a motor vehicle. It does not cover aircraft or related parts. It does not cover the property of any boarders, roomers, or other tenants. It does not cover any property located in an apartment that is typically rented out. Finally, it does not cover any business data, including both electronic and paper records.

Coverage D (Loss of Use)

Coverage D of the standard homeowners' policy pertains to the **loss of use**. It begins by explaining that the limit of liability for coverage is the sum total of all the coverage that is subsequently described. When a loss covered under coverage D makes the residence unfit for habitation, the insurance company promises to pay either **additional living expenses** or **fair rental value**. Additional living expenses are any necessary increases in expenses incurred by the insured in order to maintain the normal standard of living within the household. The fair rental value is the agreed-upon rental price for the part of the residence that cannot be used, less any expenses that will not continue to be incurred while the structure is uninhabitable. If the structure damaged is not the primary residence of the policyholder, fair rental value may not be obtained. Whether the insured receives additional living expenses or the fair rental value, the payment rendered will be for the minimum amount of time within which it is possible to replace or repair the damage, or for the insured to relocate.

Coverage D (Loss of Use) of Premises Rented to Others

The insurance company will provide **fair rental value** for loss of use to any portion of the residence premises that is rented to others. The amount of the fair rental value will be reduced by the value of any expenses that will not continue to be incurred while the premises are not fit to live in. Again, payment under coverage D will be made either for the residents to **relocate** or for the minimum amount of time necessary to **repair or replace** the damaged areas. There is also some coverage available if a civil authority prohibits the owner from using the residence premises as a result of some direct damage to neighboring premises. In order for this coverage to apply, the direct damage to the neighboring premises must be the result of a peril insured against by this policy. When payments are made as a result of this prohibition by a civil authority, they will last two weeks at the most. Coverage D will not provide payments to cover loss or expense caused by the cancellation of a lease or agreement.

Additional Coverages
Debris Removal

In addition to the four general areas of coverage provided by a standard homeowners' policy, the insurance company will typically offer some additional coverage for **debris removal**. Specifically, the insurance company will promise to pay any reasonable expense for the removal of the debris of covered property if the loss was caused by a peril named in the policy. The standard policy will also promise to pay for the removal of ash, dust, or particles when they derive from a volcanic eruption. Payment for debris removal is included in the limits of liability as they apply to the damaged

34

property. If the expense for removal of debris results in the limit of liability exceeding, the insured party may be eligible for an extra five percent of the limit of liability to be devoted exclusively to debris removal. In a similar fashion, the insurance company promises to pay up to $500 of reasonable expenses for the removal from the residence premises of any trees or neighbor's trees knocked down by windstorm, hail, ice, snow, or sleet. These payments will only be made, however, if the fallen tree damages a covered structure.

REASONABLE REPAIRS AND TREES, SHRUBS, AND OTHER PLANTS

The standard homeowners' policy will promise some additional payments to cover the costs of making **reasonable repairs** to protect against further damage after covered property has already been damaged. When these protective measures include repair to other damaged property, it will be necessary for the other damaged property to be covered by the given policy, and for the damage to have been caused by an applicable peril insured against. It should be noted that coverage for reasonable repairs does not increase the limit of liability for the covered property, and does not relieve the insured party or their duties to prevent further loss. With regard to **trees, shrubs, and other plants** on the residence premises, the insurance company will typically cover them for loss due to the following causes: fire, lightning, explosion, riot, aircraft, vandalism, and malicious mischief or theft. Payments for plants will not exceed five percent of the limit of liability for the dwelling, and no more than $500 will be paid for damage to any one plant.

FIRE DEPARTMENT SERVICE CHARGE AND PROPERTY REMOVED

Among the additional coverages offered as part of the standard homeowners' policy, the insurance company will typically offer up to $500 for any charges incurred because of a visit by the fire department to protect covered property from a peril insured against. **Fire department service charges** are not covered when the residence premises is located within the jurisdiction of the responding fire department. There is no deductible applied to the fire department service charge coverage, which is considered to be additional insurance. Covered property will be covered for damages caused by perils insured against while being **removed** from the premises. The standard limit of liability continues to apply to the property being removed.

CREDIT CARD, FUNDS TRANSFER CARD, FORGERY, AND COUNTERFEIT MONEY

Among the additional coverages offered as part of the standard homeowners' policy, the insurance company will typically offer $500 worth of coverage for losses related to credit cards, funds transfer cards, forgery, and counterfeit money. Specifically, the insurance company will promise to pay any legal obligation incurred by the insured party related to the theft or unauthorized use of **credit cards** in the name of the insured. The insurance company will also pay $500 for losses resulting from the theft or unauthorized use of a **funds transfer card** registered in the insured's name. The insurance company will provide identical coverage if the insured loses money because of **forgery, check fraud, or good faith acceptance of counterfeit United States or Canadian currency**. This coverage will not be extended if the credit card or funds transfer card was used by a resident of the insured's household, by anyone who was entrusted with either type of card, or if the insured fails to comply with all terms and conditions of the card issuer.

DEFENSE OF CREDIT CARD, FUNDS TRANSFER CARD, FORGERY, AND COUNTERFEIT MONEY DAMAGE PAYMENTS

With regard to coverage for losses related to credit cards, fund transfer cards, forgery, and counterfeit money, losses that result from multiple acts committed by the same person are classified as a **single loss**. The standard homeowners' policy typically will not provide coverage for any losses that arise during **business operations**. This coverage is considered to be additional insurance, and will not be subject to a deductible. The insurance company reserves the right to

investigate and settle any claims related to these losses. The responsibility of the insurance company to investigate and defend the claim is terminated once the **limit of liability** has been exhausted. In situations where damages are sought from the insured party for liability related to credit cards or funds transfer card coverage, the insurance company will provide a defense at its own expense. Finally, the insurance company reserves the right to pay for the defense of the insured or the bank of the insured to secure payment related to forgery coverage.

LOSS ASSESSMENT

In the additional coverages portion of the first section of the standard homeowners' policy, the insurance company will typically promise some payment for **loss assessment**. It is common for the insurance company to offer a maximum of $1000 for the insured party's share of loss assessment charged during the policy period if this assessment is related to direct loss to the covered property and the loss was caused by a peril insured against under Coverage A other than earthquake or volcanic eruption. The $1000 maximum applies to any single loss, regardless of how many assessments are conducted. Loss assessments that are charged to the insured party by a government are not covered by the standard homeowners' policy.

COLLAPSE

The standard homeowners' policy provides only limited coverage for the **collapse** of covered property. The standard policy will only cover the collapse of the building if it is caused by one of the **perils insured against in Coverage C** (personal property) or one of the following: hidden decay; hidden insect or vermin damage; the weight of possessions, equipment, animals, or people; the weight of rain; or the use of defective materials or methods during the construction or renovation process. The standard homeowners' policy will not cover collapse-related damages to a swimming pool, awning, septic tank, or retaining wall unless the loss is those directly related to building collapse. Coverage for collapse does not expand the limit of liability applied to the damaged covered property.

GLASS OR SAFETY GLAZING MATERIAL

The standard homeowners' policy offers some special additional coverage for **glass or safety glazing material**. The insurance company will typically promise to cover the breakage of glass or safety glazing that is part of a storm door, storm window, or covered building. The standard policy will also cover damage to covered property by broken glass or safety glazing material that originates in a storm door, storm window, or covered building. If the glass or safety glazing material breaks on the dwelling on the residence premises, and the dwelling has not been occupied for at least 30 days, the loss will not be covered. Also, in the calculation of the loss related to broken glass, the value of the broken glass will be calculated according to the cost of replacement glazing. Coverage for glass or safety glazing material does not increase the limit of liability applicable to the damaged property.

LANDLORD'S FURNISHINGS

Among the additional coverages offered as part of the standard homeowners' policy, the insurance company will typically offer to pay a maximum of $2500 for damage to any appliances, carpeting, or other household furnishings in an **apartment** on the residence premises that is frequently rented by an insured party. In order for this coverage to apply, the loss must be caused by one of the following perils: fire or lightning; windstorm or hail; explosion; riot or civil commotion; aircraft; vehicles; smoke; vandalism or malicious mischief; falling objects; weight of snow, ice, or sleet; accidental discharge or overflow of water or steam; sudden and accidental tearing apart, cracking, burning, or bulging of a steam or hot water heating system; freezing of a plumbing system; sudden and accidental damage from artificially generated electrical current; or volcanic eruption.

PERILS INSURED AGAINST

COVERAGE A (DWELLING) AND COVERAGE B (OTHER STRUCTURES)

The standard homeowners' policy will include a comprehensive description of the **perils** against which insurance coverage is provided for each aspect of the policy. With regard to Coverages A and B, the insurance company only provides coverage for the **direct loss to property**. Coverages A and B do not insure for loss involving collapse or loss due to the freezing, leaking, or discharge of a plumbing, heating, air conditioning, or fire-protective sprinkler system if the dwelling is vacant unless the insured party has taken reasonable steps to shut off the water supply and maintain heat in the dwelling. The insurance company will not provide coverage for loss due to freezing, thawing, or pressure to a fence, pavement, swimming pool, patio, retaining wall, or dock. The insurance company will not cover loss due to theft in a dwelling under construction, including the theft of construction materials. The insurance company will not pay for costs related to vandalism and malicious mischief at a dwelling that has been vacant for a minimum of 30 consecutive days.

In the standard homeowners' policy, the insurance company will **decline** to pay for any loss due to deterioration, marring, or wear and tear. The insurance also declines to cover any loss due to mechanical breakdown, latent defect, or inherent vice. Damage caused by smog, rust, or any other mold, corrosion, or rot is not covered by the standard homeowners' policy. Moreover, the insurance company typically will decline to pay damages for the smoke from industrial or agricultural smudging operations. The insurance company will often decline to pay damages for the dispersal, discharge, release, or escape of pollutants unless this situation was caused by a peril insured against under Coverage C. The standard homeowners' policy will not cover damage caused by animals owned or kept by an insured, though if these animals (or insects) cause damage to a water system and the water subsequently causes damage, the water damage may be covered.

COVERAGE C (PERSONAL PROPERTY)

With regard to Coverage C (personal property), the insurance company will typically cover any **direct physical loss** to property caused by fire or lightning. Coverage C will also apply to damage caused by windstorm or hail, but not by rain, sleet, snow, sand, or dust unless one of these forces enters the building through a hole created by wind or hail. The **personal property coverage** applies to losses due to explosion, riot or civil commotion, aircraft, vandalism or malicious mischief, and any smoke damage not caused by industrial operations or agricultural smudging. This coverage applies to losses from theft as well as attempted theft and likely theft. Theft loss is not covered if the theft was committed by an insured or was from a dwelling under construction. In addition, loss to theft is not covered if it occurs off of the residence premises.

Personal property coverage extends to losses caused by falling objects, although it does not apply to property losses caused by falling objects unless the roof or external walls of the building were damaged by the falling object initially. Coverage C applies to losses from the weight of ice, snow, or sleet, including when these factors damage property within a building. Coverage C applies to losses from the accidental discharge or overflow of steam or water from a plumbing, heating, or air-conditioning system, though it does not apply to loss to the system itself. Coverage C will also extend to the sudden and accidental tearing apart, bulging, cracking, or burning of a steam or hot water heating system, or of an air-conditioning system. Coverage C applies to the freezing of plumbing, heating, or air-conditioning systems, though it will not apply if the dwelling is unoccupied unless the insured can prove that he or she has used reasonable care to shut off and drain the water supply and to maintain heat in the building. Coverage C will apply to losses caused by sudden and accidental damage from artificially generated electrical current, and it will also apply to losses related to volcanic eruption.

37

EXCLUSIONS

ORDINANCE OR LAW AND EARTH MOVEMENT

Section I of the standard homeowners' policy continues by listing some of the exclusions to coverage. The insurance company will not cover any loss caused directly or indirectly by any excluded items. To begin with, the insurance company declines to cover losses relating to the enforcement of any **ordinance or law**, including those that apply to the repair, construction, or demolition of a building or other structure. There are some homeowners' policies that make a specific point of offering this coverage, but it is not offered in the standard policy. The typical homeowners' policy will refuse to cover damage related to **earth movement**, a generic phrase that includes earthquake, tremors related to volcanic eruption, mine subsidence, mudflow, or landslide. The only exceptions to this exclusion are when earth movements cause direct loss resulting from fire, explosion, or the breakage of glass or safety glazing material.

WATER DAMAGE AND POWER FAILURE

The standard homeowners' policy declines to ensure for losses directly or indirectly caused by **water damage**, an umbrella phrase that includes flood, overflow of a nearby body of water, tidal water, or waves. This exclusion also applies to water damage in situations where the water is driven by wind. The standard homeowners' policy will not cover water damage from water that is backed up in sewers or drains, or which is overflowing from a sump. The insurance company will also decline to pay for loss caused by subsurface water, including water that leaks through a building or foundation. However, if water damage leads to direct loss by theft, explosion, or fire, this loss will be covered. The insurance company will also typically decline to pay for losses due to the **failure of power or other utility service**, assuming that this failure takes place elsewhere than the residence premises. If, however, a peril insured against occurs on the residence premises, only the ensuing loss will be eligible for insurance coverage.

NEGLECT, WAR, NUCLEAR HAZARD, AND INTENTIONAL LOSS

In the standard homeowners' policy, the insurance company will decline to pay for losses that are the result of **neglect**. For the purposes of this policy, neglect is defined as the failure to use all reasonable means to preserve and maintain property during and after the event precipitating the loss. The standard homeowners' policy also contains an exclusion for **war**, meaning that the insured will not be covered for losses resulting from any military action or discharge of a military weapon. The insurance company will decline to cover loss caused by **nuclear hazard**. Finally, the standard homeowners' policy will contain an exclusion for **intentional loss**, which is defined as a loss that comes about because of an act committed by or at the behest of the insured and with the intent to cause the loss.

WEATHER CONDITIONS, ACTS, OR DECISIONS

There are some special exclusions in the standard homeowners' policy for the property described in Coverages A (dwelling) and B (other structures). To begin with, the standard homeowners' policy will exclude losses suffered to such property because of **weather conditions**. The weather conditions exclusion only applies, however, if the weather conditions combined with one of the other excluded sources of loss. Property mentioned in Coverages A and B is also not covered for losses resulting from **acts or decisions**, including an unreasonable failure to act, whether the party in question is a person, organization, or government agency. Finally, property described in Coverages A and B will not be insured for losses resulting from **faulty, defective, or inadequate planning, development, surveying, or zoning**. This property will not be insured against losses relating to **defective or faulty maintenance or construction materials**. This last exclusion applies to the property described in Coverages A or B, regardless of whether it is on or off the residence premises.

CONDITIONS

INSURABLE INTEREST, LOSS TO A PAIR OR SET, AND GLASS REPLACEMENT

The final part of the first section of the standard homeowners' policy outlines some basic conditions. To begin with, the insurance company will declare that no matter how many parties have **insurable interest** in a covered piece of property, the insurance company will not be liable for anything more than the applicable limit of liability, and will not be liable to the insured for any amount more than the insured's interest at the time of the loss. If the insured party should suffer a **loss to a pair or set of items**, the insurance company has two options: it may either pay the difference between the actual cash value of the property before and after the loss, or may repair or replace any part if that will restore the pair or set to its pre-loss value. If the insured suffers a loss because of **glass damage** caused by a peril insured against, the amount of payments will depend on the value of the safety glazing materials required by ordinance or law.

DUTIES OF THE INSURED AFTER LOSS

The standard homeowners' policy outlines some specific **duties** for the insured party after a loss. To begin with, the insured party must immediately **notify** the insurance company or its agent. If the loss is due to theft, the insured party must immediately notify the police as well. If the loss is related to credit card or funds transfer card coverage, the insured party must immediately notify the credit card or funds transfer card company. The insured party is also responsible for **protecting** the property from any more damage. When the property must be repaired immediately, the insured party should make all **reasonable and necessary repairs** and should maintain a comprehensive and accurate **record** of the repair expenses. The insured party is responsible for maintaining a complete **inventory** of all damaged personal property, including the actual cash value, quantity, description, and amount of loss.

After a loss, the insured party may be required at the request of the insurance company to **show the damaged property**, or to provide the insurance company with any **pertinent records or documents**. The insured party may be required to submit to an **examination** under oath, and may be required to sign a **statement** given under oath. Finally, the insurance company may legally request that the insured party send a signed and sworn **proof of loss** within 60 days. A proof of loss should describe when and how the loss occurred; the interest of the insured in the property; any other insurance that covers the loss; any changes in title or occupancy that have occurred during the term of the policy; specifications of damaged buildings, as well as detailed repair estimates; an inventory of the damaged personal property; any receipts related to additional living expenses or fair rental value loss; and, if the loss is related to credit card, funds transfer card, forgery, or counterfeit money coverage, sufficient evidence or affidavit to support the claim and indicate the amount and cause of loss.

LOSS SETTLEMENT

The conditions portion of the first section of the standard homeowners' policy includes a comprehensive description of the protocol for **loss settlement**. With regard to personal property, structures other than buildings, and awnings, outdoor equipment, and household appliances, the insurance company will provide coverage at the **actual value** at the time of loss, so long as this is not in excess of the amount necessary to repair or replace the property. The buildings listed under Coverages A (dwellings) and B (other structures) will be covered to the extent of replacement cost, without any deduction for depreciation. However, there are some contingencies that depend on the value of the insurance policy. If the value of the insurance policy is at least 80 percent of the full

39

replacement cost of the building immediately before the damage occurs, then the insurance company will pay whatever cost is necessary to repair or replace the property, applying the deductible but not deducting for depreciation. However, this payment will not exceed the smallest of the following three values: the applicable limit of liability for the building, the replacement cost of the damaged component of the building, and the amount actually required to repair or replace the building damage.

The amount of **replacement cost** that will be paid for buildings under Coverage A or B is subject to some conditions. If the value of the insurance policy at the time of the loss is less than 80 percent of the full replacement cost of the building prior to the loss, then the insurance company will pay the larger of the following two amounts: the actual cash value of the damaged building part, or the proportion of the cost to fix the damaged building part after application of deductible but before depreciation, up to 80 percent of the building's replacement cost. In order to make this judgment, of course, it may be necessary to determine the value of insurance that is equal to 80 percent of the full replacement cost of the building just before the loss. In this calculation, the insured should not include the value of excavations, foundations, piers, or underground pipes, wiring, or drains.

In the loss settlement portion of Section I of the standard homeowners' policy, the insurance company typically declares that it will not pay any more than the **actual cash value of damage** before the replacement or repair is complete. After the repair or replacement is complete, the insurance company will settle the loss according to the provisions already described in the **loss settlement section**. The only exception to this policy is when the cost to repair or replace the damage is both less than $2500 and less than five percent of the amount of insurance on the building. When this is the case, the insurance company will settle the loss according to the above provisions even before repair or replacement is complete. The final provision of the loss settlement section states that the insured party may disregard any of the above procedures and make a claim based on actual cash value. When the insured selects this option, he or she may also claim additional liability in the 180 days after the loss.

APPRAISAL

In the event that the insured party and the insurance company disagree about the value of the loss, there is a specific protocol for **appraisal**. Either side is legally entitled to request an appraisal. When an appraisal is to occur, each side has 20 days to select a competent **appraiser**. The two appraisers will meet and choose an **umpire**. If the two appraisers are unable to agree upon an umpire, after 15 days the parties may agree to have the umpire selected by a judge in the court of record in the state in which the residence premises is located. Once all of the parties are named, each appraiser will estimate the loss. If the appraisers agree about the value of the loss, both parties are bound to their decision. If the appraisers disagree, the umpire will render a verdict. If any two of the three agree on the value, both parties will be bound to it. Each party will be responsible for paying its appraiser, and the other costs of appraisal and the umpire will be split.

OTHER INSURANCE, SUITS AGAINST THE INSURANCE COMPANY, INSURANCE COMPANY OPTIONS, AND LOSS PAYMENT POLICY

In the standard homeowners' policy, the insurance company will typically assert that, if **other insurance policies** cover the damage covered by this policy, the insurance company will only pay a **proportion** of the loss equal to the proportion of the limit of liability to the total limits of liability for insurance covering this loss. **Legal suits** may not be brought against the insurance company unless all policy provisions have been complied with and the suit is brought within one year of the loss. The insurance company will also assert that it retains the right to **repair or replace** any part of the damaged property with like property, so long as the insurance company gives written notice no more than 30 days after receiving a signed, sworn proof of loss. All losses will be adjusted with the insured party. Unless some other party is named in the policy and is entitled to receive payment, losses will be paid directly to the named insured. Losses are payable 60 days after the insurance company receives the proof of loss and reaches an agreement with the insured, observes the entry of a final judgment, or receives an appraisal award.

ABANDONMENT OF PROPERTY AND MORTGAGE CLAUSE

The standard homeowners' policy asserts that the insurance company does not need to accept any property that has been **abandoned** by an insured. This policy will also typically include a **mortgage clause**. According to this clause, whenever a mortgagee is named in the policy, all losses payable under Coverages A or B will be paid to the mortgagee and the insured party according to fair amount of interest. When more than one mortgagee is named, the order of payments is the same as the order indicated on the mortgages. It should be noted that the denial of claims made by the insured will not necessarily mean that the claims of the mortgagee will be denied. However, in order for a mortgagee to have a claim validated despite the denial of the insured's claim, the mortgagee needs to notify the insurance company about any ownership change or alteration in risk. The mortgagee must also pay any premiums the insured has neglected, and must submit a signed, sworn statement of loss no more than 60 days after receiving notice that the insured has failed to do so.

COVERAGE OF NO BENEFIT TO THE BAILEE, NUCLEAR HAZARD CLAUSE, AND PROTOCOL FOR RECOVERED PROPERTY

The standard homeowners' policy asserts that the insurance company will not recognize any assignment or grant any coverage benefiting a person or organization that is **handling or storing property for a fee**. In addition, the standard homeowners' policy will state that losses attributable to **nuclear hazard** are not covered. The loss caused by nuclear hazard is considered separate from losses caused by smoke, fire, or explosion. Finally, the standard homeowners' policy will assert that if the insured or the insurance company should **recover** any property for which payment has already been made under this coverage, the recovering party is required to notify the other as soon as possible. The insured party may decide whether the property should be returned to or retained by him or her or the insurance company. If the insured decides to take possession of the recovered property, the payments made thus far will be adjusted based on the amount received for the recovered property.

SECTION II (LIABILITY COVERAGES)
COVERAGE E (PERSONAL LIABILITY)

Coverage E of the standard homeowners' policy applies to **personal liability**. In the typical formulation, the insurance company promises that, if a claim or suit is brought against the insured because of bodily injury or property damage caused by some event covered by this policy, the insurance company will pay damages up to the **limit of liability**. Any **prejudgment interest** awarded against the insured party is considered to be part of these damages. The insurance company also promises to pay for the **defense** of the insured party. The legal representation will be selected by the insurance company. The insurance company retains the right to investigate and settle claims and suits. However, the responsibility of the insurance company to investigate and settle suits terminates once the limit of liability is reached.

COVERAGE F (MEDICAL PAYMENTS TO OTHERS)

In the standard homeowners' policy, Coverage F relates to **medical payments to others**. Typically, the insurance company will promise to cover any necessary medical expenses that are incurred or called for by a doctor within three years of a **bodily injury**. Under the heading medical expenses,

The insurance company includes medical, surgical, x-ray, dental, ambulance, hospital, professional nursing, prosthetic devices, and funeral services. Coverage F does not apply to payments made for the insured or for regular residents of his or her household unless these residents are **employees** of the household. Generally, this coverage applies to people who are injured on the insured location, or people who are injured off the insured location but whose bodily injury is caused by the activities of the insured or in some way relates to conditions on the insured location.

EXCLUSIONS FOR COVERAGES E AND F

Section II includes some **exclusions** that apply to Coverages E and F. To begin with, these coverages do not apply to bodily injury or property damage that is **expected or intended** by the insured party. They also do not apply to injury or property damage that stems from **insurance business activities**. They do not apply to any injuries or property damage arising out of the **rental** of any part of the property by the insured. These coverages do not apply to injury or damage related to the provision of **professional services**. They also do not apply to injuries or damage related to a premises that is owned or rented by the insured, but is not itself an **insured location**. Coverages E and F do not apply to injury or damage related to the ownership, maintenance, use, or transport of **motor vehicles**. Finally, these coverages do not apply to injury or damage related to the ownership, maintenance, use, or transport of a **watercraft**.

Coverages E and F will not apply to any bodily injury or property damage arising from the use, maintenance, or transport of an **aircraft**. They also will not apply to any injury or damage caused directly or indirectly by **war** or other military action. They will not apply to any injury or property damage resulting from the transmission of a **communicable disease** by the insured party. These coverages will not apply to any injury or property damage related to physical **abuse**, mental abuse, sexual molestation, or corporal punishment. Finally, Coverages E and F will not apply to any damages or injury related to the use, sale, production, possession, or transfer of a **controlled substance**. Controlled substances are those designated as such by federal food and drug laws.

EXCLUSIONS ONLY FOR COVERAGE E

There are certain exclusions that apply only to **Coverage E** (personal liability). To begin with, Coverage E does not apply to any liability related to a **loss assessment** charged against the insured party as a member of a community, association, or corporation of property owners. It also does not apply to any liability taken on by the insured under any **contract or agreement**, except for written contracts that relate directly to the ownership, use, or maintenance of an insured location, or in which the insured party assumes liability for others before a particular event. Finally, Coverage E does not apply to any liability for **property damage** to property owned by the insured, and it does not apply to liability for property damage related to property occupied by, rented to, or used by the insured.

Coverage E does not apply to liability for any bodily injury suffered by a person who is eligible to receive **mandatory or voluntary benefits** from the insured based on occupational disease law, non-occupational disability law, or workers' compensation law. Coverage E also does not apply to liability for any bodily injury or property damage when the injury or damage is also covered by a **nuclear energy liability policy**, or when the injury or damage would also be covered by a nuclear energy liability policy were the limit of liability not exhausted for the policy. Nuclear energy liability policies are those issued by the Mutual Atomic Energy Liability Underwriters, the American Nuclear Insurers, or the Nuclear Insurance Association of Canada.

EXCLUSIONS ONLY FOR COVERAGE F

In the standard homeowners' policy, there are a few exclusions that apply only to **Coverage F** (medical payments to others). This coverage does not apply to bodily injuries suffered by residence employees when these employees are injured **away from the insured location** and the injury does not arise out of the course of the employee's normal employment. Also, Coverage F will not apply for injuries to any person who is eligible to receive **mandatory or voluntary benefits** under an occupational disease law, workers' compensation law, or non-occupational disability law. Coverage F also will not apply for injuries resulting from **radioactive contamination, nuclear radiation, or nuclear reaction**. Finally, Coverage F will not apply to any injury suffered by a person who regularly resides on the insured location but is **not a residence employee**.

ADDITIONAL COVERAGES

CLAIM EXPENSES

Section II of the standard homeowners' policy describes some additional areas of coverage. All of these areas of coverage are in addition to the limits of liability. To begin with, the insurance company promises to cover any expenses incurred during the **defense of a suit** by the insurance company. The insurance company also promises to cover any costs that are **taxed** against an insured during the defense of a suit. The insurance company will also promise to pay for the premiums on **bonds** required for a suit being defended by the insurance company. However, the insurance company will not pay more than the bond amounts indicated in Coverage E. The insurance company also will promise to pay for any **reasonable expenses** incurred by the insured at the request of the insurance company. The insurance company will even pay for **loss of pay** up to $50 per day, so long as the work time missed by the insured is due to cooperation with a defense or suit brought by the insurance company. Finally, the insurance company will promise to pay **interest** on the entire judgment accruing after the entry of the judgment but before payment has been made.

FIRST AID EXPENSES AND PROPERTY DAMAGE OF OTHERS

In **Section II** of the standard homeowners' policy, the insurance company will typically promise to pay any expenses for **first aid** required by other people, if the injuries are covered by the policy and caused by the insured. The insurance company will not pay for first aid for any insured party. If the insured **damages the property** of others, the insurance company will promise to pay up to $500 for each occurrence. However, the insurance company will not pay for damage that was caused intentionally, and will only pay to the extent of the amount recoverable under Section I of the policy. The insurance company will not make these payments for damages to any property owned or rented by the insured, and will not make payments for any damages arising out of activities related to the insurance business. Finally, the insurance company will not make these payments for any property damage arising out of the use, ownership, or maintenance of a motor vehicle, watercraft, or aircraft.

LOSS ASSESSMENT

According to the standard homeowners' policy, the insurance company will pay a maximum of $1000 for the insured party's share of a **loss assessment** charged by an association or corporation of property owners. However, it is required that the loss assessment be the result of bodily injury or property damage covered by Section II of the policy, or that the loss assessment be the result of liability on the part of a director, officer, or trustee acting in that capacity. No matter how many assessments are performed on the property, the insurance company will pay no more than $1000 for any loss arising out of a single accident, even if this accident entails continuous or repeated exposure to the same harmful condition.

LIMIT OF LIABILITY AND SEVERABILITY OF INSURANCE

The conditions portion of **Section II** begins by discussing the **limit of liability**. According to this section, the total amount of liability under Coverage E for any single occurrence will be the limit of liability indicated on the **declarations page**. This is true regardless of how many insured parties are involved, how many claims are made, and how many people are injured. Any bodily injury or property damage that results from a single accident or repeated exposure to the same harmful conditions will be treated as a single occurrence. Similarly, the total amount of liability available under Coverage F for all medical expenses payable to a single person because of one accident will be no more than the limit of liability for Coverage F indicated on the declarations page. The second condition states that this insurance policy applies **separately** to each insured party, though this will not increase the limit of liability related to any single occurrence.

DUTIES AFTER LOSS

The conditions provision of **Section II** of the standard homeowners' policy outlines the duties of the insured after a **loss**. To begin with, the insured is responsible for providing the insurance company with **prompt notice** of the accident or occurrence. This written notice should indicate the identity of the insured party and the policy, and should provide any available information about the time, location, and circumstances of the accident or occurrence. The written notice should also include the names and addresses of any witnesses and claimants. The insured party should also immediately **forward** any notices, summons, demands, or other processes related to the accident or occurrence. If the insurance company requests it, the insured should be prepared to **cooperate** in the settlement or in the investigation or pursuance of court cases related to the event. If damages are covered under damage-to-the-property-of-others coverage, the insured party is responsible for **exhibiting** the damaged property if possible, and then submitting a **sworn statement of loss** to the insurance company within 60 days. Finally, the insured is not allowed to assume any obligations or incur any expenses besides **first aid** at the moment of injury.

DUTIES OF AN INJURED PERSON AND PAYMENT OF CLAIMS UNDER COVERAGE F

Any party injured in an accident or occurrence that is covered by **Coverage F** (medical payments to others) has certain duties, according to the standard homeowners' policy. First, the injured party (or someone acting on behalf of the injured party) should provide **written proof of the claim** as soon as it is practical to do so. If required by law, this written proof should be made under oath. The injured party should also grant the insurance company authorization to receive any copies of pertinent **medical records and reports**. Finally, if the insurance company requests it, the injured party must be prepared to submit to **physical examination** by the insurance company's doctor whenever the insurance company requests it. As for the payment of claims under Coverage F, it is important to note that any payment made under this coverage does not constitute an admission of liability by either an insured party or the insurance company.

SUITS BROUGHT AGAINST THE INSURANCE COMPANY, BANKRUPTCY OF AN INSURED PARTY, AND OTHER INSURANCE (COVERAGE E: PERSONAL LIABILITY)

According to the conditions in **Section II** of the standard homeowners' policy, no legal action may be brought against the insurance company unless there has been complete and total **compliance** with the provisions of the policy. Moreover, no party may join the insurance company in an **action** brought against the insured. Any action brought against the insurance company in relation to Coverage E must be postponed until the financial obligation of the insured party has been determined and agreed upon by the insurance company. In the event that the insured party goes bankrupt, this will not affect the insurance company's obligations under the policy. Finally, with regard to Coverage E (personal liability), this coverage is considered to be excess over any other

valid and collectible insurance, with the exception of insurance that is specifically written to be in excess to the limits of liability for Coverage E.

SECTIONS I AND II (CONDITIONS)

POLICY PERIOD, CONCEALMENT OR FRAUD, AND LIBERALIZATION CLAUSE

The final part of the standard homeowners' policy is a set of conditions that apply to both **Sections I and II**. The first of these stipulates that the homeowners' policy only applies to losses under Section I coverage and bodily injury or property damage under Section II coverage, and these events must occur during the **policy period**. Another condition that applies to all coverages is that the policy will be rendered void if the insured makes **false statements**, engages in **fraudulent conduct**, or intentionally **conceals or misrepresents** any material fact or circumstance related to the insurance policy. Finally, the standard homeowners' policy will include a **liberalization clause**, which states that any time the insurance company makes a change that expands coverage under this policy without increasing the premium, such change will automatically apply to the policy on the date it is implemented in the state of jurisdiction, assuming that this implementation date is within 60 days before or during the policy period.

WAIVER OR CHANGE OF POLICY PROVISIONS, NONRENEWAL, ASSIGNMENT, AND SUBROGATION

In the standard homeowners' policy, any waiver or change of provisions must be made in **writing** by the insurance company in order to be considered valid. If the insurance company requests an appraisal or an examination, this will not waive any of its stated rights. The insurance company reserves the right to **decline to renew** the policy, but it promises to notify the policyholder of this nonrenewal a minimum of 30 days before the policy expires. The standard homeowners' policy may be assigned, but assignment will not be valid unless written consent is given by the insurance company. As for **subrogation**, the insured party is allowed to waive rights to recovery against any person before a loss occurs. However, if rights of recovery are not waived, the insurance company may force the assignment of these rights to whatever extent the insurance company has already made payment. If the insured party desires an assignment, he or she must deliver signed copies of all related papers to the insurance company. It should be noted that subrogation may not apply to the following coverages in Section II: damage to property of others or medical payments to others.

DEATH OF INSURED

The final comprehensive condition in the standard homeowners' policy pertains to the **death of the insured**. If one of the individuals named on the declarations page should die during the period of the policy, the insurance company will provide coverage to the **legal representative** of the deceased individual. This policy applies as well to **spouses** of the people named on the declarations page and **fellow residents** of the household in which the named insured lives. The coverage extended to the legal representative of the deceased only applies to the premises and property covered by the policy at the time of the death. The insurance company will also cover any person who has temporary custody of the property of the deceased during the interval before a legal representative is appointed.

Farm Property and Liability Coverage

Standard Farm Property Policy

SECTION I (COVERAGES)
COVERAGE A (DWELLINGS)

Section I of the **standard farm property policy** begins by describing the property covered by **Coverage A** (dwellings). The insurance company will typically promise to pay for any **direct physical loss** of or **damage** to covered property at the insured location listed on the declarations page, so long as the loss or damage is related to a covered cause of loss. To begin with, the standard farm property policy will cover each dwelling owned by the policyholder and accompanied by a limit of insurance on the declarations page. These listed dwellings are covered regardless of whether they are on the insured location. Coverage A will also apply to any structures attached to covered dwellings unless the structure is attached merely by a utility line or fence. The standard farm property coverage will also apply to any materials on the insured location that are meant to be used in the construction or repair of covered dwellings or structures attached to covered dwellings. Finally, Coverage A of the standard farm property policy will cover any building or outdoor equipment that is primarily used in the service of the covered dwellings, the grounds surrounding the covered dwellings, or structures attached to the covered dwellings.

PROPERTY NOT COVERED BY COVERAGE A, AND SPECIAL LIMITS OF INSURANCE UNDER COVERAGE A

Coverage A of the standard farm property policy will not apply to **land, water, or plants**. This includes the land on which the covered dwelling stands. Some plants, trees, shrubs, or lawn may be covered by the extended coverage in Section II of the standard farm property policy. The standard policy will also include a special limit of insurance under Coverage A for **outdoor radio and television satellite dishes and antennas**. These pieces of equipment are subject to a special limit of insurance of $1000 for any single event. The special limit is not added on to the general limit of insurance under Coverage A. If the insured party has negotiated a higher limit of insurance, and this is specified on the declarations page, the higher limit will apply.

LOSS CONDITIONS-VALUATION (PROPERTY)

According to **Section I** of the standard farm property policy, the basis for **loss settlement** related to Coverage A is determined by the **ratio** of the limit of insurance for the affected covered property to the full replacement cost. In the calculation of the full replacement cost, the insurance company will not consider the values of excavations, footings, foundations, piers, or other support structures below the subsurface of the lowest basement. Similarly, the calculation of replacement cost will not include the consideration of underground drains, pipes, flues, or wiring. When the limit of insurance is **at least 80 percent** of the full replacement cost of the damaged structure at the time of the loss, the loss awarded will be the smallest of the following three amounts: the applicable limit of insurance, the amount actually spent to repair or replace the structure, and the cost of replacing the damaged part with similar material.

In situations where the limit of insurance for a damaged structure is **lower than 80 percent** of the full replacement cost at the time of loss, the awarded loss will be the larger of the following two values: actual cash value of the damaged structure at the time of the loss, or a proportion of the repair or replacement cost for the damaged part of the structure. This proportion of repair or replacement cost does not include a **deduction for depreciation**. It is equal to the ratio of the limit

46

of insurance to 80 percent of the repair or replacement cost, not including any increased costs relating to the enforcement of laws or ordinances. When the loss suffered by the policyholder qualifies for payment according to the replacement cost basis, but the repair or replacement cost is greater than five percent of the limit of insurance or $2500, the insurance company will only establish the amount of loss according to actual cash value.

Covered Property Under Coverage B (Other Private Structures Appurtenant to Dwellings)

Coverage B of the standard farm property policy applies to **other private structures appurtenant to dwellings**. The insurance company promises to pay for any direct physical loss or damages to the covered property at the insured location named on the **declarations page**, so long as it is related to a covered cause of loss. Coverage B applies to all private structures that are owned by the policyholder and that are appurtenant to the covered dwelling. For the purposes of this policy, the appurtenant structures must be separated by a clear space from the covered dwelling, and may only be attached to the dwelling by a fence or utility line.

Property Not Covered Under Coverage B, and the Limits of Insurance Under Coverage B

Coverage B of the standard farm property policy does not cover **water or land**, including the land on which the appurtenant structures are located. Coverage B does not apply to any structures that are **rented** or held by individuals who are not a tenant of the covered dwelling, or that are used principally by the policyholder for farming. The only exception to this rule is **private garages**, which are covered. There are also a few **miscellaneous structures** indicated on the declarations page as other property not covered under Coverage B. Under Coverage B, the insurance company will pay no more than 10 percent of the Coverage A limit of insurance for the loss or damage related to a single occurrence. It should be noted, however, that this 10 percent is additional to the Coverage A limit. There is a special limit of insurance of $1000 for a single occurrence in which outdoor radio and television satellite dishes and antennas are damaged or destroyed. Coverage B is subject to the same valuation loss protocol as Coverage A, as well as to the common policy conditions in the farm property conditions.

Property Covered Under Coverage C (Household Personal Property)

Coverage C of the standard farm property policy applies to **household personal property**. The insurance company typically promises to pay for any **direct physical loss** of or **damage** to covered property at the insured location indicated on the declarations page, so long as it is related to a covered cause of loss. Coverage C applies to all household personal property owned or used by the insured and the members of the insured family who reside with him or her. However, this property is only covered while it is on the **insured location**. Coverage C also applies to household personal property owned by other people when it is in a covered dwelling or on the grounds **appurtenant** to that dwelling, assuming these grounds are owned by the named insured. Household personal property owned by others will only be covered at the request of the named insured.

Property Not Covered Under Coverage C

Coverage C of the standard farm property policy does not apply to any property that is specifically covered elsewhere. It also does not apply to any **aircraft** or related parts. Coverage C does not apply to **animals, birds, or fish**. It does not apply to any **plants**, including lawns, owned by the named insured as a tenant. There are some exceptions in which plants, trees, shrubs, and lawns are covered by a coverage extension in Section II of the standard farm property policy. Coverage C does not apply to any **business property** unless it is specifically included. This coverage also does not apply to any recording or storage media for **electronic data processing**. It does not apply to any electronic equipment designed to be powered by the electrical system of a **motor vehicle**. It does not cover any **farm personal property** besides office equipment, furniture, and fixtures, and it does not cover any credit cards, electronic funds transfer cards, or other devices used to deposit, withdraw, or transfer **funds**. Finally, it does not cover **motor vehicles** or their parts.

SPECIAL LIMITS OF INSURANCE

The standard farm property policy includes some **special limits** for insurance under **Coverage C**. The special limits accompany the otherwise applicable limits of insurance indicated on the declarations page. There is a limit of $200 on gold besides goldware, silver other than silverware, platinum other than platinumware, and money. There is a limit of $1500 on letters of credit, securities, passports, and manuscripts. This limit applies to both paper and electronic versions of these documents. There is a limit of $1500 on watercraft and related equipment. There is a limit of $1500 on trailers that are not used for farming or with watercraft. There is a limit of $2500 on business property found on the insured location. There is a limit of $500 on business property found off of the insured location.

With regard to Coverage C, there are special limits of insurance for certain items when they are lost due to **theft**. To begin with, there is a $3000 limit on firearms and their related equipment. There is a $2500 limit on stolen watches, jewelry, furs, and precious and semiprecious stones. There is a $2500 limit on stolen goldware, silverware, pewterware, and platinumware, as well as any implements plated with these metals, as for instance trays, trophies, tea sets, and similar items. Regardless of how the items are lost or damaged, there is a $1500 limit on electronic equipment and accessories installed on a motor vehicle and designed to be powered by the electrical system of a motor vehicle. There is also a $1500 limit on electronic equipment and accessories primarily used in the operation of a farm or business off of the insured location.

CONDITIONS

In the standard farm property policy, the discussion of **Coverage C** concludes with a description of the **conditions** that apply to this policy. There is a specific **loss condition** for Coverage C, and this coverage is also subject to the **common policy conditions** and the **farm property conditions**. The farm property conditions are outlined in the farm property section of the standard policy. The loss condition for Coverage C describes the process of **property valuation**. In it, the insurance company will promise to settle at the actual cash value at the time the loss is incurred. However, the insurance company will not make a payment greater than is necessary for repair or replacement of the covered household personal property that is damaged or lost.

COVERAGE OF ADDITIONAL LIVING EXPENSES UNDER COVERAGE D (LOSS OF USE)

Coverage D of the standard farm property policy relates to the **loss of use of personal property**. In the typical formulation, the insurance company will promise to cover the **additional living expenses** of the insured party up to the limit of insurance indicated on the declarations page. When a covered cause of loss renders the principal living quarters of the insured party uninhabitable, any required increase in living expenses will be reimbursed by the insurance company. The insured party may request such money as is necessary to maintain the normal standard of living. In order for Coverage D to apply, however, the uninhabitable area must be either a dwelling covered by Coverage A or the dwelling in which covered household personal property is found when the insured party is a tenant. The insurance company will make payment for additional living expenses under Coverage D for the minimum amount of time necessary for the insured party to repair or replace the property or relocate.

COVERAGE OF FAIR RENTAL VALUE AND LOSS AND EXPENSE DUE TO EMERGENCY PROHIBITION AGAINST OCCUPANCY UNDER COVERAGE D.

The standard farm property policy will guarantee payment under **Coverage D** of the **fair rental value** of a dwelling or appurtenant structure, under Coverages A and B, respectively, when these structures are rendered uninhabitable by a covered cause of loss. However, this reimbursement of fair rental value will not include any **expenses that do not continue** while the property is not being used. The insurance company will reimburse for fair rental value for the minimum amount of time within which the insured party can repair or replace the damaged property, such that it is fit for habitation again. The standard farm property policy will also make payment under Coverage D for any loss or expense caused by an **emergency prohibition against occupancy**. That is, additional living expenses or fair rental value loss will be reimbursed when a civil authority forbids the insured from using a structure because of direct damage to a neighboring property by a covered cause of loss. However, these payments will only be made for two weeks, and will not be made at all if they are caused by the cancellation of a lease or agreement. The term of liability under Coverage D is not limited by the expiration of the policy, and no deductible applies to this coverage.

SECTION II (COVERAGE EXTENSIONS)
TREES, SHRUBS, PLANTS, AND LAWNS

The second section of the standard farm property policy outlines some **coverage extensions**. The first of these is for **trees, shrubs, plants, and lawns**. This coverage extension applies to Coverages A and C. It declares that trees, shrubs, plants, and lawns within 250 feet of a covered dwelling are considered to be covered property, so long as loss or damage is related to one of the following: fire or lightning, civil commotion, riot, explosion, aircraft, theft, vandalism, or vehicles not owned by a resident of the covered dwelling. However, the maximum amount of payment for trees, shrubs, plants, or lawns is five percent of the Coverage A limit of insurance or 10 percent of the Coverage C limit of insurance if the dwelling is not covered by Coverage A. Moreover, the insurance company will pay a maximum of $500 for damage or destruction of any single tree, shrub, plant, or lawn. This coverage extension is considered to be additional insurance. Any trees, shrubs, plants, or lawns that are used for business or farming are not covered by this extension.

HOUSEHOLD PERSONAL PROPERTY OF THE INSUREDS AWAY FROM THE INSURED LOCATION

The standard farm property policy includes a coverage extension for the **household personal property of insureds away from the insured location**. However, this coverage extension only applies to **Coverage C**. It is considered a part of the applicable limit of insurance rather than an addition to it. For the purpose of this coverage extension, it does not matter if the insured party is the owner or the tenant of the property. This coverage extension applies to household personal property no matter where it is located, so long as it is used by the insured party or members of the insured party's family who live at the insured location. There is a special limit of insurance on this property, however, equal to either $1000 or 10 percent of the limit of insurance indicated on the declarations page for household personal property, whichever is larger. This special limit of insurance does not apply to property that is moved from the insured location during repairs or renovations, or that is located at a newly acquired principal residence.

REFRIGERATED PRODUCTS (NOT FARM PERSONAL PROPERTY)

The standard farm property policy includes a coverage extension for **refrigerated products** that are not farm personal property. However, this extended coverage only applies to **Coverage C**, and is not an addition to the applicable limit of insurance. This coverage extension applies regardless of whether the insured party is the owner or tenant of the property. It states that the insurance company will pay a maximum of $500 for damage or loss to refrigerated products in an occupied dwelling or appurtenant structure if said damage or loss is caused by the **interruption of electrical service** or a **mechanical or electrical breakdown**. However, this coverage extension will not apply to loss or damage to farm personal property or property not owned by the insured party. There is no deductible for this coverage extension.

BUILDING ADDITIONS AND ALTERATIONS

The standard farm property policy includes a coverage extension for **building additions and alterations**. However, this coverage extension for Coverage C is only applicable when the insured party is a **tenant**. The policy states that Coverage C applies to building additions, improvements, installations, alterations, or fixtures, so long as they are paid for by the insured party. This extension is considered to be additional insurance, and is limited to 10 percent of the insurance limit for household personal property. The insurance company will pay for the loss on the basis of actual cash value at the time of loss if the repair or replacement is done within a year. If the repair or replacement is done after a year, the insurance company will settle according to a proportion of the repair or replacement cost. This proportion is the ratio of the interval from the loss to the lease expiration to the interval from the repair to the lease expiration.

SECTION III (ADDITIONAL COVERAGES)
REMOVAL OF FALLEN TREES

The standard farm property policy includes some additional coverages, first of all for the cost of **removing fallen trees**. The insurance company promises to pay any reasonable expenses incurred by the insured party for removing a fallen tree from the grounds appurtenant to the principal residence. However, this coverage only applies if the tree has **damaged property** covered under Coverage A, B, or C. Also, the additional coverage only applies if the tree stands within 250 feet of a covered dwelling, and if the tree fell because of a covered cause of loss besides one of the following: theft, vandalism, fire or lightning, riot or civil commotion, aircraft, explosion, or vehicles both owned and operated by people who do not live in the covered dwelling.

CREDIT CARDS AND ELECTRONIC FUNDS TRANSFER CARDS OR OTHER ACCESS DEVICES, FORGERY, AND COUNTERFEIT CURRENCY

In the standard farm property policy, the insurance company will assert that a maximum of $500 of additional coverage will be paid to satisfy the legal obligation of an insured party related to the theft or unauthorized use of **credit cards or electronic funds transfer cards**. A similar loss will obtain for any losses related to **forgery, check alteration, or counterfeit currency**. The insurance company will not, however, make payment for any loss related to dishonest behavior or business practices of the insured. Also, no deductible applies to this additional coverage. Related to the additional coverage for fraudulent use of credit cards, electronic transfer cards, forgery, and counterfeit currency, the insurance company reserves the right to make appropriate investigations and settlements. Of course, the obligation to pursue these settlements and investigations terminates when the limit of liability has been reached.

WATER DAMAGE AND GRAVE MARKERS

The standard farm property policy declares that the insurance company will provide additional coverage in the event of **water or steam damage** related to plumbing, heating, air conditioning, or fire sprinklers. Specifically, the insurance company will pay for the expense of removing and replacing part of the structure so that the damaged system can be repaired or replaced. However, the insurance company will not cover the expense of repairing any **defect** which led to the escape of water or steam from a system or appliance containing water or steam. With regard to this additional coverage, sumps and sump pumps are not included. Finally, the standard farm property policy includes a maximum of $5000 of additional coverage for grave markers and mausoleums.

With regard to these losses, the insurance company promises to settle at actual cash value at the time of loss. The additional coverage for damage to grave markers and mausoleums is subject to the same limits of insurance that apply to other covered property.

Standard Farm Liability Policy

SECTION I (COVERAGES)

INSURING AGREEMENT FOR COVERAGE H (BODILY INJURY AND PROPERTY DAMAGE LIABILITY)

Coverage H of the standard farm liability policy covers bodily injury and property damage liability. In the insuring agreement for this coverage, the insurance company promises to pay any legal obligations of the insured related to bodily injury or property damage. The insurance company also retains the right to defend the insured in the event of a suit seeking such damages. The insurance company retains the right to investigate any relevant occurrences and to settle any related claims or suits. **Bodily injury** includes all of the damages related to death, healthcare, or loss of services. **Property damage** is defined as any loss of the use of tangible property or physical injury to the property. When property is not physically injured, but cannot be used, the property damage is deemed to have occurred at the time that use became impossible.

COVERAGE H (EXCLUSIONS)

EXPECTED OR INTENDED INJURY AND CONTRACTUAL LIABILITY

Coverage H of the standard farm liability policy does not apply to any bodily injury or property damage that could have been **expected** or was **intended** by the insured. This exclusion obtains even if the resulting injury or damage is significantly different than the insured intended, as well as if it is sustained by a different person or piece of property than was intended or expected. The exclusion for expected or intended injury does not apply to any bodily injuries that are caused by the use of reasonable force while **protecting** persons or property. There is another exclusion under Coverage H for any injury or damage for which the insured is already obligated to pay damages because of his or her assumption of liability in an agreement or contract. The contractual liability exclusion does not apply to any liability that the insured would have had were there no contract or agreement, or any liability that is assumed as part of an insured contract.

POLLUTION

Coverage H of the standard farm liability policy does not apply to any bodily injury or property damage caused by the actual or threatened discharge, release, or escape of **pollutants**. This exclusion pertains to the premises owned or occupied by the insured, as well as any site or location used by the insured or others for the handling or disposal of waste. Moreover, the pollution exclusion pertains to any site or location from which the insured or any contractors or subcontractors work directly on behalf of the insured. Moreover, Coverage H will not apply to any loss, cost, or expense related to a request or demand that the insured test for, remove, neutralize, or treat pollutants. This coverage will not apply to any losses caused by claims or suits by governmental authorities related to damages that occurred during the treatment or neutralization of pollutants.

RELEASE OR DISCHARGE FROM AIRCRAFT; AND AIRCRAFT, MOTOR VEHICLE, MOTORIZED BICYCLE, OR TRICYCLE

Coverage H of the standard farm liability policy does not apply to any bodily injury or property damage related to substances released or discharged from an **aircraft**. Similarly, this coverage does not apply to any injury or damage related to the ownership, maintenance, or use of any aircraft, motor vehicle, motorized bicycle, or tricycle by the insured. Neither does this coverage apply to any injury or damage that could result in **vicarious liability** for the actions of a minor operating such a vehicle. This exclusion does not apply to injuries or damages suffered by a residence employee who is not maintaining or operating the vehicle. Also, this exclusion does not apply to any motor vehicles that are not subject to **registration requirements**, whether because they are designed for recreational use off public roads or because they are to be used exclusively in the assistance of the handicapped.

WATERCRAFT AND MOBILE EQUIPMENT

Coverage H of the standard farm liability policy does not apply to bodily injury or property damage related to the ownership, maintenance, or use of most **watercraft**. Specifically, this exclusion applies to sailing vessels and watercraft that are principally designed to be propelled by an **electric motor or engine power**. Watercraft powered by either inboard or inboard-outdrive engines with less than 50 horsepower are not covered if they are not owned by the insured party. Watercraft powered by inboard or inboard-outdrive engines with more than 50 horsepower are not covered if they are not owned or rented by an insured party. Sailing vessels are not subject to this exclusion if they are less than 26 feet long or if they are longer than 26 feet but are not owned by or rented to an insured party. Coverage H does not apply to any bodily injury or property damage related to the transportation of mobile equipment by the insured, nor to any injury or damage related to the use of a self-propelled land vehicle as part of training or participation in a speed, strength, demolition, or stunt contest.

USE OF LIVESTOCK OR OTHER ANIMALS, BUSINESS PURSUITS, AND CUSTOM FARMING

Coverage H of the standard farm liability policy does not apply to any bodily injury or property damage related to the use of **livestock** or other animals in preparation or performance of a racing, speed, strength, or stunt activity. This exclusion applies only to those **preparatory and performance activities** that occur at the site designated for the activity or contest. An exclusion also applies to the use of livestock or other animals for providing **transportation for a fee**, as for instance at a fair or charity event. Coverage H does not apply to bodily injury or property damage related to the business pursuits of an insured, specifically the provision of services or goods for payment. This exclusion does not apply to the activities of insured parties under the age of 21, so long as these activities are related to part-time or occasional business, and the insured party has no employees. Coverage H also excludes bodily injury or property damage related to the performance or nonperformance of custom farming operations. This final exclusion is only applicable when the insured party has received more than $5000 for custom farming operations in the year immediately preceding the event.

PROFESSIONAL SERVICES, AND RENTAL OF PREMISES AND OWNERSHIP OR CONTROL OF PREMISES

Coverage H of the standard farm liability policy does not apply to any bodily injury or property damage related to the performance or nonperformance of **professional services**. An exclusion also applies to bodily injury or property damage related to acts or omissions that occur at locations owned, rented, or controlled by the insured party, but which are not listed as insured locations. However, this exclusion does not apply to bodily injury or property damage sustained by a **residence employee** during the course of his or her employment by the insured party. Coverage H also does not apply to bodily injury or property damage related to the rental or holding for rental of the insured locations. Finally, this exclusion does not apply to the rental of a farm premises for farming purposes, the rental of a residence for residential purposes, or the occupancy of part of the insured party's principal residence for use as living quarters by residence employees.

COMMUNICABLE DISEASE, WORKERS' COMPENSATION OR SIMILAR LAW, AND EMPLOYERS' LIABILITY

Coverage H of the standard farm liability policy does not apply to bodily injury or property damage related to the transmission of a **communicable disease** by an insured party. This coverage does not apply to any obligation the insured may take on as part of a workers' compensation, unemployment compensation, or disability benefits law. Similarly, Coverage H does not apply to bodily injuries sustained by **nonresidence employees** in connection with their employment. Bodily injuries sustained by residence employees are not covered unless the employee registers his or her claim within three years of the end of the policy period. Finally, Coverage H does not apply to any bodily injury sustained by an **immediate family member** of an employee as a result of a bodily injury suffered by the employee. There are certain exceptions to this exclusion, as for instance when the insured has assumed some liability as part of an insured contract.

BUILDING OR STRUCTURE UNDER CONSTRUCTION, BODILY INJURY TO AN INSURED, AND DAMAGE TO PROPERTY

Coverage H of the standard farm liability policy does not apply to any **bodily injuries** that are sustained on the premises where a building or structure is being **constructed**. However, this exclusion does not apply to bodily injuries sustained by people who are not insured, or to bodily injuries sustained by residence employees during the course of their employment. Coverage H also excludes bodily injury suffered by an insured party, as well as any claim made against an insured party to repay or share damages with a party who has been obliged to make a payment because of bodily injury suffered by an insured party. Coverage H also excludes property damage to any items owned by the insured; any property rented or occupied by the insured; any premises sold or given away by the insured; any property loaned to the insured; or any property placed in the care, custody, or control of the insured.

DAMAGE TO THE PRODUCT OF THE INSURED, TO THE WORK OF THE INSURED, AND TO IMPAIRED PROPERTY OR PROPERTY NOT PHYSICALLY INJURED

Coverage H of the standard farm liability policy does not cover damage to the product of the insured when this damage arises, even in part, from the **operations of the product**. Similarly, Coverage H does not apply to property damage to the work of the insured when this damage arises from the work itself. It also does not apply to any part or aspect of a property that must be restored, repaired, or replaced because of poor work by the insured. Finally, Coverage H does not apply to any property damage to impaired or physically uninjured property that arises out of defects, deficiencies, or inadequacies in the product or work of the insured, or when this damage arises out of the delay or failure to perform contractual obligations.

RECALL OF PRODUCTS, WORK, OR IMPAIRED PROPERTY; SEXUAL MOLESTATION, CORPORAL PUNISHMENT, OR PHYSICAL OR MENTAL ABUSE; AND CONTROLLED SUBSTANCES

Coverage H of the standard farm liability policy does not apply to any damages claimed by the insured because of the **withdrawal, repair, inspection, or recall** of the insured's product, work, or impaired property, so long as this action is based on a **known or suspected** defect, deficiency, or inadequacy. Coverage H also does not apply to any bodily injury or property damage related to **sexual molestation, corporal punishment, or physical or mental abuse**. Finally, Coverage H does not apply to any bodily injury or property damage related to the use, sale, manufacture, possession, or delivery of a **controlled substance**. Controlled substances are those defined as such by the federal food and drug laws. Common examples are narcotics, marijuana, and cocaine. The exclusion of injuries or damages related to controlled substances does not apply to the legal use of prescription drugs with the permission of a licensed physician.

PERSONAL INJURY, DISTRIBUTION OF MATERIAL IN VIOLATION OF STATUTES, AND WAR

Coverage H of the standard farm liability policy does not apply to any bodily injury that is the result of **personal injury**. Personal injury is related to one of the following offenses: false arrest, detention, or imprisonment; malicious prosecution; wrongful eviction from or invasion of a private occupancy; or oral or written publication of slanderous, libelous, or confidential materials. Coverage H also excludes any bodily injury or property damage directly or indirectly related to violations of the **Telephone Consumer Protection Act or CAN-SPAM Act of 2003**. Finally, Coverage H excludes bodily injury or property damage arising directly or indirectly out of **war** or other military action.

SECTION I (COVERAGES)

INSURING AGREEMENT FOR COVERAGE I (PERSONAL AND ADVERTISING INJURY LIABILITY)

Coverage I of the standard farm liability policy relates to personal and advertising injury liability. The insuring agreement for this coverage states that the insurance company will pay any amounts for which the insured party becomes legally obligated because of **personal injury or advertising injury**. Advertising injury is related to the following offenses: oral or written publication of slander or libel, oral or written publication of private information, unauthorized use of another party's advertising idea in an advertisement, or infringement upon copyright or slogan in an advertisement. This coverage only applies to obligations that arise out of personal activities or operations typical of farming.

SECTION I (EXCLUSIONS)

KNOWING VIOLATION OF THE RIGHTS OF ANOTHER, MATERIAL PUBLISHED WITH KNOWLEDGE OF FALSITY, MATERIAL PUBLISHED PRIOR TO THE POLICY PERIOD, AND CRIMINAL ACTS

Coverage I of the standard farm liability policy does not apply to any personal injury or advertising injury that is the result of the insured's actions when the insured has the understanding that the act to be committed would **violate another person's rights** and inflict either personal injury or advertising injury. This coverage also does not apply to personal injury or advertising injury caused by **oral or written publication** by the insured when the insured has knowledge of the falsity of the information being published. This coverage does not apply to personal injury or advertising injury related to the oral or written publication of any material that was first published **before the initiation of the policy period**. Also, this coverage does not apply to personal injury or advertising injury related to **criminal acts** committed by the insured. However, the insurance company still has the duty to defend the insured before criminal liability has been established.

CONTRACTUAL LIABILITY, POLLUTION, DISTRIBUTION OF MATERIAL IN VIOLATION OF STATUTES, AND WAR

Coverage I of the standard farm liability policy does not apply to any personal injury or advertising injury for which the insured party has already assumed liability and a **contract or agreement**. However, the liability for damages that the insured would have had in the absence of a contract or agreement is not excluded. Coverage I does not apply to personal injury or advertising injury related to the actual or threatened discharge, release, or escape of **pollutants**. Coverage I also does not apply to personal injury or advertising injury directly or indirectly related to violations of the **Telephone Consumer Protection Act or the CAN-SPAM Act of 2003**. Finally, Coverage I does not apply to personal injury or advertising injury directly or indirectly related to **war** or other military actions.

Business Pursuits, Civic or Public Activities for Pay, and Personal Injuries to Insured

There are some exclusions that are specific to damages for **personal injury** under Coverage I of the standard farm liability policy. To begin with, **Coverage I** of the standard farm liability policy does not apply to personal injuries related to the **business activities** of the insured party. This exclusion generally applies to any activity related to the provision or promise of a service or product as part of normal business operations. Coverage I also does not apply to personal injuries related to the **civic or public activities** that the insured performs for compensation. Coverage I also does not apply to personal injuries sustained by any **insured party**. Finally, Coverage I does not apply to any **claims** made against an insured party to repair or share damages with another party who is required to pay damages because of personal injury.

Breach of Contract; Quality or Performance of Goods; Wrong Quotation or Description of Prices; and Business Advertising, Broadcasting, Publishing, or Telecasting

There are some exclusions specific to damages for **advertising injury** under Coverage I of the standard farm liability policy. To begin with, Coverage I does not apply to advertising injuries related to a **breach of contract**, except in cases where the insured party had an implied contract to use the advertising idea of another party in his or her promotional materials. It also does not apply to any advertising injuries related to the failure of goods or services to conform with **statements of quality** made in the insured parties advertising. Coverage I does not apply to advertising injuries related to an **incorrect quotation or description of pricing** in an advertisement. Finally, Coverage I does not apply to any offenses by an insured party whose business includes **advertising, broadcasting, publishing, or telecasting**.

Pollution-Related Loss, Cost, or Expense

Coverage I of the standard farm liability policy has a special exclusion related to **pollution**. Coverage I will not apply to any **loss, cost, or expense** related to a request or order for monitoring, removal, or treatment of pollutants. Similarly, Coverage I does not apply to any loss, cost, or expense related to claims or suits made by or on behalf of a government in relation to damages sustained during the testing, monitoring, removal, containment, treatment, or neutralization of pollutants. When tests are required to assess the effects of pollutants, any loss, cost, or expense that arises from the tests will not be reimbursed under Coverage I.

Coverage J (Medical Payments)
Insuring Agreement

Coverage J of the standard farm liability policy relates to **medical expenses**. According to the insuring agreement for Coverage J, the insurance company will promise to pay for reasonable medical expenses. **Reasonable medical expenses** are those that are deemed necessary by a doctor within three years of the event that caused the bodily injury. Under Coverage J, the insurance company promises to reimburse the insured for medical expenses no matter who was responsible for the accident. By reasonable medical expenses, the insurance policy means first aid at the scene of the accident; required medical, surgical, x-ray, and dental services; and required ambulance, hospital, nursing, and funeral services. Coverage J only applies to individuals besides the insured who are on the insured premises with permission, individuals besides the insured who are injured because of a condition on the insured location or because of the actions of an insured or an insured's farm employee in the course of his or her employment, or a residence employee in the course of his or her employment. This coverage also applies to injuries caused by animals owned or being cared for by an insured.

COVERAGE J (EXCLUSIONS)

PROFESSIONAL SERVICES AND BUSINESS PURSUITS; AND LOCATIONS RENTED, LOANED, OR CONTROLLED BY THE INSURED

Coverage J of the standard farm liability policy does not apply to expenses for bodily injuries to people who are on the insured location for the purpose of **providing professional services or engaging in business**. However, this coverage does apply to bodily injuries suffered by residence employees. There is another exclusion to Coverage J for bodily injuries that occur on locations that are **owned, rented, or controlled** by the insured, but which are not insured locations. Again, there is an exception to this exclusion for bodily injuries suffered by residence employees while performing the duties associated with their employment.

FARM EMPLOYEES OR OTHERS MAINTAINING THE FARM, WORKERS' COMPENSATION OR SIMILAR LAW, AND INJURY TO RESIDENT

Coverage J of the standard farm liability policy does not cover expenses for bodily injuries suffered by farm employees or other individuals engaged in work that is typical of the **use or maintenance** of the insured location as a farm. There are exceptions to this exclusion for bodily injuries sustained by residence employees or others on the insured location during the performance of neighborly assistance for which payment is not expected. Coverage J does not apply to any individuals who are eligible to receive benefits from the insured or from the government as part of a **worker's compensation, nonoccupational disability, or occupational disease law**. Finally, Coverage J does not apply to any injuries suffered by any person who regularly **resides** at the insured location or who is a presiding member of the named insured's household. There is an exception to this exclusion for bodily injuries suffered by residence employees. It should also be noted that any bodily injuries excluded under Coverage H are also excluded under Coverage J.

COVERAGES H AND I (SUPPLEMENTARY PAYMENTS)

ADDITIONAL COVERAGES

The standard farm liability policy offers some additional coverages for **supplementary payments** under **Coverages H and I**. To begin with, the insurance company guarantees some additional payments related to the **investigation or settlement of claims** made against an insured. The insurance company promises to pay any expenses it incurs during an investigation or settlement, as well as all of the costs that are taxed against the insured as part of a suit. The insurance company also promises to pay any prejudgment interest that is charged to the insured in relation to a judgment paid by the insurance company. The insurance company promises to pay up to $250 towards the cost of bail bonds that are required because of the use of a vehicle covered under Coverage H. The insurance company will pay the costs of any bonds necessary to release attachments, so long as these bond amounts are less than the relevant limit of insurance. Finally, the insurance company promises to pay any interest on a judgment that accrues after the judgment has been rendered but before the insurance company has made the required payment. None of these supplementary payments will reduce the limits of insurance.

ADDITIONAL PAYMENTS FOR DAMAGE TO THE PROPERTY OF OTHERS

The standard farm liability policy includes some additional coverage for **damage to the property of others**. The insurance company typically will promise to pay a maximum of $1000 for each instance of property damage caused by an insured to the property of others. The insurance company retains the option to pay the **actual cash value** of the property or to **replace or repair** the property. The insurance company will not pay for property damage to the property of others when it is caused on purpose by an insured party who is at least 13 years old. Also, the insurance company will not extend this additional coverage for damage to property owned by or rented to an insured or a member of his or her household. Finally, this additional coverage will not be extended to property damage to the property of others that is related to the ownership, operation, or use of motor vehicles, motorized bicycles, farm machinery, watercraft, or aircraft.

LIMITS OF INSURANCE

In the standard farm liability policy, the **limits of insurance** listed on the declarations page constitute the maximum payment that will be made by the insurance company, regardless of the number of claims or suits, the number of insured parties involved, or the number of parties making claims or bringing suits. The **general aggregate limit** indicated on the declarations page is the maximum payment for damages under Coverages H and I and medical expenses under Coverage J. The **each-occurrence limit** indicated on the declarations page is the maximum payment that will be made for damages under Coverage H and medical expenses under Coverage J related to a single occurrence. Any bodily injury or property damage that is caused by continuous or repeated exposure to the same harmful conditions will be treated as a single occurrence. Most farm liability policies also include special limits for fire damage, advertising injury, and medical expenses.

LOSS CONDITIONS

BANKRUPTCY, INSURANCE UNDER TWO OR MORE COVERAGES, AND LEGAL ACTION AGAINST THE INSURANCE COMPANY

The insurance company will not be relieved of any obligations it has as part of the standard farm liability policy should the insured or the estate of the insured declare **bankruptcy** or become insolvent. In situations where the same loss or damage is covered by **multiple coverages** of the standard farm liability policy, the insurance company is not obliged to pay any more than the actual amount of loss or damage. The standard farm liability policy also asserts that no person or organization has the right to involve the insurance company in a **suit** requesting damages from an insured party. Also, no one can sue the insurance company on the basis of this insurance policy unless all of the terms of the policy have been honored.

CONDITIONS

DUTIES IN THE EVENT OF OCCURRENCE, OFFENSE, CLAIM, OR SUIT

In the standard farm liability policy, the insured party has certain **duties** in the event of an occurrence, offense, claim, or suit. To begin with, the insured party must **notify** the insurance company as soon as is practicable if an event occurs that may result in a claim. The insured party is responsible for communicating the location, time, and circumstances of the event. The insured party should also provide the names and addresses of all **injured persons** and any available **witnesses**. If it is likely that a violation of law has been committed, the insured party is responsible for notifying the **police**. The insured party should not make any **payment** or incur any expenses on behalf of the insurance company without receiving permission. Finally, with regard to claims for medical expenses under Coverage J, the insured party must provide **written proof** of the claim, and must do so under oath if requested. The insured party should also submit to any requested **physical examinations** and should provide any relevant records.

NO ADMISSION OF LIABILITY WITH MEDICAL PAYMENTS, OTHER INSURANCE, AND TRANSFER OF RIGHTS OF RECOVERY AGAINST OTHERS TO THE INSURANCE COMPANY

The standard farm liability policy asserts that any payments made under Coverage J do not constitute an **admission of liability** by the insured party or the insurance company. When the insured party has **other insurance** that covers an occurrence covered by the standard farm liability policy, the insurance company is only obliged to pay the proportion of the covered damages and related defense costs that the applicable limit of insurance has to the total amount of insurance that provides the same coverage. This condition does not apply to occurrences related to the ownership, maintenance, or use of a motor vehicle, watercraft, or piece of mobile equipment. Finally, any rights held by the insured to recover payments made by the insurance company under the standard farm liability policy will be **transferred** to the insurance company. The insured party may do nothing that will impair the ability of the insurance company to exercise these rights.

LIBERALIZATION, REPRESENTATIONS, AND SEPARATION OF INSUREDS

If at any point the insurance company revises the standard farm liability policy in such a way that the coverage is broadened without increasing the premium, this revision (known as a **liberalization**) will immediately apply to the policy. Acceptance of the terms of the policy by the insured party is taken as assurance that all of the statements on the declarations page are complete and accurate. The insured party acknowledges that the policy was issued based on the information he or she provided. The final additional condition of the standard farm liability policy declares that coverage applies to each insured party individually when claims or suits are made against multiple parties. The insurance policy will treat each named insured as if he or she were the **only named insured**.

Auto Insurance

OWNERSHIP OF PRIVATE PASSENGER AUTO AND COVERED AUTO

In the standard personal auto policy, a person is considered to own a **private-passenger automobile** if he or she has leased it under a written agreement and has held the automobile for a continuous period of at least six months. For the purposes of this policy, a **covered automobile** indicates any vehicle listed on the declarations page. Also, the policy applies to any private passenger autos, pickup trucks, or vans of which the insured party becomes owner. Pickup trucks or vans are only covered if they weigh less than 10,000 pounds and are not used for the transportation or delivery of materials and goods unless this use is for farming or ranching or is incidental to the insured party's business of installing or repairing equipment or furnishings.

Standard Personal Auto Policy

PART A (LIABILITY COVERAGE)
INSURING AGREEMENT

Part A of the standard personal auto policy outlines **liability coverage**. Typically, the insurance company will agree to pay damages for property damage or bodily injury caused by the insured party in an automobile accident. The cover damages include any prejudgment interest the insured party is ordered to pay by a court. As in other insurance policies, the insurance company reserves the right to settle or defend any claim or suit for damages. All of the costs incurred during this defense will be paid by the insurance company, in addition to the limits of liability. Once the insurance company has reached the limits of its liability for this coverage, its responsibility to defend or settle it is finished. If the bodily injury or property damage is not covered by this personal auto policy, the insurance company has no responsibility to defend or settle any related claims.

WHO IS INSURED

With regard to the liability coverage outlined in Part A of the standard personal auto policy, the insurance company will typically assert that the insured party is the **named insured** as well as any **family member** for the purposes of ownership, maintenance, or use of automobiles or trailers. Liability coverage is also extended to any person who is using a **covered automobile** owned by the insured party. Essentially, any person or organization whose acts arise from the use of a covered automobile and whose acts are covered by this part of the insurance form are deemed to be covered. Finally, the insurance company allows that there may be some instances in which coverage may be afforded to a person or organization operating a vehicle other than the covered automobile or trailer.

SUPPLEMENTARY PAYMENTS

The protocol for supplementary payments under liability coverage is outlined in Part A of the standard personal auto policy. Typically, the insurance company will promise to pay up to $250 for the cost of **bail bonds** stemming from an accident, including any associated traffic law violations. Note that these supplementary payments are made in addition to the normal limits of liability. In order for the insured party to receive supplementary payments for bail bonds, the associated accident must involve a bodily injury or property damage covered by the policy. The insurance company will also promise to make supplementary payments for any premiums on **appeal bonds** or bonds to release attachments related to a suit that is being defended. The insurance company will also typically promise to pay any **interest** that accrues after the judgment has been entered. Typically, the insurance company will decline to pay any more interest after offering to pay the

59

portion of the judgment that does not exceed the limits of liability related to this coverage. Finally, the insurance company will typically agree to pay up to $50 a day for **loss of earnings** incurred because of attendance at hearings or trials at the request of the insurance company.

EXCLUSIONS

In Part A of the standard personal auto policy, the insurance company will typically decline to provide liability coverage for any person who causes bodily injury or property damage **on purpose**. The insurance company will also decline to provide liability coverage for property damage to property that is owned or being transported by one of the **named insured**. The insurance company will not provide liability coverage for any property that is used by, rented to, or in the care of the insured party, with the only exception being property damage to a private garage or residence. The insurance company typically will also decline to provide liability coverage for bodily injury to an **employee** of the named insured during the course of employment. This exclusion does not apply to bodily injury suffered by domestic employees unless those domestic employees are eligible for workers' compensation benefits.

In a standard personal auto policy, the insurance company will decline to extend coverage for the insured party's liability if the insured party is operating a vehicle as a **public conveyance**. Public conveyances are distinct from carpools. The coverage also does not apply to the insured parties while they are employed or otherwise occupied in the sale, repair, service, storage, or parking of vehicles that are mainly used on **public highways**. The standard personal auto policy also will not extend liability coverage to insured parties while they are using **business vehicles**. The auto policy will not apply to individuals who are using a vehicle without a reasonable belief of being entitled to do so. Also, the personal auto policy will not provide liability coverage for the ownership, maintenance, or use of motorized vehicles with **fewer than three wheels**.

LIMIT OF LIABILITY

Part A of the standard personal auto policy describes the **limit of liability** with regard to liability coverage. Typically, the limit of liability indicated on the declarations page is the maximum limit of liability for all damages arising from a **single accident**. This is the maximum limit of liability regardless of the number of insureds, the number of vehicles involved in the accident, the number of vehicles or premiums indicated in the declarations page, and the number of claims made as a result of this accident. The limit of liability will be applied by the insurance company to create any separate limits related to bodily injury or property damage liability. Any of the separate applications will not affect the overall limit of liability.

OUT-OF-STATE COVERAGE

According to the standard personal auto policy, the insurance company will use a special protocol for determining coverage for accidents that occur in a **different state**. In situations where the accident occurs in a state or province where there is a similar law setting higher limits of liability for property damage or bodily injury than those specified on the declarations page, the insurance company will pay up to the **higher specified limit**. For accidents that occur in states or provinces where a compulsory insurance law requires nonresidents to have insurance, the insurance company will provide the **required minimum amount** and type of coverage for that state or province. The out-of-state coverage section of Part A concludes by noting that the insured party will never be entitled to duplicate payments for the same elements of loss.

FINANCIAL RESPONSIBILITY AND OTHER INSURANCE

Part A of the standard personal auto policy describes the protocols for **financial responsibility** and situations in which **more than one insurance policy** may apply. To begin with, the insurance

60

company will typically state that, in situations where this policy is certified as a future proof of financial responsibility, it promises to comply with the law to whatever extent is required of it. With regard to other insurance policies, the standard personal auto policy will typically only promise to pay its fair share of the loss. This **fair share** is the portion of the liability coverage's limit of liability within the total of all applicable limits. Part A concludes by noting that any insurance provided for a vehicle not owned by the insured party should be considered access over any other collectible insurance.

PART B (MEDICAL PAYMENTS COVERAGE)
INSURING AGREEMENT

Part B of the standard personal auto policy describes the **medical payments coverage**. It begins with a discussion of the **insuring agreement**. In the standard policy, the insurance company promises to pay all reasonable expenses incurred for necessary and appropriate medical and funeral services arising from bodily injury caused by an accident and suffered by an insured party. However, it is typical for the insurance company to limit these payments to expenses incurred within the **three years** following the date of the accident. For the purposes of medical payments coverage policy, the insured is defined as the individual named on the declarations page, as well as any of their family members, while occupying any motor vehicle designed for use on public roads. This coverage also applies to the named insured and his or her family members when they are pedestrians struck by a motor vehicle designed for use on public roads. The medical payments coverage also applies to any other person occupying the covered automobile of the insured.

EXCLUSIONS

The second section of Part B of the standard personal auto policy lists a number of **exclusions** from this coverage. To begin with, the insurance company will typically decline to provide medical payments coverage arising from bodily injury sustained by an insured party occupying a motorized vehicle with **fewer than four wheels**. The insurance company will also usually decline to pay for injury sustained while occupying a covered auto that is being used as a **public conveyance** (this does not apply to carpools). The standard personal auto policy will not extend medical payments coverage to those who are injured while occupying a vehicle being used as a **residence or premises**. Also, the insurance company will decline to extend coverage if the bodily injury occurs during the course of **employment** and could also be covered by workers' compensation benefits. In the standard personal auto policy, the insurance company will decline to extend medical payments Coverage A for bodily injuries sustained while occupying a vehicle that is owned or available for the regular use of the insured party, but is **not a covered auto**.

The exclusions related to medical payments coverage will continue by stating that the insurance company declines to pay for any bodily injuries sustained while occupying a vehicle despite having the reasonable belief that the insured party is entitled to occupy that vehicle. In other words, insured parties cannot receive medical payments coverage for injuries sustained while riding in a **stolen car**. Neither will the insurance company provide medical payments coverage for individuals who are riding in a vehicle that is being used for **business purposes** by the insured unless that vehicle is a private passenger auto, pickup, or van. The standard personal auto policy does not cover bodily injuries arising from nuclear weapons, war, or other **military actions**. Finally, the medical payments coverage does not extend to bodily injuries stemming from **radioactive** contamination, radiation, or nuclear reaction.

LIMIT OF LIABILITY

After outlining the exclusions from medical payments coverage, the standard personal auto policy will describe the **limits of liability**. Specifically, the standard policy will state that the limit of medical payments coverage indicated on the **declarations page** represent the maximum liability for each person injured in a single accident. This is asserted by the insurance company regardless of the number of insureds involved in the accident, the number of claims made, the number of vehicles or premiums indicated on the declarations page, and the number of vehicles involved in the accident. Moreover, the insurance company will typically state that any amounts payable for coverage under the medical payments policy are reduced by any amounts paid or payable by liability coverage or uninsured motorists' coverage. Finally, the insurance company asserts that no payments will be made unless the injured party or his or her legal representative gives written agreement that the payment shall be applied toward any judgment or settlement received by the insured party under liability coverage or uninsured motorists' coverage.

OTHER INSURANCE

The last section of Part B of the standard personal auto policy describes the protocol for handling medical payments coverage when **other insurance policies** are applicable. To begin with, the insurance company will typically declare that it shall only pay its share of the loss when other auto medical payments insurance applies. Moreover, the insurance company will define its **share** as the proportion of its limit of liability within the total of all applicable limits. At the same time, any insurance provided that is related to a vehicle not owned by the insured party will automatically be defined as **excess** to any other collectible auto insurance that offers payments for medical or funeral expenses.

PART C (UNINSURED MOTORISTS' COVERAGE)

INSURING AGREEMENT

Part C of the standard personal auto policy discusses **uninsured motorists' coverage**. It typically begins by outlining the **insuring agreement** for this coverage. The insurance company will promise to pay any compensatory damages that an insured party is legally entitled to recover from the owner or operator of an uninsured motor vehicle because of bodily injury. In order for this coverage to apply, however, the bodily injury must have been caused by an accident and must have been sustained by a listed insured party. Moreover, the liability of the owner or operator must be related to his or her ownership, use, or maintenance of the uninsured motor vehicle. The insurance company asserts that it is not bound by any judgment for damages arising out of a suit that is brought without the written consent of the insurance company.

UNINSURED MOTOR VEHICLES

The first section of Part C of the standard personal auto policy defines **uninsured motor vehicles**. A motor vehicle is considered to be uninsured if no **bodily injury liability bond or policy** applies to it at the time of the accident in question. A vehicle is also considered to be uninsured if it is covered by a bodily injury liability bond or policy at the time of the accident, but the limit of this liability is less than the **minimum limit** specified by the financial responsibility law of the state in which the vehicle is covered. Hit-and-run incidents, in which the owner or operator cannot be identified, are considered to be uninsured motor vehicles. Finally, vehicles to which a bodily injury liability bond or policy applies may be defined as uninsured if the wanting or insuring company **becomes insolvent or denies coverage**. Vehicles that are designed to be used mainly off of public roads or are currently being used as a residence or premises may not be defined as uninsured motor vehicles.

EXCLUSIONS

The standard personal auto policy lists several **exclusions** to uninsured motorists' coverage. To begin with, the insurance company typically will decline to provide uninsured motorists' coverage for bodily injury suffered by any person occupying or struck by a vehicle owned by the insured or one of the insured's family members when this vehicle is not insured for **uninsured motorists' coverage**. In addition, the insurance company will decline to provide uninsured motorists' coverage if the injured party or his or her legal representative settles the injury claim **without the consent of the insurance company**. The insurance company will not provide coverage if the injured party is occupying his or her vehicle as a **public conveyance** at the time of the accident. Uninsured motorists' coverage will not be provided for **punitive or exemplary damages**. Finally, **disability benefits laws and workers' compensation laws** may not be used as a justification for coverage under an uninsured motorists' policy.

POLICY: LIMIT OF LIABILITY

As it did with the other forms of coverage offered in the standard personal auto policy, the insurance company will declare that the **limit of liability** associated with uninsured motorists' coverage is the amount indicated on the **declarations page**, regardless of the number of insureds, claims made, vehicles involved in the accident, or vehicles or premiums indicated on the declarations page. In addition, any amounts that are otherwise payable for damages under uninsured motorists' coverage will be reduced by amounts equal to any sums paid because of the bodily injury by **other legally responsible persons or organizations**. The limits of liability for uninsured motorists' coverage will also be diminished by any sums paid or payable for bodily injury under **disability benefits law or workers' compensation law**. Similarly, any amount of payment made for **uninsured motorists' coverage** will reduce the amount of liability coverage under Part A.

OTHER INSURANCE AND ARBITRATION

Part C of the standard personal auto policy indicates that the usual protocol for handling **multiple insurance coverages** will apply to uninsured motorists' coverage. In other words, the insurance company will only pay its share of the loss when there is other applicable insurance. The uninsured motorists' coverage share is the portion of its limit of liability related to the total of all applicable limits. Part C also explains the protocol for **arbitration of disputes** between the insured party and the insurance company. In the event that the insured party and the insurance company disagree about whether the insured is entitled to damages, or about the amount of damages, either party may request arbitration in writing. Each party will be permitted two arbitrators, who in turn will select a third. If the three arbitrators cannot reach an agreement within 30 days, a final decision may be rendered by the judge or a court with jurisdiction. If arbitration is necessary, but each side will be responsible for the expenses incurred, the expenses of the third arbitrator will be split.

PART D (COVERAGE FOR DAMAGE TO YOUR AUTO)
INSURING AGREEMENT

Part D of the standard personal auto policy outlines the coverage for **damage to the insured's automobile**. The first section of Part D is the **insuring agreement**. The insurance company typically will promise to pay for any direct or accidental loss to the covered auto or any non-owned auto, including replacement or repair of equipment. The insurance company will typically assert, however, that any applicable deductible indicated on the declarations page will be subtracted from the payment. The insurance company will promise to pay for losses caused by collision, so long as collision coverage is indicated on the declarations page, and for losses caused by events other than collisions only if other-than-collision coverage is indicated on the declarations page. For the purposes of this policy, collision is defined as the upset of the auto or its impact with another vehicle or object. Loss for reasons other than collision may be caused by fire; theft or larceny; explosion or earthquake; missiles or falling objects; windstorm; riot or civil commotion; hail, water, or flood; malicious mischief or vandalism; contact with birds or animals; or breakage of glass.

DEFINITION OF NON-OWNED AUTO

In the insuring agreement related to Part D, the insurance company typically will promise to pay for some direct and accidental losses to "**non-owned autos**." The end of the insuring agreement offers a comprehensive definition of non-owned autos. For the purposes of this coverage, a non-owned auto is any private passenger auto, pickup truck, van, or trailer that is being operated by the named insured or a family member but which is not owned by or furnished for the regular use of the named insured or family member. In addition, the policyholder may receive coverage for any auto or trailer that he or she does not own but that is being used as a **temporary substitute** for his or her covered automobile, while the covered automobile is not being used because of breakdown, loss, repair, servicing, or destruction.

TRANSPORTATION EXPENSES

The standard personal auto policy will include some additional payments for **transportation expenses**. These do not trigger the application of the deductible. In standard arrangement, the insurance company will offer to pay up to $30 per day, with a maximum payment of $900. These payments are made to reimburse the insured party for transportation expenses incurred after the **total theft** of a covered automobile. Of course, these transportation expenses are only reimbursed if the insurance policy includes **other-than-collision coverage** on the declarations page. The insurance company will also pay these transportation expenses for any loss of use for which the insured party becomes legally responsible after the theft of a non-owned automobile. Again, payment for loss of use expenses requires other-than-collision coverage. The insurance company will often decline to pay any expenses incurred more than 48 hours after the theft, and will not pay for any subsequent expenses after the stolen automobile is restored or the insurance company has paid for the loss.

EXCLUSIONS

The standard personal auto policy enumerates the **exclusions** from coverage for damage to the automobile of the insured party. To begin with, the insurance company typically will decline to pay for any loss incurred by the covered auto while it is being used as a **public conveyance**. The coverage provided in this section does not extend to damage due and limited to **freezing, normal wear, mechanical failure, electrical problems, or road damage to tires**. Coverage for damage to the automobile of the insured party will not apply to losses caused by **radioactive contamination, nuclear weapons, war, or other military action**. This policy will not provide coverage for any non-owned auto that is being used by the insured or one of his or her family members without the **reasonable belief** that the user is entitled to do so. This coverage will not reimburse for losses to **radar detection equipment, custom furnishings, or special decorations**.

LIMIT OF LIABILITY AND PAYMENT OF LOSS

Part D of the standard personal auto policy describes the **limit of liability** for coverage related to damages to the insured party's automobile. Specifically, the limit of liability for loss will be either the **actual cash value** of the stolen or damaged property, or the amount required to **replace or repair** the property, whichever is smaller. It is noted that the insurance company will pay a maximum of $500 for damages to trailers that are not owned by the insured. With regard to the payment of losses, the insurance company reserves the right to either compensate the insured monetarily or to replace or repair the damaged or stolen property. The insurance company also reserves the right to return any stolen property to the named insured. The costs of this shipment will be borne by the insurance company. Moreover, the insurance company promises to pay for any damages that were caused by the theft. Finally, the insurance company reserves the right to keep all or part of the property in exchange for an agreed-upon or praised price.

BENEFITS TO BAILEE, OTHER SOURCES OF RECOVERY, AND APPRAISAL

The insurance policy that provides coverage for damage to the automobile of the insured shall not directly or indirectly **benefit any carrier or other bailee for hire**. As it has for other coverages in the personal auto policy, the insurance company states that it will only pay its share of the loss when **other sources of recovery** are available to the insured. This policy's share is the proportion of its limits of liability to the total of all applicable limits. With regard to non-owned autos, the insurance provided by this coverage will be considered excess over coverage provided by the owner of the auto, any other applicable physical damage insurance, and any other source of recovery. If the insurance company and the insured party do not agree on the value of the loss, either side is entitled to request an **appraisal**. The protocol for appraisal is that both sides select an appraiser, and these two appraisers select an umpire. The two appraisers will submit independent estimates, and if they fail to agree, the difference will be mediated by the umpire. Any decision agreed upon by two of the three arbitrators will be binding to all parties.

PART E: (DUTIES AFTER AN ACCIDENT OR LOSS)
GENERAL DUTIES

Part E of the standard personal auto policy outlines the **duties** of the insurance company and the insured after an accident or loss. To begin with, the insurance company will declare that it has no obligation to provide coverage unless the insured party has **fully complied** with the terms of the policy. For instance, the insured party must **notify** the insurance company immediately of the location, time, and circumstances of the accident or loss. The insured party should also provide the names and addresses of all **injured persons** and all available **witnesses**. Insured parties seeking coverage are required to **cooperate** during the investigation, defense, or settlement of any claims or suits. The insured party should also deliver copies of any **notices or legal papers** associated with the loss or accident as soon as possible. If requested, the insured should submit to **physical examination**, the expense of which will be borne by the insurance company. The insured must also authorize the insurance company to obtain any **medical reports** or relevant records.

DUTIES RELATED TO UNINSURED MOTORISTS' COVERAGE

There are some special duties required by the insured party who seeks **uninsured motorists' coverage** or coverage for damage to his or her auto. If the insured party is seeking uninsured motorists' coverage, he or she must also immediately notify the **police** in the event of a hit-and-run situation. If a suit is brought related to this situation, the insured party is required to send copies of all **legal papers** to the insurance company promptly. If the insured party is seeking coverage for damage to his or her automobile, he or she must also take reasonable steps to protect the automobile in question from **further loss**. Any reasonable expenses required to prevent further loss will be reimbursed by the insurance company. If the automobile is **stolen**, the insured party must promptly notify the police. Finally, in order to receive coverage for damage to his or her auto, the insured party must permit the insurance company to **inspect and appraise** the damaged property before it is thrown away or fixed.

PART F (GENERAL PROVISIONS)
BANKRUPTCY AND CHANGES TO THE POLICY

The final part of the standard personal auto policy, which covers **general provisions**, typically begins by declaring that the **bankruptcy** or insolvency of the insured party will not relieve the insurance company of any obligations under this policy. The general provisions section continues by stating that the sum total of the policy is expressed in the form, and any alteration or waiver of terms requires an **endorsement** issued by the insurance company. The insurance company will also assert the right to **change** the information used to calculate the premium, even when these changes will increase the amount of premium. The specific changes in circumstance that may result in a premium adjustment include the number, type, or use classification of insured vehicles; the drivers of insured vehicles; the place where insured vehicles are garaged; and the coverage, limits, or deductible. Whenever the premium needs to be adjusted, the adjustment will be in accordance with the rules of the manual. If the adjustment period is going to broaden coverage without adding to the premium, the change will be implemented automatically.

FRAUD

Part F of the standard personal auto policy asserts that the insurance company will not provide any coverage for an insured party who has made **fraudulent statements** or participated in **fraudulent behavior** related to any accident or loss for which he or she is seeking coverage under this policy. Furthermore, the insurance company will assert that no **legal action** may be brought against it unless the insured has complied with all of the terms of the insurance policy. With regard to the liability coverage, no legal action may be brought against the insurance company before the insurance company agrees in writing that the insured party has an obligation to pay, and before the amount of the insured's obligation has been determined by judgment. In addition, no person or group has the rights to take legal action against the insurance company in order to determine the insured's degree of liability.

INSURANCE COMPANY'S RIGHT TO RECOVER PAYMENTS

In the general provisions section of the personal automobile policy, the insurance company will typically declare that if it should make a payment and subsequently determine that the person to or for whom the payment was made is entitled to damages from a third party, the insurance company shall be **subrogated** to that right. Moreover, the person to whom payment was originally made is required to **cooperate** in whatever way is necessary, and to perform no actions that would prevent the insurance company from exercising its rights after the loss. It should be noted that these rights to recover payments do not apply under the coverage for damage to the automobile of the insured, so long as the person using that automobile had a reasonable belief that he or she was entitled to do so. This provision continues by stating that if the insurance company makes a payment under this policy and the person to or for whom payment is made recovers damages from another, then the person who receives damages is required to hold in **trust** the recovered damages and reimburse the insurance company for whatever it is paid.

CANCELLATION OF THE POLICY

The final provision in Part F describes the protocol for **cancellation of the policy**. Typically, the insurance company will allow the named insured on the declarations page to cancel the policy by **returning** it to the insurance company or giving the insurance company **advanced written notice** of the date on which the policy will be canceled. The insurance company, on the other hand, is allowed to cancel the policy by **notice** to the named insured at the address indicated on the declarations page. If the insurance company is canceling the policy due to nonpayment of premium, or if the policy is canceled within its first 60 days, the insurance company is only required to give 10 days of notice. In all other situations, the insurance company must use at least 20 days of notice before policy is canceled. Once a personal automobile policy has been in effect for 60 days, it will only be canceled for nonpayment of premium, the revocation of the driver's license of the insured, or if it is determined that the policy was obtained through material misrepresentation.

NONRENEWAL OR AUTOMATIC TERMINATION

The final general provision outlined in Part F of the standard personal auto policy describes the protocols for **nonrenewal and automatic termination of the policy**. If the insurance company decides not to renew or continue the policy, it is required to mail **notice** to the named insured party at least 20 days before the end of the policy period. For policy periods other than one year, the insurance company may only renew on the anniversary of the original effective date. If an offer of renewal is made by the insurance company but is not accepted by the named insured, the policy automatically ends at the conclusion of the current policy period. If the named insured fails to pay the mandatory renewal or continuation premium, this is interpreted as refusal to continue the policy.

Business Auto Policy

BASIC STRUCTURE OF THE DECLARATIONS PAGE

Business auto coverage forms typically come with a special **declarations page**. There are two versions of this declarations page: one that is used when coverage is issued as a **monoline policy**, and one that is used when coverage is issued as part of a **package policy**. The typical declarations page is divided into six sections, or **items**. Item 1 contains general information about the risk. Item 2 explains some coverages, coverage symbols, limits of liability, and the required premium for each coverage. Item 3 is a schedule of the automobiles owned by the business. Item 4 is a schedule of the automobiles that have been hired or borrowed by the business. Item 5 is a schedule for non-ownership liability, and Item 6 is a schedule of gross receipts or mileage for liability coverage for leasing rental or public auto concerns.

BASIC STRUCTURE OF A BUSINESS AUTO POLICY

The typical business auto policy is divided into **five sections**. Section 1 describes the covered automobiles. Section 2 describes the liability coverage, and Section 3 describes the physical damage coverage. Section 4 describes the business auto conditions, and Section 5 is devoted to definitions. The typical business auto policy coverage form does not include provisions for medical payments or uninsured motorists' coverage. In order for these coverages to go into effect, **endorsements** must be attached. After listing the sections of the coverage form, the insurance company will typically alert the policyholder of the necessity of reading the entire policy carefully. Moreover, the insurance company will indicate that the policyholder should refer to the fifth section for precise definitions of any words or phrases that appear in quotation marks.

SECTION 1 (COVERED AUTOS)

INTRODUCTION AND DESCRIPTION OF A COVERED AUTO DESIGNATION SYMBOLS

Section 1 of the standard business auto policy reminds the policyholder that the particular automobiles covered by each version of the policy are indicated in **Item 2** of the declarations page. The policy will then describe the **symbols** that are used to designate various covered automobiles. A one denotes any automobile. A two denotes automobiles that are owned by the business. Any automobile that is acquired by the business after the initiation of the policy is included in designation two. A three denotes an owned private passenger automobile only. A four denotes all owned automobiles besides private passenger automobiles. A five denotes all of those automobiles that are required to have no-fault benefits in the state where they are principally garaged or licensed. A six denotes all owned automobiles that are subject to a compulsory uninsured motorists' law. A seven denotes only those automobiles that are specifically described in item 3 of the declarations page, and for which a special premium charge is indicated. An eight indicates only those automobiles that are leased, hired, rented, or borrowed. Finally, a nine indicates only those automobiles that are used in connection with the business but which are not owned, leased, hired, rented, or borrowed by the business.

SECTION 2 (LIABILITY COVERAGE)

COVERAGE

Section 2 of the standard business auto policy begins by defining the **basic coverage** to be provided. The insurance company declares that it will pay all of the sums an insured party must legally pay because of any **bodily injury or property damage** caused by an accident and resulting from the ownership, use, or maintenance of a covered automobile. Moreover, the insurance policy promises to pay all of the amounts legally owed by the insured as **pollution costs or expenses**. The insurance company only promises to pay for covered pollution costs or expenses when the same accident that incurred the expense caused property damage or bodily injury. The insurance company reserves the right and duty to defend any **suit** asking for damages related to a covered pollution cost or expense, though this right may be waived. Moreover, the duty of the insurance company to defend or settle claims comes to an end once the payment of judgments has reached the **limits of liability coverage**.

WHO IS INSURED

The **second section** of the standard business auto policy includes a brief list of those parties who qualify as an **insured** for the policy. To begin with, the named party is considered an **assured** for any covered automobile. Second, in most cases any person who is using a covered automobile with the permission of the named party is also covered. There are a few exceptions to this coverage. For instance, the owner or anyone else from whom the named insured party **hires or borrows** a covered auto is not covered by the insurance. Neither is an **employee** of the insured party if the covered automobile is owned by that employee or a member of his or her household. Individuals using covered automobiles who are working in a **business** of selling, servicing, parking, repairing, or storing automobiles are not covered unless that business is the business of the insured party. Any person who is **moving** property to or from a covered automobile is not covered unless they are an employee, partner, lessee, or borrower of the employer. Finally, **partners** of the named insured are not covered if he or she or a member of his or her household owns the automobile. The final group to be covered by the standard business auto policy is any person liable for the conduct of the insured party. This coverage only extends to the limits of that liability.

SUPPLEMENTARY PAYMENTS

Section 2 of the standard business auto policy goes on to describe the protocol for **supplementary payments**. The insurance company promises to pay for all **expenses** it incurs. It also promises to pay for up to $250 off the cost of **bail bonds** required because of covered accidents. These bonds do not have to be furnished by the insurance company, however. The insurance company also promises to pay the cost of bonds needed to release attachments related to any suits defended by the insurance company. However, this promise only extends to bond amounts within the limit of insurance. The insurance company promises to pay all **reasonable expenses** incurred by the insured party at the request of the insurance company. This includes reimbursement for loss of earnings up to $100 per day because of time off from work. The insurance company promises to pay all costs that are **taxed** against the insured related to any suit defended by the insurance company. Finally, the insurance company promises to pay all **interest** on the full amount of any judgment that accrues after the judgment has been entered in a defended suit.

OUT-OF-STATE COVERAGE EXTENSIONS

Section 2 of the standard business auto policy explains the **out-of-state coverage extensions**. Namely, the insurance company will typically promise to **increase** the limit of insurance for liability coverage to meet the minimum requirements of the compulsory or financial responsibility law of the jurisdiction in which the automobile is being used. However, this extension of limits does not apply to the limits imposed by laws related to **motor carriers** of property or passengers. The insurance company also promises to provide the **minimum** amounts of coverage required for out-of-state vehicles in the jurisdiction in which the covered automobile is being used. However, the insurance company will not make **redundant payments** for the same elements of loss because of out-of-state coverage extensions.

LIABILITY EXCLUSIONS

Section 2 of the standard business auto policy describes some **liability exclusions**. To begin with, the insurance company does not cover any **expected or intended** injury or property damage. That is, any bodily injury or property damage expected or intended by the insured party is not covered by this policy. The insurance also does not apply to any liability assumed by the insured party under any **contract or agreement**. However, the insurance company does cover liability for damages related to **insured contracts**. The standard business auto policy does not cover the obligations of the insured party under any **workers' compensation, disability benefits, or unemployment compensation law**. This insurance policy will not cover bodily injuries to **employees** of the insured that are related to the normal course of employment. The insurance company also will not cover any bodily injury to a **fellow employee** of the insured that occurs in the course of the fellow employee's employment. These last exclusions are meant to ensure that the business auto policy does not have to provide coverage that should be provided by a workers' compensation policy.

Section 2 of the standard business auto policy continues its list of liability exclusions by declaring that the insurance policy will not be applied to any property damage to a covered **pollution cost or expense** related to property owned or transported by the insured. The basic business auto policy does not cover any bodily injury or property damage caused by the **handling of property** before or after it is in the covered automobile. Moreover, this insurance policy does not cover any bodily injury or property damage related to the **operation of a mechanical device** unless that mechanical device is connected to the covered automobile. The insurance policy does not cover any bodily injury or property damage related to the **operation of mobile equipment**, as for instance the self-propelled vehicles upon which cherry pickers are mounted.

Section 2 of the standard business auto policy continues its list of liability exclusions by declaring that the policy will not apply to any bodily injury or property damage that occurs after work has been **completed or abandoned**. For the purposes of the business auto policy, work is defined as complete when all of the tasks indicated in the contract have been completed, when all the work at a particular job site has been completed, or when the relevant part of the work at a job site has been put to its intended use by someone besides another contractor or subcontractor. Work is considered to be complete even if it requires ongoing service, maintenance, correction, repair, or replacement.

POLLUTION AND WAR LIABILITY EXCLUSIONS

Section 2 of the standard business auto policy declares that the policy does not cover bodily injury or property damage that arises out of the actual or threatened discharge, release, or escape of **pollutants** if these pollutants are being transported into, onto, or from the covered vehicle. The insurance policy also does not cover bodily injury or property damage related to pollutants before the pollutants are moved into or onto the covered auto. The insurance policy also doesn't cover any injury or damage related to pollutants after they have been moved from the auto. The final liability exclusion in the standard business auto policy is related to **war**. The insurance policy does not cover any bodily injury or property damage caused by war, though this exclusion is limited to liability assumed under a contract or agreement.

69

LIMIT OF INSURANCE

Section 2 of the standard business auto policy includes a description of the **limit of insurance**. Here, the insurance company declares that it will not make payments in excess of the maximum amount of liability coverage indicated on the **declarations page**. Any bodily injury, property damage, learned covered pollution cost or expense that is caused by continuous or repeated exposure to the same conditions will be considered by the insurance company as resulting from a **single accident**. In other words, the policyholder may not receive duplicate payments for the same elements of loss. There is a single limit of insurance for each individual accident, no matter how many covered vehicles are involved, how many insured individuals are involved, or how many premiums have been paid.

SECTION 3 (PHYSICAL DAMAGE COVERAGE)

LOSS COVERAGE

At the beginning of the **third section** of the standard business auto policy, which has to do with **physical damage coverage**, the insurance company will typically define the coverage. The standard iteration is that the insurance company will provide **comprehensive coverage** for losses to covered automobiles unless the cause is the covered automobile's collision with another object or the covered automobile is overturned. The insurance company will pay for losses under **specified causes** of loss coverage, specifically fire, lightning, or explosion; theft; windstorm, hail, or earthquake; flood; mischief or vandalism; or the sinking, burning, collision, or derailment of any conveyance that is transporting the covered automobile. Finally, the insurance company will assert that losses will be paid under **collision coverage** when the injury or property damage is caused by the covered auto's collision with another object or the covered auto is overturned.

TOWING AND GLASS BREAKAGE COVERAGE

Section 3 of the standard business auto policy will outline the coverage related to **towing and glass breakage**. Typically, the insurance company will promise to pay up to the limit published in the declarations for any **towing and labor costs** incurred when a covered auto is disabled. In order for the towing charges to be covered, however, all labor must be performed at the site of the breakdown. Section 3 will also describe the coverage provided related to **glass breakage**. Generally, it will state that if the automobile in question has comprehensive coverage, then the insurance company will pay for any glass breakage, any loss caused by hitting a bird or other animal, and any loss caused by missiles or falling objects. In the event that the glass breaks during a collision or when the vehicle is overturned, the policyholder may have this defined as a loss under collision coverage.

COVERAGE EXTENSION

It is typical for the **third section** of the standard business auto policy to include a brief description of the protocol for **coverage extension**. This relates to the theft of covered vehicles. The standard for the insurance company is to promise maximum payment of $30 per day, with the largest overall payment being $900, for transportation expenses incurred because of the **theft** of a private passenger automobile. This coverage extension only applies for those vehicles for which the owner carries either comprehensive or specified causes of loss coverage. The insurance company typically promises to pay for all **transportation expenses** incurred within the first 48 hours of the vehicle's theft. The insurance company will stop paying for incurred transportation expenses when the vehicle is returned or its loss has been fully reimbursed by the insurance company, regardless of when the business auto policy expires.

EXCLUSIONS

Section 3 of the standard business auto policy describes some of the **policy exclusions**. The business will not be reimbursed for losses resulting from any of these excluded causes, even when some other cause or event contributes concurrently or in any other way to the loss. To begin with, any losses suffered as a result of **nuclear hazard** are excluded from coverage. This includes the explosion of any weapon employing atomic fission or fusion, or nuclear reaction or radiation, or radioactive contamination. The insurance company also refuses to pay for losses caused by **war**, even when that war is undeclared. This exclusion also applies to insurrections, rebellions, revolutions, and any warlike actions by military force. The exclusion relates to military actions regardless of whether they are aggressive or defensive.

OTHER EXCLUSIONS

Section 3 of the standard business auto policy outlines a few other **exclusions** besides nuclear hazard and military action. The insurance company will typically refuse to pay for any losses related to **sound reproducing equipment** unless it has been permanently installed in a covered automobile. Likewise, the insurance company will not pay for loss of CDs, tapes, records, or other sound reproducing devices. It will also not pay for losses to **sound receiving equipment** like citizens band radio, two-way mobile radio, or scanning monitor receivers unless these devices are permanently installed in the dashboard. Finally, the insurance company will decline to pay for losses to equipment designed or used for the **detection or location of radar**. The business auto policy does not cover **wear and tear, freezing, mechanical breakdown, or electrical problems** unless they are caused by another loss covered by the insurance policy. Finally, the insurance company will not pay for punctures, blowouts, or general road damage to **tires**.

LIMIT OF INSURANCE AND DEDUCTIBLE

Section 3 of the standard business auto policy provides a basic summary of the **limits of insurance**. Typically, the insurance company will state that the maximum payment for any single accident is either the **actual cash value** of the damaged or stolen property at the time of the loss, or the cost of **repairing/replacing** the damaged or stolen property, whichever is less. With regard to the policy deductible, the insurance company states that for each covered automobile, the obligation to repair, reimburse, return, or replace damaged or stolen property will be reduced by the **deductible** amount indicated on the declarations page. Losses caused by **fire or lightning** are not subject to the comprehensive coverage deductible shown on the declarations page.

SECTION 4 (BUSINESS AUTO CONDITIONS)
APPRAISAL FOR PHYSICAL DAMAGE LOSS

The **fourth section** of the standard business auto policy outlines the **business auto conditions**. The conditions described in this section accompany the **Common Policy Conditions**. The conditions listed here are divided into two sections: loss conditions and general conditions. The **loss conditions section** begins by describing the protocol for **appraisal of physical damage loss**. Namely, if the insurance company and the policyholder disagree about the amount of a loss, either party may request an appraisal. This appraisal condition is much the same as the one found on a standard property insurance policy. Each side will be charged with selecting a competent appraiser, and so two estimations of actual cash value and loss will be generated. If the appraisers disagree, their differences will be submitted to an umpire. If the appraisers agree, their decision is automatically binding. Each party will be responsible for paying the appraiser it selects, and the other costs of appraisal and umpiring will be split equally. Submitting to an appraisal does not waive the insurance company's rights to deny a claim.

ACCIDENT, CLAIM, SUIT, OR LOSS DUTIES

Section 4 of the standard business auto policy continues by outlining the duties of the policyholder in the event of **accident, claim, suit, or loss**. To begin with, the policyholder is responsible for **alerting** the insurance company as soon as possible. There are certain pieces of information that the policyholder is required to provide. The policyholder will need to provide the **location and time** of the incident, as well as the **sequence of events** that led to it. The policyholder will also need to provide his or her **name and address**. In addition, the policyholder will need to provide, if possible, the names and addresses of any **other injured parties or witnesses**. The policyholder also has some duties designed to minimize the extent of the loss. The policyholder should assume no **obligation** and pay no **expense** without the consent of the insurance company unless this obligation or expense is intended to be borne by the policyholder. The policyholder should promptly send the insurance company copies of any **request, demand, notice, order, legal paper, or summons** related to the claim or suit. The policyholder should also **cooperate** with investigation or defense of the claim or suit. Finally, the policyholder must authorize the insurance company to obtain **medical records** or any other information that is relevant.

LEGAL ACTION AGAINST THE INSURANCE COMPANY AND LOSS PAYMENT

The **fourth section** of the standard business auto policy outlines the scenarios in which **legal action** may be brought against the insurance company. There are only a few of these. For instance, legal action may only be brought against the insurance company if every term of the **Coverage Form** has been complied with completely. Also, it is necessary for the insurance company to have agreed in writing that the insured has an **obligation to pay**. In other words, the insurance company may not be brought into court to determine the liability of the insured party. The fourth section of the standard business auto policy also outlines the protocol for payment of losses under **physical damage coverage**. The insurance company reserves the right to take any of the following actions: return the stolen property at the expense of the insurance company; pay for, replace, or repair damaged or stolen property; or accept all or any of the damaged or stolen property at an appraised or agreed-upon value.

TRANSFER OF RIGHTS OF RECOVERY AGAINST OTHERS TO THE INSURANCE COMPANY

The **fourth section** of the standard business auto policy outlines the protocol for the **transfer of rights of recovery** against others to the insurance company. According to this section, the right of any party to or for whom the insurance company makes payment to recover damages from a third party is transferred to the **insurance company**. The person or group to or for whom the insurance company has made payment is obliged to **protect the rights** of the insurance company and should do nothing to impair these rights. This final loss condition is a standard **subrogation clause**. With it, the insurance company secures the ability to receive the right payment from anyone who has received payment from the insurance company and is subsequently owed money.

BANKRUPTCY, CONCEALMENT, MISREPRESENTATION, OR FRAUD; AND LIBERALIZATION

After outlining the loss conditions, **Section 4** of the standard business auto policy continues by describing the **general conditions**. To begin with, the standard policy will state that the **bankruptcy or insolvency** of the insured or the state of the insured does not relieve the insurance company of any of the obligations indicated by the coverage form. The insurance company will go on to state that the coverage form is rendered void by any **fraud** by the policyholder, so long as this fraud relates in any way to the terms of the insurance policy. The coverage form is also rendered void by any intentional concealment or misrepresentation of material facts related to the coverage form, covered automobiles, the policyholder's interest in the covered automobiles, or claims under this coverage form. The next of the general conditions is that, in the event that the insurance company revises the **coverage form** in such a way that more coverage is provided without raising

72

the premium, the policy will be automatically adjusted on the same day that this revision goes into effect in the policyholder's state.

PHYSICAL DAMAGE COVERAGES WHEN THERE IS NO BENEFIT TO THE BAILEE

Section 4 of the standard business auto policy describes the protocol for **physical damage coverages when there is no benefit to the bailee**. Specifically, this section declares that the insurance company will not recognize any assignment or grant any coverage that benefits a person or organization that is holding, storing, or transferring property for a fee. This provision is asserted despite any other possibly contradictory provision in the coverage form. Section 4 goes on to describe the protocol for **other insurance**. This coverage form provides primary insurance for any automobile owned by the policyholder. However, for any covered automobile that is not owned by the policyholder, the insurance provided by this policy is simply the excess over any other collectible insurance. Despite this provision, the liability coverage of the standard business policy is considered primary for any liability assumed under an insured contract.

PREMIUM AUDIT

Section 4 of the standard business auto policy describes the calculation of the **estimated premium**. Specifically, the insurance company typically states that the original estimated premium is based on the **reported exposures** at the time of the policy's initiation. Once the actual exposures are determined, the final premium can be calculated. The estimated total premium is credited against the final premium due, and either the insured or the insurance company will receive whatever difference exists. When the standard business auto policy is issued for a period of more than one year, the premium for it is computed every year based on the rates or premiums that have been established at the beginning of that year.

POLICY PERIOD, COVERAGE TERRITORY, AND TWO OR MORE COVERAGE FORMS

Section 4 of the standard business auto policy includes a brief summation of the **policy period** and the **coverage territory**. Specifically, the insurance company will typically state that the coverage form promises coverage for accidents and losses that occur within the dates specified on the declarations page and within the coverage territory. The usual coverage territory is the United States of America and all territories and possessions of the United States of America, Puerto Rico, and Canada. In most cases, the insurance company will also cover any loss or accident related to covered vehicles that are being transported between any of these covered territories. The last provision of the fourth section relates to accidents that are covered by **more than one insurance policy**. The insurance company will typically declare that the aggregate maximum limit of insurance under all the coverage forms or policies may not be higher than the highest applicable limit of insurance for any one coverage form or policy. The only exception to this rule is when one of the insurance policies has been issued specifically as excess insurance.

SECTION 5 (DEFINITIONS)
ACCIDENT, AUTO, BODILY INJURY, AND INSURED

The **fifth section** of the standard business auto policy is devoted to **definitions**. In a standard business auto policy, an **accident** is any exposure to conditions that result in property damage or bodily injury. An **automobile** is a land motor vehicle, trailer, or semi-trailer that was designed to travel on public roads. Mobile equipment, as for instance the devices that are used to move cherry pickers, does not count as an automobile. **Bodily injury** is defined in the standard business auto policy as any personal injury, sickness, or disease. Death that results from injury, sickness, or disease is also classified as bodily injury. The standard business auto policy defines the **insured** as any person or organization who qualifies to receive the coverage. The coverage described in this form applies separately to each insured party who seeks coverage or against whom a suit or claim is brought, except with regard to the limit of insurance.

COVERED POLLUTION COST OR EXPENSE

The **fifth section** of the standard business auto policy offers an extremely detailed definition of **covered pollution cost or expense**. To begin with, the standard policy will state that covered pollution cost or expense refers to any cost or expense that arises out of any request, demand, order, or any claim or suit by a **government authority** for the insured to cleanup or dispose of pollutants. The policy then goes on to provide an extensive list of situations that would not be considered as covered pollution costs or expenses. The primary intention of this language is to limit strictly the coverage provided for the cleanup and removal of pollutants that are part of an automobile's **normal operations**, namely motor oil or gasoline. The standard business auto policy will refuse to offer coverage for any pollution that escapes from the covered vehicle while it is being transported or stored.

INSURED CONTRACT

In the **fifth section** of the standard business auto policy, an **insured contract** is defined as any of the following: sidetrack agreement, last of premises, any easement or license agreement, an obligation to indemnify a municipality when required by ordinance, part or all of any other business-related contract or agreement in which the insured party assumes the tort liability of another to pay for injury or damage to a third party, or any business-related contract or agreement pertaining to the rental or lease of automobiles. For the purposes of the standard business auto policy, however, an insured contract does not include the section of any contract or agreement that **indemnifies** any person or organization for injury or damage related to construction or demolition operations. Also, the insured contract's classification does not include contracts or agreements related to the **loan, lease, or rental** of an auto if a driver is included in the loan, lease, or rental.

MOBILE EQUIPMENT

The **fifth section** of the standard business auto policy provides a comprehensive definition of **mobile equipment**. Mobile equipment includes any of the following: bulldozers, forklifts, farm machinery, or other vehicles designed to be used off public roads; vehicles that are propelled on crawler treads; and vehicles that are maintained for use entirely on or adjacent to premises owned or rented by the insured party. Moreover, mobile equipment includes any equipment that has the primary purpose of providing **mobility** to permanently mounted road construction equipment, resurfacing equipment, powertrains, shovels, diggers, drills, and any vehicles that are maintained primarily for purposes other than the transport of cargo or people. Some exceptions to this definition include equipment designed primarily for snow removal, street cleaning, and road maintenance, though not construction or resurfacing. These forms of equipment are classified as **autos**.

POLLUTANTS, PROPERTY DAMAGE, SUIT, AND TRAILER

The **fifth section** of the standard business auto policy defines **pollutants** as any solid, liquid, gaseous, or thermal irritant or contaminant. Among the forms of pollutants are smoke, vapor, soot, fumes, acids, alkalis, chemicals, and waste. **Waste** is defined as any material that is to be reconditioned, reclaimed, or recycled. In the context of the standard business auto policy, **property damage** is any loss of use or diminution in value of tangible property. A **suit** is defined as any civil proceeding in which it is alleged that damages to which this insurance applies have occurred because of property damage, covered pollution cost or expense, or bodily injury. An arbitration proceeding to which the insured party submits or is required to submit is also defined as a suit. Finally, in a standard business auto policy the term "**trailer**" includes semi-trailers.

74

Commercial Package Policy (CPP)

Standard Commercial General Liability Policy

SECTION 1 (COVERAGES)

INSURING AGREEMENT

The standard commercial general liability policy devotes its **first section** to **coverages**. To begin with, the policy will help outline the **bodily injury and property damage liability**. This provision typically begins by declaring that the insurance company promises to pay any sums for which the insured becomes legally obligated to pay because of applicable bodily injury or property damage. The insurance company does reserve the right to defend any **suit** seeking these damages, as well as to investigate precipitating events and settle any resulting claims or suits. The amount paid by the insurance company only extends up to the **limits of insurance** described in the third section of the policy. Also, the insurance company's responsibility and right to defend **expire** when the insurance company has paid the applicable limit of insurance.

REQUIREMENTS FOR BODILY INJURY AND PROPERTY DAMAGE LIABILITY

The **first section** of the standard commercial general liability policy outlines some of the **requirements for bodily injury and property damage liability**. Specifically, this insurance will only apply to bodily injury and property damage if the injury or damage is the result of an occurrence that takes place **within the coverage territory**. Also, precipitating occurrence must not have occurred before the **wreck drawback due date** or after the **conclusion of the policy period**. Finally, bodily injury and property damage are only covered if the claim for damages is originally made against the insured party during either the **declared policy** or any **extended reporting period** provided by the insurance company. When determining the time of a claim by a person or organization seeking damages, the insurance company will assert that the claim was made either when settlement is made or when notice of the claim was received and recorded by the insured or the insurance company, whichever comes first.

EXCLUSIONS

Section 1 of the standard commercial general liability policy describes some of the **policy exclusions**. To begin with, the standard commercial general liability policy does not apply when the bodily injury or property damage could have been **expected or intended** from the standpoint of the insured party. However, this exclusion does not apply when bodily injury or property damage could have been expected, but the claimant was required to use reasonable force to protect persons or property. This insurance policy also will not cover bodily injury or property damage for which the insured party is obliged to pay damages because of the **assumption of liability** and a **contract or agreement**. This exclusion does not apply to insured contracts. The standard commercial general liability policy also will not cover any injury or damage for which the insured party may be held liable because he or she contributed to the **intoxication** of another person, or furnished alcoholic beverages to an intoxicated person or a person under the legal drinking age.

Section 1 of the standard commercial general liability policy typically declares that the insurance company will refuse to pay any obligation of the insured party stemming from a **workers' compensation, unemployment compensation, or disability benefits law**. The insurance company also refuses to pay for any bodily injury to an employee of the insured that arises out of or during the course of **employment** by the insured, regardless of whether the insured may be liable as an employer or in any other capacity. Also, this exclusion applies to any obligation to cooperate in the payment of damages with **another party**. However, this exclusion does not apply to liability that the insured party assumes as part of insured contract. Finally, the standard commercial general liability policy contains a long provision eliminating coverage for basically any type of exposure to **pollution**. In most cases, businesses are required to purchase a separate environmental impairment liability insurance policy to cover the risks of pollution.

The list of exclusions in the **first section** of the standard commercial general liability policy continues by asserting that the insurance company will not pay for bodily injury or property damage that results from the ownership, use, or maintenance of any **aircraft, automobile, or watercraft**. Also, the insurance company will not pay for bodily injury or property damage that results from the transportation of **mobile equipment** by an auto owned or operated by the insured. The standard commercial general liability policy does not cover bodily injury or property damage caused by **war** or other military actions. The insurance company also refuses to pay for property damage to property **owned, rented, or occupied** by the insured. Finally, the insurance company will not pay for damage to **property loans** to the insured, or property that has been **given away or abandoned** by the insured.

The compendium of exclusions in the **first section** of the standard commercial general liability policy continues by asserting that the insurance company will refuse to pay for property damage to the **product** of the insured if the property damage is caused by any part of the product. In like fashion, the insurance company will refuse to pay for property damage to the **work** of the insured party if the damage is the result of the work itself. It will also refuse to pay for property damage to property that is impaired or that has been physically injured because of a **defect or delay**. Finally, the insurance company will decline to pay for damages that are claimed for any loss, expense, or cost incurred by the insured party for the loss of use, removal, repair, inspection, or disposal of the product, work, or impaired property when this product, work, or property is taken off the market because of a **defect or suspected deficiency**.

PERSONAL AND ADVERTISING INJURY LIABILITY INSURING AGREEMENT

The standard commercial general liability policy includes a brief description in Section 1A of the **insuring agreement for personal and advertising injury liability**. Namely, the insurance company will promise to pay for any damages legally owed by the policyholder because of applicable **personal or advertising injury**. Again, the insurance company reserves the right to investigate the precipitating event and dispute any claims in court. The responsibility and right to investigate is abandoned when the applicable limit of insurance has been reached in the payment of judgments or settlements. This insurance applies to any personal injury caused by an offense that occurs in the course of the policyholder's **business**, as well as to any **advertising injury** (that is, injury caused by an offense arising from the advertisement of the policyholder's goods, products, or services). Of course, the insurance only applies if the offense was committed in the coverage territory and in the interval between the retroactive date and the end of the policy period. In the view of the insurance company, the date of the claim by the person or organization seeking damages will be either the date on which notice of the claim is received and recorded by the insured party or the insurance company, or when the insurance company makes settlement, whichever comes first.

EXCLUSIONS TO PERSONAL AND ADVERTISING INJURY LIABILITY

There are some special exclusions in the standard commercial general liability policy with regard to **personal and advertising injury coverage**. To begin with, the insurance company will not pay expenses under this policy for **bodily injury** to the insured party, or to any person hired to do work for or on behalf of the insured party. Furthermore, this coverage will not apply to bodily injury to

76

persons who could receive coverage as well from **workers' compensation, disability benefits, or similar law**. The insurance company will not pay the policyholder for the expenses related to persons who normally **occupy** a part of the premises owned or rented by the insured party. This policy will not apply to injury suffered during **athletic competition, war, or other military action**.

SUPPLEMENTARY PAYMENTS

The final provision of the **first section** of the standard commercial general liability policy has to do with **supplementary payments**. Specifically, the insurance company typically will promise to pay **all expenses incurred** with respect to any claim or suit it defends. It will also pay up to $250 for the cost of **bail bonds** required because of traffic law violations or accidents related to the use of vehicles that receive coverage under the bodily injury liability policy. It is not necessary, however, for the insurance company to supply these bonds. The insurance company will also promise to pay the cost of any bonds required to release attachments, so long as these bonds' amounts are within the applicable limit of insurance. Again, it is not necessary for the insurance company to actually furnish these bonds.

In the standard commercial general liability policy, the insurance company will typically promise to pay all reasonable expenses that are incurred by the policyholder at the request of the insurance party during the investigation or defense of any **claim or suit**. This will typically include up to $100 a day in compensation for loss of earnings because of **time missed from work**. The insurance company will also pay all costs **taxed** against the insured in the suit, as well as any **prejudgment interest** awarded against the policyholder on the part of the judgment paid by the insurance company. However, if the insurance company offers to pay the applicable limit of insurance, it will not make any payments for prejudgment interest based on the interval after this offer is made. Finally, the insurance company will pay all of the **interest** on the full amount of any judgment that accrues after the entry of the judgment but before payment by the insurance company, so long as this is within the applicable limit of insurance. None of the supplementary payments made by the insurance company reduce the limits of insurance.

SECTION 2 (WHO IS AN INSURED)
BASIC DESIGNATION

Section 2 of the standard commercial general liability policy defines the **people and companies** who are covered by this insurance policy. Specifically, the section will typically state that all individuals named on the declarations page, as well as their spouses, are insured with respect to the actions of a **business** for which the individual is the sole owner. In addition, **partnerships and joint ventures** that are named in the declarations are defined as insured parties. The members, partners, and spouses of those designated in the declarations as a partnership or joint venture are also considered to be insured, but only with respect to the operations of the business. Finally, any other organizations besides a partnership or joint venture that are designated in the **declarations** are insured. All of the executive officers and directors of such an organization are defined as an insured, though only in respect to the operations of the business. Similarly, stockholders are considered to be insured, but only to the extent of their liability.

OTHER INSURED PARTIES

Besides the individuals and groups named on the declarations page, there are some **other parties** who are insured by the standard commercial general liability policy. To begin with, the **employees** of a named insured party are insured with respect to actions taken as part of their employment. However, employees are not covered for injuries or damages they suffered. In addition, any person acting as the **real estate manager** of the named insured is covered by the standard commercial general liability policy. Finally, there are a couple of contingencies in the event that the insured party dies. If the named insured dies, any person or organization with **temporary custody** of the property of the insured is covered during the interval before a legal representative is appointed, though only with respect to liability related to the maintenance or use of that property. Also, if the named insured party should die, his or her **legal representative** will be covered by the insurance with respect to his or her duties as a legal representative.

USERS OF MOBILE EQUIPMENT AND NEWLY FORMED OR ACQUIRED BUSINESSES

The standard commercial general liability policy asserts that any person driving **mobile equipment** that is owned by the named insured is covered while doing so, as long as he or she is driving on public roads and with the permission of the named insured. At the same time, any other person or organization that is **responsible for the conduct of a driver** of the insured parties' mobile equipment is covered, assuming that he or she has no other operable coverage and that the coverage provided by the commercial general liability policy is limited to liability related to the operation of the equipment. As with the employees of the named insured, **operators** of mobile equipment owned by the insured are not covered with respect to bodily injury to themselves or damage to the property of the named insured. Finally, any **organization** that is formed or acquired by the named insured is afforded temporary insurance, assuming there is no other insurance available to that entity. This coverage lasts for 90 days at the most after the formation or acquisition of the organization.

SECTION 3 (LIMITS OF INSURANCE)
GENERAL AGGREGATE LIMIT

The **third section** of the standard commercial general liability policy is devoted to the **limits of insurance**. To begin with, the insurance company will assert that the limits of insurance indicated on the declarations page and further explicated below represent the **maximum payment** regardless of the number of insured parties, claims or suits, or persons or organizations making claims or suits. With regard to the **general aggregate limit**, the insurance company asserts that this is the most it will pay for the sum of the following: medical expenses under Coverage C, damages under Coverage A (except those included in the products-completed operations hazard), and damages under Coverage B. The **products-completed operations aggregate limit** is defined as the maximum payment under Coverage A for bodily injury and property damage classified as products completed operations hazard.

PERSONAL AND ADVERTISING INJURY, OCCURRENCE, FIRE DAMAGE, AND MEDICAL EXPENSE LIMITS

Section 3 of the standard commercial general liability policy declares that the **personal and advertising injury limit** is the maximum payment under Coverage B for the sum total of the damages related to the personal injury and advertising injury suffered by a single person or organization. The personal and advertising injury limit is subject to adjustment based on the general aggregate limit. The **occurrence limit** is the maximum amount the insurance company will pay for the sum of medical expenses stemming from any particular occurrence under Coverage C and damages under Coverage A. The **fire damage limit** is the maximum payment under Coverage A for property damages related to a single fire. It is subject to the occurrence limit. The **medical expense limit**, finally, is the maximum amount of payment under Coverage C for all medical expenses related to bodily injury suffered by a single person. Again, this limit is subject to the occurrence limit.

SECTION 4 (COMMERCIAL GENERAL LIABILITY CONDITIONS)

BANKRUPTCY

The **fourth section** of the standard commercial general liability policy describes the **commercial general liability conditions**. To begin with, it indicates that the **bankruptcy or insolvency** of the insured or the estate of the insured will not relieve the obligations of the insurance company. The insured party is obliged to **notify** the insurance company as soon as is practicable of any occurrence or offense which could possibly result in a claim. This notice should include the time, location, and circumstances of the occurrence. It should also include the names and addresses of more than one insured person or witness, as well as the nature of any injury or damage caused by the occurrence. If an insured party receives a **claim**, it should immediately record the date and the specifics, and notify the insurance company as soon as practicable. If the insured party receives **notice of a suit**, it should immediately send copies of any connected papers, demands, summonses, or notices, and should authorize the insurance company to obtain records and other information. The insured party is responsible for cooperating with the insurance company in the investigation, settlement, or defense of all claims and suits.

LEGAL ACTION AGAINST THE INSURANCE COMPANY

The **fourth section** of the standard commercial general liability policy describes the rights and responsibilities of the policyholder in the event of **legal action brought against the insurance company**. To begin with, the insurance company will typically state that no person or organization has the right under this coverage part to enjoin or partner with the insurance company in a suit requesting damages from an insured party. Similarly, no person or organization has the right to sue the insurance company related to this coverage part unless all of the terms have been complied with fully. The insurance company does grant the right of people and organizations to sue them to recover on an agreed settlement or final judgment after an actual trial, but the insurance company refuses to be held liable for payments that are not described in this coverage part or are in excess of the limit of insurance.

OTHER INSURANCE

Section 4 of the standard commercial general liability policy describes how the responsibilities of the insurance company are limited when the insured party has access to **other valid and collectible insurance**. In situations where this commercial general liability policy is **primary**, its coverage will not be limited unless the other applicable insurance is primary as well. In that case, the responsibilities are shared by the policies. There are situations, though, in which the standard commercial general liability policy is considered to be an **excess** over any of the other applicable insurance policies. For instance, this insurance is considered an excess to any other insurance policy that applies to bodily injury or property damage on something besides a claims-made basis, so long as this insurance policy was effective before the beginning of the commercial general liability policy period. The standard commercial general liability policy is also considered to be an excess with regard to fire, extended coverage, elders, risk, installation risk, or any similar coverage related to the work of the named insured.

EXCESS INSURANCE AND INSURANCE COMPANY RESPONSIBILITY

The **fourth section** of the standard commercial general liability policy outlines the responsibilities of the insurance company in situations when this policy is considered to be **excess insurance**. In this scenario, the insurance company has **no duty** under Coverages A or B to defend against any suit or claim which another insurer is required to defend. This is not to say that the insurance company will not defend against such suits or claims. Also, in situations where the standard commercial general liability policy is deemed an excess over other insurance, it will only pay the share of the amount of the loss greater than the sum of the total of all deductible and self-insured amounts under the other shoe insurance policies and the total amount that would be paid by all other insurance in the absence of the commercial general liability policy.

METHOD OF SHARING

The **fourth section** of the standard commercial general liability policy describes the **method for sharing payments** among applicable policies. If the other insurance policies allow for a **contribution of equal shares**, then this will be the preferred method. Namely, each insurer will contribute equal amounts until each is paid either its applicable limit of insurance or the full amount of loss, whichever comes first. In the event that the other insurance policies do not permit contribution by equal shares, it will be necessary to **contribute by limits**. When this is the case, the share of each insurer is calculated from the ratio of its applicable limit of insurance to the total applicable limits of insurance for all of the insurers.

PREMIUM AUDIT

The **fourth section** of the standard commercial general liability policy outlines the **premium audit protocol**. To begin with, the insurance company will assert that all premiums for this coverage part will be computed in accordance with the **rules and rates** of the company. The next note indicates that the premium amount shown in this coverage part as an advanced premium should be understood only as a **deposit premium**. In other words, at the end of each audit period, the insurance company will calculate the earned premium for that period. All audit premiums are due and payable to the named insured party. When the total amount of the advance and audit premiums paid for a particular policy term is greater than the earned premiums, the **difference** will be returned to the named insured party by the insurance company. The final provision of this section is that the named insured must maintain **records** of whatever information will be required to compute premiums, and should be able to send copies of this information upon the insurance company's request.

REPRESENTATIONS AND SEPARATION OF INSUREDS

The **fourth section** of the standard commercial general liability policy includes some basic assurances about the **representations** on the declarations page. To begin with, it states that by accepting this policy, the named insured agrees that all of the statements in the declarations page are accurate and comprehensive. The acceptance of the policy also indicates agreement that those statements are based upon representations made by the insured party to the insurance company, and that the policy was issued because of the insurance company's reliance upon these representations. The fourth section goes on to describe the protocol for **separation of insured parties**. Namely, the insurance company will declare that this policy applies as if each named insured were the only named insured. Also, the policy will apply separately to each insured party against whom a suit is brought or claim is made. The only exceptions to this policy regarding separation of insureds are with respect to the limits of insurance, and any rights or duties that are explicitly assigned to the first named insured party.

TRANSFER OF RIGHTS OF RECOVERY AND NONRENEWAL OF POLICY

The **fourth section** of the standard commercial general liability policy describes the protocol for the **transfer of rights of recovery** against other parties to the insurance company. Specifically, it declares that whenever the insured party has the right to recover part or all of any payment made by the insurance company under this policy, those rights are immediately transferred to the insurance company. Moreover, the insured party may not do anything to impair the exercise of those rights by the insurance company. At the request of the insurance company, the insured party must file suit or cooperate with the insurance company as it files suit. In the event that the

80

insurance company decides not to **renew** this coverage part, it typically will promise to mail or deliver written notice at least 30 days before the expiration date. This written notice will be sent to the first named insured on the declarations page. If the notice is mailed, the mailing will be sufficiently proved by a proof of mailing.

INSURED PARTY'S TO CLAIM AND OCCURRENCE INFORMATION

The **fourth section** of the standard commercial general liability policy includes a description of the rights of the insured party to **claim and occurrence information**. To begin with, the insurance company will promise to provide the first named insured party on the declarations page with certain basic information. In addition, the insurance company will provide a list or some other record of each occurrence that the insurance company has discovered and which has not been reported before to any other insurer. This report will include the date of the occurrence and a brief description. The insurance company will also provide a summary of all payments made and amounts reserved under any applicable products-completed operations aggregate limit or general aggregate limit. This report will be itemized by policy year. The insurance company admits that the amounts reserved are estimated and subject to change.

CANCELLATION OF POLICY BY THE INSURANCE COMPANY

Section 4 of the standard commercial general liability policy concludes by describing the protocol for **cancellation or nonrenewal** of this coverage by the insurance company. Specifically, the insurance company promises that if it cancels or decides not to renew this coverage, it will provide **notice** at least 30 days before the end of the policy period. This notification can be given even earlier if the policyholder requests it. If the policyholder elects to cancel or not renew the policy, he or she must provide written notice to the insurance company within 60 days of the termination date. If this is done, the insurance company promises to respond within 45 days of receiving this written request. The insurance company goes on to state that claim and occurrence information are retained for business purposes.

SECTION 5 (EXTENDED REPORTING PERIODS)
EXTENDED REPORTING PERIODS

Section 5 of the standard commercial general liability policy outlines the protocol for **extended reporting periods**. To begin with, the insurance company will typically declare that one or more extended reporting periods will be provided if the commercial general liability coverage is **canceled or not renewed**. One or more extended reporting periods may also be provided if the insurance company elects to renew or replace the commercial general liability insurance with an insurance with a retroactive date later than the retroactive date indicated on the declarations page of the given commercial general liability policy, and the replacement insurance does not apply to bodily injury, personal injury, advertising injury, or property damage on a claims-made basis. These extended reporting periods do not lengthen the policy, or alternatively, scope of coverage, and only apply to claims for property damage or bodily injury occurring before the end of the policy period, but not before the retroactive date indicated on the declarations page. In addition, these extended reporting periods (which may not be canceled once in effect) may apply to personal injury or advertising injury caused by an offense that occurs before the end of the policy period, but not before the retroactive date indicated on the declarations page.

BASIC EXTENDED REPORTING PERIODS

The **fifth section** of the standard commercial general liability policy is devoted to **extended reporting periods**. It is typical in these policies for a **basic extended reporting period** to be offered. The basic extended reporting period is provided automatically and without the policyholder incurring any additional charge. The basic extended reporting period begins at the end of the normal policy period, and lasts for **five years** for claims related to property damage and bodily injury, so long as the precipitating occurrences were reported within 60 days of the end of the policy period. The basic extended reporting periods may also last for five years for claims related to advertising injury and personal injury caused by an offense reported to the insurance company within 60 days of the end of the policy period. The basic extended reporting period only lasts for **60 days** for all other claims. This basic ERP does not apply to claims covered by any insurance purchased subsequently.

SUPPLEMENTAL EXTENDED REPORTING PERIODS

Most standard commercial general liability policies make a **supplemental extended reporting period (ERP)** available, though the policyholder will be required to receive an **endorsement** and pay an extra charge. The supplemental extended reporting period begins at the termination of the basic extended reporting period. In order to receive the endorsement for this supplemental ERP, the policyholder must submit a written request within 60 days after the end of the policy period. Supplemental ERP is not initiated until the premium for it is paid. The amount of additional premium will be calculated according to the standard rules and rates of the insurance company. In addition, the insurance company may take into account the exposures insured, the previous types and amounts of insurance, and the limits of insurance available under this coverage part for future payment of damages. A supplemental ERP premium will not be more than twice the amount of the annual premium for this coverage part.

EFFECTS ON LIMITS OF INSURANCE

In the standard commercial general liability policy, the basic extended reporting period will not **reinstate or increase** the limits of insurance. However, supplemental extended reporting periods may create a **different limits amount**. Specifically, the **separate aggregate limits** of insurance will be equal to the dollar amount indicated on the declarations page in effect at the end of each policy period. This is true for the **general aggregate limit** and the **products-completed operations aggregate limit**. The granting of a supplemental ERP will then require the amendment of paragraphs two and three of the limits of insurance. The personal and advertising injury limit, the fire damage limit, and the each occurrence limit will continue to apply as originally set forth in Section 3.

SECTION 6 (DEFINITIONS)
ADVERTISING INJURY AND IMPAIRED PROPERTY

There are a few key **definitions** elucidated in **Section 6** of the standard commercial general liability policy. To begin with, an **advertising injury** is defined as any injury that arises from the slanderous or libelous or oral or written publication, whether it relates to a person, an organization, or a person or organization's goods, products, or services. Advertising injury may also stem from the oral or written publication of material that violates a person's right of privacy; the misappropriation of advertising ideas or business procedure; or the infringement of copyright, slogan, or title. **Impaired property** is defined as tangible property that is either useless or less useful because it incorporates the insured party's product or work that is known or believed to be defective, inadequate, deficient, or dangerous. Property may also be impaired if it is less useful because the insured party has failed to fulfill the terms of an agreement or contract. Property impairment is only covered by the commercial general liability policy if the repair, replacement, adjustment, or removal of the insured parties work or product can restore the property to use, or if the property can be restored to use by the insured parties' fulfillment of the contract or agreement terms.

PRODUCTS-COMPLETED OPERATIONS HAZARD

Section 6 of the standard commercial general liability policy offers a comprehensive definition of **products-completed operations hazard**. For the purposes of the standard policy, products-completed operations hazard includes all of the property damage and bodily injury that is caused by the insured parties work or product but that occurs away from any premises owned or rented by the insured party. The only exceptions to this are for products still in the physical possession of the insured party or work that has not yet been finished or abandoned. For the purposes of this definition, the work of the insured party is considered to be **complete** when all of the work called for in the contract has been completed or, if the insured party is meant to work at more than one site, when all the work to be done at a particular site has been completed. Similarly, work is considered to be finished once it has been put to its intended use by any party other than the insured or another contractor or subcontractor working on it.

PROPERTY COVERED BY THE STANDARD COMMERCIAL PROPERTY POLICY

The standard commercial property policy covers any **building or structure** described on the **declarations page**. This coverage includes any completed additions, fixtures, and permanently installed machinery and equipment. This coverage also includes any personal property that is owned by the insured party and used to maintain or service the building or structure. The standard commercial property policy also covers any of the following business property located on or within 100 feet of the covered location: furniture and fixtures, machinery and equipment, inventory, materials or services, and leased personal property. Finally, the standard commercial property policy covers any personal property of another party that is in the care or control of the insured and that is located in or on a named building or within 100 feet of the named premises.

PROPERTY NOT COVERED BY THE STANDARD COMMERCIAL PROPERTY POLICY

The standard commercial property policy does not cover the loss of **accounts, bills, currency, or food stamps**. This policy does not cover **animals**, with two exceptions: animals that are owned by other people and boarded by the named insured, and animals that are owned as stock by the insured. The standard commercial property policy does not cover any **automobiles** on consignment or any paved surfaces, as for instance bridges, patios, roadways, or walks. The policy does not cover any **contraband** or other property that is being traded or transported illegally. It does not cover any expenses for **excavating, filling, grading, or backfilling**. It does not cover any damage to the **foundations** of buildings, structures, or machinery located below the lowest basement floor or, if there is no basement, below the ground. The policy does not cover any **water, crops, lawns, or land**, even the land on which the property is situated.

The standard commercial property policy does not cover the personal property of the insured while it is **airborne or waterborne**. The policy does not cover **bulkheads, docks, pilings, or piers**. The standard commercial property policy does not cover any property that is covered by **another insurance policy** more specifically, except as excess insurance. Commercial property policies do not cover **retaining walls** that are external to a building. They do not cover **underground drains, flues, or pipes**. These policies do not cover **electronic data**, nor do they cover the cost of replacing or restoring records or other papers. Standard commercial property policies do not cover **vehicles** or self-propelled machines if these are licensed for operation on public roads or are operated primarily away from the named premises. Finally, the standard commercial property policy does not cover grain, straw, hay, or other **crops** while they are outside of the buildings on the premises.

ADDITIONAL COVERAGES

DEBRIS REMOVAL

In the standard commercial property policy, the insurance company will pay for any expense related to the **removal of the debris** of a covered property if the damage to the covered property is caused by a covered loss. In order for debris removal to be covered, it must be reported in writing to the insurance company within 180 days. The additional coverage for debris removal does not include any expenses related to the removal of **pollutants** from land or water, or any expenses incurred to restore or replace polluted water or land. Moreover, the coverage for debris removal does not increase the overall limit of liability unless one or both of the following scenarios exists: the actual debris removal expense is greater than 25 percent of the sum of the direct physical loss payment and the deductible, or the sum of the actual debris removal expense and the amount paid for direct physical loss or damage is greater than the limit of insurance for the covered property in question. When one or both of these scenarios occurs, the insurance company will pay up to an additional $10,000 for the expense related to debris removal for each location.

PRESERVATION OF PROPERTY, FIRE DEPARTMENT SERVICE CHARGE, AND POLLUTANT CLEANUP AND REMOVAL

When it is necessary to **move** covered property in order to keep it from being damaged or lost, the insurance company will pay for any direct physical loss or damage that occurs while the property is being moved or temporarily stored, so long as this loss or damage occurs within 30 days of the original movement of the property. In situations where the **fire department** must come to save or protect a covered property from a covered cause of loss, the insurance company will pay a maximum of $1000 for any liability incurred by the insured party. There is no deductible for the additional coverage for the fire department service charge. The insurance company will also provide some additional coverage for the expense of **removing pollutants** when the release of these pollutants is caused by a covered cause of loss.

INCREASED COST OF CONSTRUCTION

In cases where the replacement cost optional coverage applies, there may also be some additional coverage under the standard commercial property policy for an **increased cost of construction**. If a building listed as covered property is damaged by a covered cause of loss, the insurance company will pay any extra costs incurred by the insured party in order to comply with the enforcement of an **ordinance or law** while rebuilding, repairing, or replacing the damaged property. This additional coverage will not pay for any costs related to ordinances or laws that applied before the loss (that is, before the building was damaged), and that the insured party failed to comply with. Moreover, this additional coverage does not apply to expenses for the enforcement of any ordinance or law requiring the demolition, repair, reconstruction, or remediation of property that has been contaminated by pollutants, fungus, rot, or bacteria.

ELECTRONIC DATA

As part of the standard commercial property policy, the insurance company will provide some additional coverage for the replacement or restoration of covered **data**. The value of a loss of electronic data that cannot be replaced will be calculated as the cost of replacing the **blank media** on which the data was stored. The covered causes of loss of electronic data are generally the same as the covered causes of loss for commercial property unless the policy indicates otherwise. Furthermore, losses of electronic data will receive this additional coverage if they are due to viruses, destructive codes, or other programming interventions designed to damage, destroy, or disrupt the system. However, the standard commercial property policy will not provide additional coverage for electronic data lost because of intentional manipulation of a computer system by an employee. The maximum amount of additional coverage provided for electronic data is $2500 per year.

COVERAGE EXTENSIONS
NEWLY ACQUIRED OR CONSTRUCTED PROPERTY

In most cases, the **coverage extensions** listed on the standard commercial property policy apply to any property located in or on a named building, or within 100 feet of the named premises. The coverage extensions may be applied if the declarations page indicates either a value reporting period symbol or if the coinsurance percentage is 80 percent or more. The first coverage extension applies to **newly acquired or constructed property**. The insured party may extend his or her coverage to include new buildings being constructed on the described premises, as well as any buildings acquired elsewhere and intended for a similar use. The maximum payment for loss or damage to newly acquired or constructed buildings is $250,000 for each building. If the standard commercial property policy applies to the business personal property of the insured, it is possible to receive an extension to have it cover property that is newly acquired, though the maximum payment for loss or damage under this extension for each building is $100,000. These coverage extensions for newly acquired property will expire 30 days after the property has been acquired.

PERSONAL EFFECTS AND THE PROPERTY OF OTHERS, VALUABLE PAPERS AND RECORDS (OTHER THAN ELECTRONIC DATA), AND PROPERTY OFF THE PREMISES

The holders of a standard commercial property policy may extend this insurance such that it applies to any **personal effects** owned by the insured or his or her employees, partners, officers, or members. This coverage may also be extended to the **personal property of other people** while it is in the care, custody, or control of the named insured. However, the maximum payment for this extension is $2500 for each location. A similar extension may be applied to the **valuable papers and records** of the business. This extension only applies to physical records, not to **electronic data**. Again, the maximum coverage under this extension is $2500. There is a third extension available for covering the property of the insured while it is **off of the described premises**. For instance, the property of the insured may receive coverage while it is temporarily in storage, at a tradeshow, or briefly at a location not owned or operated by the insured. The maximum payment for loss under this extended coverage is $10,000.

OUTDOOR PROPERTY AND NON-OWNED DETACHED TRAILERS

The standard commercial property policy may be extended to include **outdoor property**, as for instance fences, antennas, signs, and plants when this property is damaged or lost due to a covered cause. The maximum amount of payments that will be made under this coverage extension is $1000, though in the case of plants, the coverage is limited to $250 for each individual plant. There is a similar coverage extension for **non-owned detached trailers**, so long as these trailers are used by the insured business and are in the care or control of the insured at the named premises. Also, it is mandatory for the insured to have a contractual responsibility to pay for any damage or loss to the trailer. This coverage extension will not apply to loss or damage that occurs while the trailer is attached to a vehicle, or during the hitching or unhitching operations. The maximum amount of payment under this coverage extension is $5000.

LIMITS OF INSURANCE AND DEDUCTIBLE

The standard commercial property policy indicates the **maximum payment** for loss or damage for a single occurrence on the declarations page. With regard to loss or damage to outdoor signs that are attached to buildings, the **limit of insurance** is $1000 for each sign per occurrence. The fire department service charge and additional coverage for pollutant cleanup and removal are considered to be excess insurance to the other limits of insurance. Similarly, any payments that are made under the preservation of property additional coverage do not expand the otherwise applicable limits of insurance. As for the **deductible**, losses with an adjusted value of less than the deductible listed on the declarations page will not be reimbursed. If a given occurrence involves a loss to more than one piece of covered property, such that multiple limits of insurance apply, these losses will not be grouped together for the purposes of the deductible. Instead, the deductible will be applied once for each occurrence.

LOSS CONDITIONS

ABANDONMENT, APPRAISAL, AND DUTIES IN THE EVENT OF LOSS OR DAMAGE

In the **loss conditions** section of the standard commercial property policy, it will typically state that there is no **abandonment** of property to the insurance company by the insured. In situations where property value or loss valuation is disputed, the insurance company and the insured may submit a written request for **appraisal**. The usual protocol is followed: both sides select an appraiser, the appraisers select an umpire, and agreement by any two of these parties constitutes a binding judgment. Each side is responsible for paying its own appraiser and its share of the appraisal and the umpire expenses. When loss or damage occurs, the insured party is responsible for **notifying** the insurance company and providing **comprehensive information** about the occurrence. If it is possible that a law has been broken, the insured party needs to notify **law enforcement**. The insured party should take any reasonable steps to **prevent further damage**, and should submit to an **examination and inspection** whenever the insurance company requests.

LOSS PAYMENT AND RECOVERED PROPERTY

When making payments under the standard commercial property policy, the insurance company reserves the right to pay the value of the property, pay the cost of repairing or replacing the property, assume ownership of all or part of the property at an agreed-upon value, or repair or rebuild the property with property of a similar kind or value. The **value of property** will be set by the insurance company according to the terms of the policy. The cost of repairing, replacing, or rebuilding it does not include any expenses associated with compliance with a **law or ordinance**. The insurance company typically will promise to provide notice of how payment will be made within 30 days after receiving the proof of loss. The insured party should not expect to receive more than his or her **financial interest** in the covered property. The insurance company reserves the right to defend the insured party against **suits** related to the claims of property owners. The expense for this will be borne by the insurance company. In the event that property is recovered after the settlement of loss, the party that recovers the property must provide prompt notice. It may be necessary for one side to return the property or make payment to the other.

VACANCY AND VALUATION

In the standard commercial property policy, there are special provisions for **vacant buildings**. The building is considered vacant if it is suitable for habitation but has 30 percent or less of its square footage occupied. If a building is under construction or renovation, it may not be considered vacant. When a building has been vacant for more than 60 days before loss or damage, the insurance company will not pay for any expenses related to vandalism, sprinkler leakage, glass breakage, water damage, or theft. Moreover, any loss or damage caused by a covered cause of loss will be subject to a payment reduction of 15 percent. Property will typically be valued at its **actual cash value** at the time of loss or damage. There is an exception for stock that has been sold but not yet delivered: it is valued at the selling price minus any foreseeable discounts and expenses. Glass breakage may be paid for at the price of installing safety glazing material when this material is required by law.

ADDITIONAL CONDITIONS

COINSURANCE

On some commercial property policies, a **coinsurance percentage** will be indicated on the declarations page. In these cases, the insurance company will decline to pay the full value of a loss if the coinsurance percentage multiplied by the value of the property at the time of loss exceeds the property's limit of insurance. Instead, the insurance company will calculate the maximum payment by multiplying the value of the property at the time of loss by the coinsurance percentage, dividing the limit of insurance by this product, multiplying the resulting quotient by the total amount of loss before removal of the deductible, and then subtracting the deductible. If this amount is less than the limit of insurance, it represents the **maximum payment**. Otherwise, the limit of insurance represents the maximum payment. Any remaining expenses must be borne by the policyholder.

MORTGAGE HOLDERS

For the purposes of the standard commercial property policy, trustees are considered to be **mortgage holders**. In the standard policy, the insurance company will promise to compensate all mortgage holders listed on the declarations page in the appropriate **order of priority**. The insurance company grants the right of the mortgage holder to receive loss payment even in situations where he or she has initiated **foreclosure** on the relevant building. The mortgage holder will still have the right to receive payment for losses even if the claim of the named insured is **denied**, so long as the mortgage holder pays any premium amounts that are due, submits a signed and sworn proof of loss within 60 days of receiving a request for such from the insurance company, and notifies the insurance company of any relevant changes in ownership or occupancy. If the insurance company elects to cancel the policy, written notice of this decision must be provided at least 10 days (when cancellation is based on nonpayment of premium) or 30 days (for all other reasons) prior to the effective date of cancellation.

OPTIONAL COVERAGES

INFLATION GUARD AND EXTENSION OF REPLACEMENT COST TO THE PERSONAL PROPERTY OF OTHERS

The standard commercial property policy will include optional coverage of loss of value due to inflation. The **inflation guard** works by automatically increasing the limit of insurance for selected property by an annual percentage indicated on the declarations page. The amount of the annual increase is calculated by multiplying the limit of insurance at the most recent policy inception date by the percentage of annual increase and by the number of days that have passed since the beginning of the policy period. When the optional coverage for replacement cost is indicated on the declarations page, the **extension of this replacement cost to the personal property of others** may also apply. The extended coverage for replacement cost for the personal property of others is limited to the amount of liability assumed by the insured party.

REPLACEMENT COST

Some commercial property policies will include optional coverage for **replacement cost**. When this is indicated, the replacement cost will take the place of the **actual cash value**. The optional coverage for replacement cost, unless otherwise specified, does not apply to the contents of a residence, the personal property of others, any works of art, or any stock. The insured party may request this additional coverage even when the original loss or damage has been settled on the actual cash value basis. However, the replacement cost basis may not be used if the lost or damaged property has not yet been repaired or replaced, or if the repair or replacement does not occur immediately after the loss or damage. **Improvements** made by tenants are still considered to be the property of the insured, and are therefore eligible for replacement cost coverage.

INSURING AGREEMENTS OF COMMERICAL CRIME POLICY
EMPLOYEE THEFT, FORGERY, AND ALTERATION

The standard commercial crime policy provides coverage for specific occurrences during the period of the policy. With regard to **employee theft**, the standard commercial crime policy will cover any loss or damage to money, securities, or other property directly caused by employee theft. This coverage applies regardless of whether the specific employee is identified, or whether the employee is acting in cooperation with non-employees. The standard commercial crime policy will also cover losses caused by the **forgery** or **alteration** of promissory notes and checks or other money orders. This applies to financial documents drawn by or drawn upon the insured, as well as those drawn by an agent of the insured. The insurance company will also typically promise to cover any legal expenses incurred when the insured is sued for refusing to pay the obligation established by a forged or altered document.

THEFT OF MONEY AND SECURITIES, ROBBERY, AND SAFE BURGLARY INSIDE THE PREMISES

The standard commercial crime policy covers the **theft of money and securities** inside the business premises, even if the business is a bank. This policy also covers damages to the premises that occurred during the theft or attempted theft of money or securities. The standard commercial crime policy will cover loss or damage to cash drawers, cash registers, safes, and vaults when the loss or damage results directly from an actual or attempted theft. In a related agreement, the standard commercial crime policy will cover loss of or damage to other property that is related to the actual or attempted **robbery** of an employee or an actual or attempted safe burglary. Finally, the insurance company will promise to pay for the loss of or damage to any **locked safe or vault** inside the premises when this loss or damage is a direct result of an actual or attempted robbery or safe burglary.

LOSS AND DAMAGE OUTSIDE THE PREMISES, COMPUTER FRAUD, FUNDS TRANSFER FRAUD, MONEY ORDERS, AND COUNTERFEIT MONEY

The standard commercial crime policy will cover the insured for the loss of money or securities, as for instance when these items are in possession of a messenger or in an armored motor vehicle. The **loss of money or securities outside the premises** is covered when it results directly from disappearance, destruction, or theft, and the loss of or damage to other property outside the premises is covered when it is the direct result of an actual or attempted robbery. The standard commercial crime policy will also cover the loss of or damage to money, securities, and other property when this results from the **fraudulent use of a computer**. Similarly, the standard commercial crime policy will cover the loss of funds after a fraudulent instruction to **transfer these funds** out of the insured's account. The standard commercial crime policy will also cover any losses sustained when the named insured exchanges merchandise, money, or services for **money orders** that are not paid upon presentation. Similarly, the insured may be reimbursed for merchandise, money, or services that he or she exchanges for **counterfeit money**.

LIMIT OF INSURANCE AND DEDUCTIBLE

The standard commercial crime policy states that the insurance company will not pay any more for a single loss than is indicated on the **declarations page**. If a particular loss is covered by more than one of the coverages or insuring agreements in the policy, then the maximum payment will be the greatest **limit of insurance** for any one of those coverages or insuring agreements. The standard commercial crime policy includes a **deductible**, and the insurance company will typically decline to pay for a covered loss unless the amount of loss is greater than the deductible indicated on the declarations page. When the amount of loss is greater than the deductible, the insurance company will pay the difference, with a maximum payment equal to the described limit of insurance.

Exclusions Under the Standard Commercial Crime Policy

Acts Committed by the Insured, Partners, Members, Employees, Managers, Directors, Trustees, or Representatives

The standard commercial crime policy does not cover any **acts committed by the named insured, his or her members, or his or her partners**. This includes acts committed by these people singly or in cooperation with others. The policy does not cover any acts committed by employees that the named insured discovered before the initiation of the policy. Similarly, the policy does not cover any losses caused by employees who had been discovered to have committed theft or other dishonest acts before the effective date of the policy. The standard commercial crime policy does not cover loss resulting from theft or any other dishonest act committed by an **employee, manager, director, trustee, or authorized representative**. The only exception to this exclusion is for instances of employee theft specifically covered in the first insuring agreement.

Confidential Information, Governmental Action, and Indirect Loss

The standard commercial crime policy does not cover losses that are the result of disclosure of **confidential information** without the permission of the insured. Examples of this confidential information include patents, trade secrets, customer lists, or operational protocols. The standard commercial crime policy will also not cover any losses related to the unauthorized use of another party's confidential information when it is held by the named insured. Some examples of this type of confidential information are credit card numbers, personal information, and financial information. The standard commercial crime policy also will not cover any losses that are the result of destruction or seizure of property on the orders of a **governmental authority**. The insurance policy will also not cover any losses that are an **indirect result** of events covered by this policy. For instance, the standard commercial crime policy will not reimburse an insured party who is unable to realize income that would have been obtained were it not for a covered loss. Similarly, the insurance company will not cover the payment of damages when the named insured is found to be legally liable. Finally, the insurance company will not cover any costs or expenses incurred by the insured party for the purpose of establishing the presence or value of a loss related to the policy.

Legal Fees, Nuclear Hazard, Pollution, and War

The standard commercial crime policy will not cover any **legal fees or expenses** incurred by the named insured. The only exception to this exclusion is that the standard commercial crime policy will pay for legal fees and expenses that are specifically covered under the insuring agreement related to forgery and alteration. The standard commercial crime policy will not cover loss or damage that is the result of **nuclear radiation or reaction**. In like fashion, the standard commercial crime policy will not cover loss or damage that is the result of **pollution**. For the purposes of this policy, pollution is defined as the release, discharge, seepage, or dispersal of any irritant or contaminant, whether solid, liquid, or gas. Finally, the standard commercial crime policy will not cover any loss or damage that is the result of **war** or other military action.

Employee Theft

The standard commercial crime policy has some specific exclusions for losses due to **employee theft**. To begin with, the standard commercial crime policy will not cover inventory shortages when the proof of the loss, or the proof of the amount of the loss, is dependent upon either an **inventory computation** or a **profit and loss computation**. However, the inventory records may be used as supporting documents when an inventory shortage has been demonstrated through other means. The insuring agreement for employee theft in the standard commercial crime policy also excludes losses resulting from trading, as well as losses caused by the fraudulent or dishonest signing, issuing, or canceling of warehouse receipts or related paperwork.

THEFT OF MONEY, SECURITIES, AND OTHER PROPERTY

The standard commercial crime policy contains some specific exclusions related to the insuring agreements for **theft of money, securities, and other property**, whether on or off the business premises. To begin with, the standard commercial crime policy states that these insuring agreements do not cover **errors or omissions** related to accounting or arithmetic. These insuring agreements also do not cover the loss caused by the **sacrifice or surrender** of property as part of an exchange or purchase. These insuring agreements do not cover loss or damage that is the result of **fire** unless it is damage to or loss of money, securities, a safe, or a vault. Finally, these insuring agreements do not cover the loss of property contained in **money-operated devices** (e.g., vending machines) unless the amount of money contained in the device is continuously recorded.

The insuring agreements for the theft of money, securities, and other property under the standard commercial crime policy do not cover any loss of or damage to **motor vehicles, trailers, or related equipment**. These insuring agreements also do not cover losses or damage to property that has been transferred or surrendered to another party off the premises when this transfer or surrender was **unauthorized** or the result of **coercion**. These insuring agreements do not cover any losses or damage that are the result of **malicious mischief or vandalism**. Finally, these insuring agreements do not cover any losses that are the result of the insured party or an agent of the insured party being persuaded by a **dishonest act** to sign over or surrender possession.

COMPUTER FRAUD AND FUNDS TRANSFER FRAUD

The standard commercial crime policy has specific exclusions for the insuring agreements related to computer fraud and funds transfer fraud. The coverage for **computer fraud** does not include losses that are caused by the use of credit, debit, charge, or identification cards. Similarly, this insuring agreement does not cover **funds transfer fraud**, in which a fraudulent instruction is given to a financial institution to move money out of the insured account. Finally, the insuring agreement related to computer fraud does not cover **inventory shortages** when they can only be proved by inventory computation or profit and loss computation. Just as the insuring agreement for computer fraud does not cover funds transfer fraud, neither does the insuring agreement for funds transfer fraud cover computer fraud. Any loss suffered by the insured from the use of a computer to transfer money or securities fraudulently will not be covered by the funds transfer fraud insuring agreement of the standard commercial crime policy.

CONDITIONS FOR THE STANDARD COMMERCIAL CRIME POLICY
ADDITIONAL PREMISES OR EMPLOYEES, AND CANCELLATION OF POLICY

There are certain conditions that are applicable to all of the insuring agreements in the standard commercial crime policy. To begin with, any **additional premises or employees** obtained by the business during the period of the policy will be covered automatically. The only exceptions to this condition are for premises and employees acquired through consolidation or merger with another business. The insured is not required to notify the insurance company of these acquisitions. Another condition of the standard commercial crime policy deals with the protocol for **cancellation**. If the named insured on the declarations page wants to cancel the policy, he or she must provide advanced written notice to the insurance company. The insurance company, on the other hand, may cancel the policy by providing written notice to the named insured. If the policy is being canceled because the insured has failed to pay the premium, the insurance company only needs to give 10 days of notice before the effective date of cancellation. If the policy is being canceled for another reason, the insurance company must give 30 days of notice. Upon policy cancellation, any premium refund that is owed will be supplied.

CHANGES TO THE POLICY; CONCEALMENT, MISREPRESENTATION, OR FRAUD; AND CONSOLIDATION (MERGER OR ACQUISITION)

The standard commercial crime policy can only be changed if certain protocols are followed. The insured party named on the declarations page is authorized to change the terms of the policy, so long as he or she receives the consent of the insurance company. In order for the terms of the policy to be amended or waived, the changes must be endorsed by the insurance company. If the insured party commits **fraud** related to the policy at any time, the policy is void. This includes any **misrepresentation or intentional concealment** of material facts related to the policy, the covered property, or a claim made under the policy. The standard commercial crime policy also has a specific set of conditions for handling **business consolidations** (that is, mergers or acquisitions). When the named insured party consolidates with another business, written notice must be provided to the insurance company as soon as possible. The insurance company must approve the request for coverage to extend to the acquired business. In such an event, the insurance company reserves the right to require additional premium payment.

COOPERATION, DUTIES IN THE EVENT OF LOSS, AND EMPLOYEE BENEFIT PLANS

The standard commercial crime policy asserts that the insured party must **cooperate** with the insurance company in every matter indicated by the policy terms. For instance, the insured party has specific **duties** after discovering a loss. The insured is responsible for notifying the insurance company as soon as possible. If the insured believes that the loss is related to a violation of law, the law enforcement authorities should be notified as well. The insured is also obliged to submit to an examination under oath at the request of the insurance company. The insured may be required to provide pertinent records to the insurance company. The insured must provide a detailed, sworn proof of loss in the first 120 days after the event. The standard commercial crime policy covers any **employee benefit plans** indicated on the declarations page, but only with regard to employee theft.

EXAMINATION OF THE INSURED'S BOOKS AND RECORDS, EXTENDED PERIOD FOR LOSS DISCOVERY, AND INSPECTIONS AND SURVEYS

One of the conditions of the standard commercial crime policy stipulates that the insurance company has the right to **examine and audit the books** of the named insured for any reason relating to the policy. This right is effective both during the period of the policy and in the three years thereafter. The standard commercial crime policy will cover some **losses discovered after the cancellation of the policy** when those losses can be demonstrated to have occurred during the period of the policy. However, such a loss must be discovered no more than a year after the date of the cancellation. The insurance company also reserves the right to make **surveys and inspections** at any time, and to provide reports and recommendations to the insured business. However, these inspections do not guarantee that conditions are safe or in conformance with legal standards. Furthermore, the insurance company is not obliged to make any inspections, reports, or recommendations.

JOINT INSURED AND LEGAL ACTION AGAINST THE INSURANCE COMPANY

The standard commercial crime policy asserts that when the declarations page indicates more than one insured party, the **first named insured** is responsible for handling the policy. Any knowledge related to the policy is considered to be held by **all named insureds**, even if it is actually only known to one named insured. An employee of one insured party is considered to be an employee of every insured party. The insurance company will decline to pay a greater compensation for losses sustained by more than one insured than it would have for losses of equal value sustained by a single insured. With regard to **legal action brought against the insurance company**, this is not permitted unless the insured parties have complied with all the terms of the policy. Moreover, the policyholder may not bring legal action against the insurance company within 90 days of filing a proof of loss with the company. However, the legal action must be brought within two years of the date of loss discovery.

LIBERALIZATION AND LOSSES SUSTAINED PARTLY DURING THIS INSURANCE AND PARTLY DURING PRIOR INSURANCE

The standard commercial crime policy has a specific protocol for revisions that broaden the scope of coverage without increasing premiums. This type of revision is known as a **liberalization**. Whenever the insurance company liberalizes the policy during the 45 days before or during the policy period, these revisions are applied to the policy immediately. With regard to **losses sustained partly during this policy and partly during prior insurance**, the insurance company will typically promise to cover the amount of loss sustained during the period of this policy. If there is any remaining loss to be covered after the prior insurance has paid its obligations, the insurance company will settle the remainder up to the limit of insurance.

LOSSES SUSTAINED DURING PRIOR INSURANCE

The standard commercial crime policy describes the protocol for handling **losses sustained entirely during a prior insurance period**. Typically, the insurance company will promise to cover any losses that took place during a prior insurance period, provided that the prior insurance was issued by that insurance company or an affiliate. In order for these events to be covered, however, there must be **no gap** between the termination of prior coverage and effective date of current coverage, and the event must be one that would be covered under the current policy. With regard to losses sustained entirely during prior insurance, the insurance company will pay a maximum equal to the **highest single limit of insurance** applicable to the period in which the event occurred. Also, the **deductible** indicated on the declarations page will be applied to the loss.

PROTOCOL FOR HANDLING OTHER INSURANCE POLICIES

The standard commercial crime policy includes a description of the protocol for **overlapping insurance coverage**. The appropriate procedure depends on whether the standard commercial crime policy is the primary insurance or excess insurance. If the standard commercial crime policy is defined as the **primary insurance**, and the named insured has other insurance policies that are subject to the same terms and conditions, the insurance company will promise to pay a share of the covered loss equal to the proportion of the applicable limit of insurance on the declarations page to the total limits of all insurance covering the same loss. However, this policy only applies if the loss is related to employee theft. For all other losses that are covered by **additional insurance policies**, the standard commercial crime policy will only cover the amount of loss greater than the limit of insurance and deductible amount of the other insurance, even if this amount is uncollectible, or the deductible amount indicated on the declarations page, whichever is greater.

PROTOCOL WHEN THE STANDARD COMMERCIAL CRIME POLICY IS EXCESS TO OTHER INSURANCE

The policy for insurance payments when the standard commercial crime policy is **excess to other insurance** is slightly different than from when the standard commercial crime policy is the primary insurance. If the standard commercial crime policy is defined as excess to other insurance, the insurance company will only agree to pay the amount of the loss greater than the **deductible** and **limit of insurance** for that other policy. This rule holds true even when the other insurance is uncollectible. Also, the payments made by the standard commercial crime policy are subject to all the normal terms and conditions. In situations where the covered loss is subject to a deductible, the deductible amount will be reduced by the grand total of all other insurance and any deductibles applicable to that other insurance.

92

OWNERSHIP OF PROPERTY, INTERESTS COVERED, PREMIUMS, AND RECORDS

The standard commercial crime policy establishes some limits for the property to be covered by the policy. The only property covered by the standard commercial crime policy is property **owned or leased by the named insured**, or property **held by the named insured for others**. Property held for others is covered even when the named insured is not legally liable for the loss of that property. All **premium payments** are the responsibility of the named insured, and any return premiums will be paid to the named insured. Also, the named insured is responsible for maintaining **records** of all the property covered by the standard commercial crime policy. These records may be requested by the insurance company to verify the amount of any loss.

RECOVERIES AND TERRITORY

The protocol for handling **payment recoveries** under the commercial crime policy is the same regardless of whether the payments were made by the insurance company or the insured. Recoveries are applied net of the expense of the recovery effort. Recoveries are applied first to the **named insured** to satisfy any covered losses greater than the amount paid under the policy. Recoveries are then applied to the **insurance company** to satisfy the amounts paid in the process of settling the claim. Third, recoveries are paid to the named insured in satisfaction of any **deductible** amount. Finally, recoveries are paid to the insured to satisfy any **loss that is not covered** by the standard commercial crime policy. The recoveries outlined in the standard commercial crime policy do not include those taken from insurance, reinsurance, security, or indemnity taken for the benefit of the insurance company. The **territory** in which the named insured is covered is the United States of America, Puerto Rico, and Canada.

TRANSFER OF RIGHTS AND DUTIES

The standard commercial crime policy asserts that the rights and duties of the named insured under the policy may not be **transferred** except with the written consent of the insurance company. The only exception to this rule is when the named insured **dies**. Upon the death of the named insured, all of his or her rights and duties are transferred immediately to his or her **legal representative** for the interval during which the legal representative is acting on behalf of the deceased. If any other party has **temporary custody** of the property of the named insured after the death of the named insured, he or she has the rights and duties of the named insured with respect to the property. The named insured is obliged to transfer all rights of recovery against other parties for losses sustained by the named insured and settled by the insurance company.

Standard Commercial Property Policy

SPECIAL FORM FOR CAUSES OF LOSS
COVERED CAUSES OF LOSS AND EXCLUSIONS RELATED TO ORDINANCES OR LAWS

The special form for causes of loss in the standard commercial property policy begins by describing the **covered causes of loss**. It should be noted that the provisions outlined on this form are only applicable when "**special**" is indicated on the declarations page. When this is the case, all covered causes of loss are equivalent to risks of direct physical loss, except when countermanded by a specific exclusion or limitation. The first exclusion on the special form states that the insurance company will not compensate for any loss related to the enforcement of an **ordinance or law** associated with the construction or repair of any property, or any ordinance or law that requires part or all of that property to be **removed**. This exclusion applies even for situations in which the insured incurs extra expenses related to compliance with the ordinance or law.

EXCLUSION FOR EARTH MOVEMENT

The special form for causes of loss in the standard commercial property policy includes an exclusion for **earth movement**. This exclusion refers to any loss or damage caused by **earthquake**, as well as any earth movement related to an earthquake. It also includes loss and damage related to **landslide** and related events. Loss or damage related to **mine subsidence** is excluded, even in situations where the mining activity is no longer ongoing. This exclusion also covers damages related to **earth sinking**, including the resulting soil conditions of contraction, expansion, cracking, and erosion. Finally, the exclusion for loss and damage related to earth movement applies to **volcanic eruptions and explosions**, as well as resulting ash, dust, or lava flow. However, if a volcanic eruption results in fire or glass breakage, the insurance policy may cover loss or damage caused by the secondary occurrences.

EXCLUSIONS FOR GOVERNMENTAL ACTION, NUCLEAR HAZARD, AND UTILITY SERVICES

The special form for causes of loss in the standard commercial property policy has an exclusion for any loss or damage related to the seizure or destruction of property on the orders of a **government**. However, if these orders are issued during a fire with the intention of preventing further spread, the resulting loss or damage will be covered by the insurance company. The special form has an exclusion for **nuclear hazard**, by which is meant nuclear radiation or reaction, as well as radioactive contamination. The special form also has an exclusion for loss or damage caused by the failure or incapacity of **utility services**, so long as this failure occurs off of the named premises. When utility problems lead to a covered cause of loss, this loss will be covered by the insurance policy.

EXCLUSIONS FOR WAR AND MILITARY ACTION; WATER; AND FUNGUS, WET ROT, DRY ROT, AND BACTERIA

The special form for causes of loss in the standard commercial property policy contains an exclusion for loss or damage related to **war and military action**, even when the war is undeclared. The special form also has an exclusion for damage or loss caused by **water**, including flood, waves, tidal waves, surface water, overflow, and spray. The water exclusion also applies to loss or damage caused by mudslide or mudflow, as well as any loss or damage from water that overflows or backs up out of a sump, sewer, or drain. The exclusion applies to surface water and water that flows up through foundations, basements, floors, doors, or windows. However, if any of these sources of water damage results in sprinkler leakage, explosion, or fire, these resulting damages or losses will be covered by the insurance company. The final general exclusion in the special form for causes of loss in the standard commercial property policy applies to damage and loss due to the presence, growth, or spread of **fungus, wet rot, dry rot, or bacteria**. This exclusion does not apply if the fungus, wet rot, dry rot, or bacteria is the result of fire or lightning.

MISCELLANEOUS EXCLUSIONS

The special form for causes of loss in the standard commercial property policy lists a series of **miscellaneous exclusions**. Any losses or damages caused by the following events will not be covered by the insurance company: artificially generated electrical current; loss of market; smoke or gas from agricultural or industrial operations; smog; rust; nesting or infestation by insects, rodents, birds, or other animals; mechanical breakdown; explosion of steam pipes, engines, boilers, or turbines; leakage of water from plumbing, heating, or air conditioning equipment; dishonest or criminal act by the insured or the employees of the insured; rain, snow, ice, or sleet when personal property is left outside; release of pollutants; or failure to take all reasonable steps to save and preserve property from further loss.

94

LIMITATIONS

The special form for causes of loss in the standard commercial property policy outlines certain **limitations** which, unless otherwise stated, will apply to all policy forms and endorsements. To begin with, this policy will not apply to loss or damage to steam boilers, pipes, engines, or turbines, so long as the loss or damage is caused by the equipment itself. This policy also will not cover loss or damage to hot water boilers or other heating equipment unless the loss or damage is caused by an explosion. The policy will not cover damage to the inside of any building or structure, or to personal property inside a building or structure, if the damage is caused by rain, sand, ice, snow, or sleet. The policy will not cover loss or damage to any building materials or supplies that are not attached to the building or structure and which are stolen. Finally, the insurance company will not pay for the repair cost for any defective systems or appliances that release water, another liquid, or powder.

Standard Commercial Inland Marine Policy

COVERED PROPERTY

Under the standard commercial inland marine policy, the insurance company promises to pay any legal obligations for direct damage or loss to **covered property**, so long as the loss or damage is the result of a covered cause of loss. **Commercial inland marine policies** are for businesses that serve as motor carriers as defined by **Title 49 of the United States Code**. For the purposes of this policy, covered property is defined as any shipment named on the declarations page that has been confirmed for transportation by a bill of lading, written contract, tariff, or shipping receipt. The coverage provided by this policy terminates when the named property is accepted at its final destination or at the conclusion of the policy period. In the meantime, property is covered while it is in containers or on land vehicles.

NOT COVERED PROPERTY

There are certain types of property that are **not covered** by the standard commercial inland marine policy. To begin with, **valuable documents** are not covered. These include passports, bills, currency, coins, securities, stamps, and accounts. **Precious metals** like gold, silver, and platinum are not covered, and neither are precious or semi-precious stones. **Works of art** such as paintings, drawings, sculptures, tapestries, and historic documents are not covered by the standard commercial inland marine policy. **Jewelry, watches, and furs** are not covered. **Live animals**, including fish and birds, are not covered. If the insured party is legally liable for a piece of **property** as a freight forwarder or warehouse operator, this property is not covered. Any property that has been tendered to another motor carrier for transportation or delivery is not covered by the standard commercial inland marine policy. Finally, any **illegal property or contraband** is not covered.

ADDITIONAL COVERAGES

CLAIM MITIGATION EXPENSE, INTERMODAL SHIPPING CONTAINERS, LOADING AND UNLOADING, AND POLLUTANT CLEANUP AND REMOVAL

In the standard commercial inland marine policy, the insurance company will agree to pay for any **necessary expenses** incurred by the insured party to protect covered property from loss or damage. However, the maximum additional payment for each event is $5000, and this coverage only applies to expenses incurred within 12 hours of the covered cause of loss. The insurance company typically will offer an additional $2500 of coverage for damage or loss to **intermodal shipping containers** when these are the property of others but in the care or control of the named insured. When the insured party is in charge of **loading or unloading** property before or after transport, any loss or damage that occurs during these processes will be covered. The standard policy will also include additional coverage of $10,000 for **pollutant cleanup and removal**, so long as the discharge or release of these pollutants is the result of a covered cause of loss. The additional coverage for pollutant cleanup and removal does not cover the costs of assessing environmental conditions unless these tests are a necessary part of the cleanup or removal.

SUPPLEMENTARY PAYMENTS AND UNCOLLECTIBLE FREIGHT CHARGES

The standard commercial inland marine policy has a typical formulation for the handling of **supplementary payments**. If the insurance company decides to investigate, settle, or defend against a suit on behalf of the named insured, all of the **related expenses** will be covered by the policy. The insurance company will also pay the costs of **bonds** required to release attachments, so long as these bonds amounts are within the applicable limit of insurance. The insurance company is not required to provide these bonds. The insurance company will also cover any costs **taxed** against the insured party in the suit, so long as these costs are taxed because of a direct physical loss or damage. Any prejudgment interest awarded against the insured party will be paid. Any **interest** on the full amount of the judgment that accrues will be paid, so long as it is within the limit of insurance. Finally, the costs of **necessary appeal bonds** will be covered by the insurance company when the insurance company elects to appeal. There is no applicable deductible on additional coverage for supplementary payments. The insurance company will usually offer $5000 of additional coverage for freight charges that become uncollectible because of loss or damage to property.

EXCLUSIONS

GOVERNMENTAL ACTION, NUCLEAR HAZARD, WAR AND MILITARY ACTION, AND LOSS OF MARKET VALUE

The standard commercial inland marine policy does not cover the legal liability of the insured for loss or damage caused by **governmental action** (meaning the seizure or destruction of property on the orders of a governmental authority). The only exception to this exclusion is when the property is destroyed at the behest of a governmental authority in order to prevent the spread of **fire**. The standard commercial inland marine policy also excludes loss or damage caused by **nuclear hazard**, which may be related to weapons, nuclear reaction, or radiation. The standard commercial inland marine policy excludes loss or damage that is the result of **war** or other military actions. Finally, the standard commercial inland marine policy will not cover any legal liability caused by the **delay, loss of market, or loss of market value** of property.

MISCELLANEOUS EXCLUSIONS

The standard commercial inland marine policy will not cover any loss or damage that is caused by **dishonesty or criminal behavior** on the part of the named insured or anyone else with an interest in the property. The only exception to this exclusion is for destructive acts committed by employees during the course of their employment. This policy also excludes loss or damage related to the discharge, release, or escape of **pollutants** unless these problems are the result of a covered cause of loss. The standard commercial inland marine policy does not cover damages caused by **wear and tear**, or by any **spoilage** caused by the failure of refrigeration equipment. If the named insured takes on liability beyond that which is imposed by law on motor carriers, the insurance company will not pay for any **subsequent liabilities**. The insurance company will also not pay for any fines or penalties that are incurred because of **legal violations**.

LIMITS OF INSURANCE AND DEDUCTIBLE

The standard commercial inland marine policy has a pre-established limit. The **limit of insurance** is the maximum payment, no matter how many insured parties are involved, how many claims or suits are brought, or how many parties bring claims or suits. The insurance company will not pay

96

for any losses or damages until the amount of the loss or damage has exceeded the **deductible** indicated on the declarations page. The insurance company will then pay the difference between the actual value of the loss or damage than the deductible, so long as this does not exceed the limit of insurance. In most cases, the deductible indicated on the declarations page will also apply to additional coverages. However, if multiple coverages or additional coverages are involved in an incident, the insurance company will use the largest applicable deductible.

ADDITIONAL COVERAGE CONDITIONS

COVERAGE TERRITORY, EARNED PREMIUM, RECORDS, AND DUTIES OF THE NAMED INSURED IN THE EVENT OF A LOSS OR SUIT

The standard commercial inland marine policy applies to property anywhere within **the United States, Puerto Rico, or Canada**. The premium indicated on the declarations page will be considered to be fully **earned** as soon as the described property leaves the shipping point. The insured party is responsible for maintaining accurate **records**, including documentation of the premium base. The insured party must maintain these records for three years after the conclusion of the policy period. In the event of a loss or suit, the insured party must provide **notice** as soon as possible to the insurance company. If a law may have been broken, the insured party must also alert the **police**. The insured party should also provide the insurer with a **comprehensive description** of the incident. The insured must take any reasonable steps to **prevent further damage**, and may not assume any **obligations** or incur any **expenses** without the consent of the insurance company. The insured party must provide the insurance company with **total access** to books and records, as well as the opportunity to **interview** the insured party under oath.

LEGAL ACTION AGAINST THE INSURANCE COMPANY

If a lawsuit or claim is brought against the insured party under a standard commercial inland marine policy, the insured party must cooperate with any investigation, settlement, or defense by the insurance company. However, no party may bring a **legal action against the insurance company** unless the terms of the policy have been fully honored. Also, the standard commercial inland marine policy asserts that no person or organization has the right to join with the insurance company in **pursuit of damages** from the named insured. This would not prevent other parties from pursuing the insurance company to receive part or all of an agreed settlement or final judgment against the named insured. However, the insurance company will not pay any damages in excess of the applicable limit of insurance.

STANDARD EQUIPMENT BREAKDOWN POLICY

COVERED CAUSE OF LOSS

The **standard equipment breakdown policy** covers losses caused by accidents. In the context of this policy, an **accident** is defined as an unfortunate event that causes direct physical damage to covered equipment. **Covered equipment** is anything that creates, transmits, or utilizes energy, or which operates under vacuum or pressure power. **Electronic communications** and **data processing equipment** are both covered. There are **six types of accidents** covered by the standard equipment breakdown policy: mechanical breakdown; artificially generated electrical current that damages electrical components; destructive explosion of steam boilers, piping, engines, or turbines; other events that damage steam boilers, pipes, engines, or turbines; events that damage water boilers or other water heating equipment; and bursting, splitting, or cracking.

PROPERTY DAMAGE, OFF-PREMISES PROPERTY DAMAGE, BUSINESS INCOME, EXTRA EXPENSE, SERVICE INTERRUPTION, AND CONTINGENT BUSINESS INCOME

The standard equipment breakdown policy covers any physical damage to **covered property** on an insured location. The policy also covers **transportable equipment** that is within the coverage territory or at another location owned or leased by the insured at the time of the accident. The insurance company will pay any actual loss of business income sustained by the insured party while the damaged equipment is being restored. The insurance company will pay whatever expenses are necessary during this interval of restoration to minimize the loss. The insurance company also promises to pay any reasonable extra expenses incurred by the insured party for the **operation of business** during the interval of restoration. The insurance company promises to pay any loss or expense related to an **interruption of service** or an **interruption of supply**.

PERISHABLE GOODS AND DATA RESTORATION

The standard equipment breakdown policy includes coverage for **perishable goods** that spoil. The spoilage of perishable goods is covered when it is the result of an interruption of service or of contamination by refrigerant. In addition, the standard equipment breakdown policy guarantees reimbursement for any necessary expenses incurred during the interval of restoration with the intention of minimizing the total amount of loss. The insurance company will cover these expenses within the policy's limit of liability. The standard equipment breakdown policy also covers any reasonable and required cost of **researching or restoring lost data**. In addition, the insurance company will promise to pay for any lost business income or extra expenses that are necessitated by the process of data restoration.

DEMOLITION, AND ORDINANCE OR LAW

The standard equipment breakdown policy covers accidents that damage covered buildings that subsequently must be **demolished** according to an ordinance or law, and that are not otherwise covered by hazardous substances coverage. The standard equipment breakdown policy will also cover any additional and unnecessary costs required to comply with an **ordinance or law** that mandates the demolition, site clearing, and/or reconstruction of a covered property. This policy will also cover additional expenses that are incurred because of an ordinance or law that regulates the construction or repair of buildings or building parts, and that is not subject to demolition coverage or hazardous substances coverage. The insurance company will pay for any additional costs required to comply with the ordinance or law that mandates reconstruction or repair of a damaged portion of the building.

EXPEDITING EXPENSES AND HAZARDOUS SUBSTANCES

The standard equipment breakdown policy will cover any reasonable extra cost for temporary repairs or the **expediting of permanent repairs or replacement**. In addition, the standard equipment breakdown policy will cover any additional cost that is required to repair or replace covered property that has been contaminated by a **hazardous substance**. This coverage for hazardous substances includes any expenses required to clean up or dispose of contaminated property. However, this coverage does not apply to contamination of commercial goods by refrigerant because that damage is addressed in the coverage for perishable goods. Moreover, the equipment breakdown coverage will pay for any loss or expense related to business income or extra expense coverage when it is related to contamination by hazardous substances.

NEWLY ACQUIRED LOCATIONS AND CONSTRUCTION

In the standard farm liability policy, the insurance company asserts that the insured party must provide prompt notification of any locations that are purchased or leased during the policy period. **Newly acquired property** is covered in the same way as those properties that are already owned.

Coverage is initiated at the time of property acquisition. **Newly built properties** are only considered to have been acquired when the finished project has been accepted by the new owner or lessor. The coverage for newly acquired locations terminates at the same time as the coverage for previously insured locations. In cases where the limit or deductible varies by location, newly acquired locations will be assigned the highest limits and deductibles. The insurance company will assess an additional premium for newly acquired properties from the date of acquisition. Whenever the insured party plans to **expand or rehabilitate** part of the named location, he or she is responsible for notifying the insurance company promptly. If notification is given, the expanded or rehabilitated property will receive full coverage under the equipment breakdown policy. However, the insured will be charged an additional premium for any newly acquired equipment.

FIRE AND EXPLOSION, ORDINANCE OR LAW, EARTH MOVEMENT, AND NUCLEAR HAZARD

The standard equipment breakdown policy does not cover losses, damages, or expenses caused by **fire and explosion**. This includes fire, smoke from a fire, combustion explosions, and other explosions. There is also an exclusion for losses caused by the enforcement or alteration of an **ordinance or law**. The standard equipment breakdown policy does not cover losses caused by **earth movement**, regardless of whether this phenomenon is natural or man-made. Examples of earth movement include earthquake, tremors, landslide, tsunami, and sinkhole collapse. Finally, the standard equipment breakdown policy does not cover losses caused by **nuclear hazard**, including nuclear reaction, radioactive contamination, nuclear detonation, or nuclear radiation.

WAR AND MILITARY ACTION, WATER, FAILURE TO PROTECT PROPERTY, FINES, MOLD, AND DELIBERATE ACTS

The standard equipment breakdown policy does not apply to losses caused by **war** or any other military action. The policy also does not provide coverage for damages caused by **water**, including floods, waves, tidal waves, or spray from a nearby body of water. There is no coverage provided for losses caused by mudslide or mudflow. Moreover, there is no coverage provided for damage caused by water that is backed up or overflows from a drain, sump, or sewer. The standard equipment breakdown policy also excludes losses caused by the failure of the insured to use all reasonable means to **protect his or her property after an accident**. The policy does not cover any **fines**, penalties, or punitive damages assessed against the insured party. The policy does not cover damages caused by **mold**, fungus, or mildew. Finally, the standard equipment breakdown policy does not cover losses caused by the **deliberate act** of any person, such as vandalism or sabotage.

ACCIDENT CAUSES EXCLUSIONS

There are certain **accident causes** that are **excluded** from the standard equipment breakdown policy. To begin with, the standard equipment breakdown policy will not cover any accidents caused by lightning, windstorm, or hail. The only exception to these exclusions occurs when covered equipment inside the building is damaged by wind-driven rain, snow, sand or dust, and the equipment was not damaged because of original damage to the building. Moreover, the standard equipment breakdown policy will not cover losses resulting from collision with a vehicle, or from objects that fall from an aircraft. The equipment breakdown policy does not cover damages from riot, civil commotion, discharge or leakage from an automatic sprinkler system, volcanic action, or electrical insulation breakdown test. In addition, the standard equipment breakdown policy will not cover losses caused by elevator collision; hydrostatic, gas, or pneumatic pressure tests; or water that is used to extinguish a fire.

ACCIDENT CAUSES EXCLUSIONS WHEN COVERED BY OTHER INSURANCE

There are some accident causes that will not be covered by the standard equipment breakdown policy if they are covered by **any other insurance policy**. These exclusions pertain even when the other insurance is not collectible, and even when the other insurance provides a much different scope of coverage. Accidents caused by falling objects or the collapse of structures are not covered by the standard equipment breakdown policy if they are covered by any other insurance policy. Accidents caused by the weight of snow, ice, or sleet are not covered by this policy except as excess insurance. Moreover, if accidents caused by the breakage of glass or the discharge of molten material from equipment are covered by another policy, they will not be covered by the standard equipment breakdown policy. There is a similar exclusion for accidents caused by freezing or water damage. For the purposes of this policy, water damage is defined as any discharge or leakage of steam or water because of the disintegration or cracking of a system or appliance.

DEDUCTIBLES

In the standard equipment breakdown policy, it is possible for **multiple deductibles** to apply to a single accident unless the declarations page indicates that the deductible is to be combined for all coverages. The insurance company declines to pay for any damages, losses, or expenses until the value of the covered damage or loss is greater than the deductible amount indicated for that coverage on the declarations page. The insurance company then promises to pay the **difference** between the applicable deductible and the total amount of loss, damage, or expense, so long as this difference is within the limit of insurance indicated on the declarations page. In situations where different deductibles apply to several pieces of covered equipment that are involved in an accident, the **highest deductible** for each coverage applies.

DIRECT AND INDIRECT COVERAGES

In many standard equipment breakdown policies, there will be a distinction between direct coverages deductibles and indirect coverages deductibles. **Indirect coverages deductibles** typically apply to business income and extra expense losses, while **direct coverages** typically apply to any remaining losses, damages, or expenses covered by the equipment breakdown policy. With regard to the application of **time deductibles**, the insurance company usually will not pay for any loss that occurs during the specified number of hours or days after an accident. If the deductible is a multiple of the average daily value deductible, it is calculated by determining the business income that would have been earned each day had there been no accident. This value is then multiplied by the number of working days in the interval following the accident. Calculations of **average daily value** take into account the business income of the entire location, even when the loss does not affect the entire location. The period of interruption may not be any longer than the period of restoration. A final way to express a deductible is as a **percentage of loss**. When this format is used, the insurance company is not liable for the indicated percentage of the gross amount of damage, loss, or expense.

ABANDONMENT, BRANDS AND LABELS, AND COINSURANCE

According to the standard equipment breakdown policy, the insured party is not allowed to **abandon** any property to the insurance company. There is a special protocol for damaged property with a salvage value when this property is **branded or labeled**. The insured party may either remove the brands or labels (assuming this will not physically damage the merchandise), or may stamp the word "salvage" on the merchandise. If taking either of these actions diminishes the value of the merchandise, the insurance company will pay the difference. In most cases, the business income coverage provided as part of the standard equipment breakdown policy is subject to **coinsurance**, meaning that the insurance company will not reimburse all of the business income loss if the actual annual value of business income is greater than the estimated annual value of income. The maximum payment that will be made in the circumstances is calculated by dividing the estimated annual value of business income by the actual annual value of business income at the time of the accident, then multiplying the quotient by the total amount of covered business income loss, and then subtracting the applicable deductible. If this amount is less than the business income limit, it represents the maximum payment.

COINSURANCE (COVERAGES OTHER THAN BUSINESS INCOME) AND DEFENSE

In the standard equipment breakdown policy, some of the coverages besides business income coverage may be subject to **coinsurance**. When this is the case, it will be indicated on the declarations page. When a **coinsurance percentage** is listed, the maximum payment will be calculated by multiplying the value of the covered property at the time of the accident by the coinsurance percentage, then dividing the applicable limit by this product, and then multiplying the total amount of loss (before adjustment with the deductible) by the resulting quotient. Finally, this product is diminished by the amount of the deductible. If this resulting value is less than the applicable limit, then it represents the maximum payment. If the applicable limit is less, it represents the maximum payment. Any remaining cost will be borne by the insured party. When the insured party is subject to lawsuits by the owners of property in the care or control of the insured party, the insurance company has the right, but not the obligation, to **defend** the insured party at the expense of the insurance company.

DUTIES IN THE EVENT OF LOSS OR DAMAGE

The standard equipment breakdown policy outlines specific **duties** of the insured party in the event of loss or damage. To begin with, the insured party must **notify** the insurance company of the loss or damage as soon as possible. This notification should include a full description of the property involved. The insured party should also take whatever measures are necessary to **reduce loss, damage, or expense**, whether by protecting property from future damage, resuming business as quickly as possible, and using any other resources that are available. The insured party must give the insurance company a reasonable amount of time to **examine** the damaged property and premises before initiating repair or replacement. The insured party should never make any statements that acknowledge **liability or obligation** on the part of the insurance company. The insured party should immediately forward any **relevant legal papers or notices** to the insurance company, and should cooperate with the investigation and settlement of the claim. Finally, the insured party must permit the insurance company to perform any desired **examinations** and receive any useful statements, even under oath.

ERRORS AND OMISSIONS

The standard equipment breakdown policy contains some basic loss conditions related to **errors and omissions**. To begin with, if the insured party makes any error or unintentional omission related to the **location or description of covered property**, and this error or omission is the only reason why a loss is not covered, the insurance company will make good the loss. The insurance company will also pay for any losses when the insured party makes an error and fails to include **listings of premises** he or she owned or occupied at the beginning of the period of the policy. The insurance company will also pay for any **damages** that are otherwise not payable only because of errors or unintentional omissions that lead to a cancellation of coverage. The insurance company, however, will not provide any coverage as a result of errors or unintentional omissions by the insured party with regard to requested coverage or values of property. Any errors or unintentional omissions should be reported as soon as they are discovered so that the premiums may be adjusted retroactively.

PROVING YOUR LOSS AND SALVAGES AND RECOVERIES

According to the standard equipment breakdown policy, the insured party must take specific steps when **proving loss**. To begin with, the insured party must provide documentation that indicates that the loss, damage, or expense is the result of a covered accident. The insured party must also provide documentation that outlines the dollar amount of the loss, damage, or expense. All of this proof must be provided at the expense of the insured party. In situations where the insured party receives some **salvage or recovery payment** after the insurance company and is provided compensation for loss or damages, the amount of the loss will be recalculated to include the eventual amount of salvage or recovery payment. If either the insurance company or the insured party is found to owe money as a result of this recalculation, it should be paid promptly.

VALUATION

In the standard equipment breakdown policy, the protocol for determining the **value** of covered property is outlined among the conditions. In general, the amount of payment for damaged property will be the smallest of the following three values: cost of **replacing** the damaged property, cost of **repairing** the damaged property, or the **actual cost** required to repair or replace the damaged property. The insurance company will always base in valuation on the most cost-effective means of restoring the **capacity** of the damaged property. This will not always mean replacement or repair with new equipment. If the insured party wants to replace damaged property with property of greater quality or capacity, the extra expense will be borne by the insured. However, the insurance company will cover the extra cost of new or replacement equipment that is better for the environment or more energy-efficient, provided that this new equipment is no more than 125 percent of the cost of the most cost-effective option.

Under the standard equipment breakdown policy, certain types of property are evaluated on an **actual cash value** basis. These include any properties that do not currently serve a necessary or useful function for the insured party, any covered property that is not repaired or replaced in the two years following an accident, and any property for which actual cash value coverage is indicated on the declarations page. There are also some situations in which the property held for sale by the insured party will be assigned the **value of the sale price** as if there had been no loss or damage. This valuation occurs when the property was manufactured by the insured party, when the replacement cost of the property is greater than the sales price, or when the insured party cannot replace the property before it is expected to be sold. With regard to **data restoration coverage**, value is assigned at either the replacement cost (for commercially available software) or the cost of reproducing records on blank media.

ADDITIONAL INSUREDS; BANKRUPTCY; CONCEALMENT, MISREPRESENTATION, OR FRAUD; AND JURISDICTIONAL INSPECTIONS

When parties are listed on the declarations page as **additional insureds**, they receive coverage under the standard equipment breakdown policy only to the extent of their interest in the covered property. Neither the insurance company nor the insured party is relieved of its obligations by the **bankruptcy** or insolvency of the insured. The insurance company will decline to compensate the insured for any losses, damages, or expenses that are intentional. The insurance company will also refuse to make payments when the insured party has intentionally **concealed or misrepresented** any material fact related to the policy, the covered property, his or her interest in the covered property, or a claim. Finally, the insured party is responsible for complying with all applicable state and federal regulations, and for submitting to any required **inspections**.

LEGAL ACTION AGAINST THE INSURANCE COMPANY, LIBERALIZATION, AND LOSS PAYABLE

With regard to the standard equipment breakdown policy, no one is allowed to bring a **legal action against the insurance company** unless the insured party has complied fully with the terms of the policy. Also, any legal action must be brought within two years of the accident unless the insurance company agrees in writing that the insured party is obliged to pay for damage to the property of others. Whenever the insurance company revises the standard equipment breakdown policy such that coverage is broadened without adding to the premium, the **liberalization** will apply as soon as they are effective in the relevant jurisdiction. The insurance company will promise to pay the insured party and the loss payee indicated on the declarations page for any **losses** covered by the policy in proportion to their interest. When the insurance company makes payment to a loss payee, the insurance company secures their rights against any other party.

PROPERTY AND EQUIPMENT MAINTENANCE, AND MORTGAGE HOLDERS

According to the standard equipment breakdown policy, it is the responsibility of the insured party to **maintain all property and equipment**. The insurance company is not responsible for the expense of maintaining, enhancing, or protecting covered property. Under the standard equipment breakdown policy, the term "**mortgage holder**" includes all trustees. The insurance company will promise to pay for any direct damage to covered property both to the insured party and to each mortgage holder in the order of precedence indicated on the declarations page. In addition, the mortgage holder has the right to receive payment for loss even when the mortgage holder has already begun a foreclosure of the covered property. The mortgage holder may have the right to receive loss payment even when the claim of the insured party is denied, so long as the mortgage holder pays any requested premium that has not been paid by the insured party, and so long as the mortgage holder submits a signed and sworn proof of loss within 60 days of receiving notice from the insurance company.

OTHER INSURANCE, COVERAGE TERRITORY, AND PRIVILEGE TO ADJUST WITH OWNER

When **another insurance policy** applies to the same loss, damage, or expense as the standard equipment breakdown policy, the latter will only apply as excess insurance after all other policies have reached their limit of liability. The **coverage territory** for the standard equipment breakdown policy is the United States (including all possessions and territories thereof), Puerto Rico, and Canada. In situations where property that belongs to others is damaged or destroyed while in the care or control of the insured party, the insurance company retains the rights to **settle with the property owner**. If this settlement is reached, it will serve to satisfy any claims made by the insured party.

SUSPENSION AND TRANSFER OF RIGHTS OF RECOVERY AGAINST OTHERS TO THE INSURANCE COMPANY

In the standard equipment breakdown policy, the insurance company retains the right to **suspend coverage** immediately for covered equipment that is discovered to be in or be exposed to a dangerous condition. This suspension may be indicated by delivery of written notice. The only way to **reverse** such a suspension is to have the equipment in question reinstated by a specific **endorsement**. While the suspension is effective, the insurance company will reduce the amount of premium on a pro rata basis. Whenever a party to whom the insurance company has made payment under the standard equipment breakdown policy has the right to recover damages from some other party, the insurance company receives those rights of recovery. The rights of recovery of the insurance company terminate once the amount of payment originally made by the insurance company has been matched.

103

Businessowners Policy

APARTMENT AND OFFICE ASSOCIATIONS COVERAGE

The standard business owner policy is a multi-peril policy providing coverage for all **small businesses** in retail locations, offices, apartments, residences, and condominiums. The standard business owner policy does include selected **processing and servicing risk protection**. There are certain restrictions for **apartment and residential condominium associations**. In order to obtain business owners' coverage, these buildings may not be more than six stories tall, and may not have more than 60 units. Any incidental occupancies of a mercantile nature must receive permits. Also, permits must be issued for processing or service occupancies that take up less than 25,000 square feet. In order to be covered by a business owners' policy, an office condominium association may not exceed six stories or 100,000 square feet. The incidental occupants of an office condominium may be mercantile operators or apartments, or selected processing and service locations, so long as these are 25,000 square feet or less.

MERCANTILE SERVICE OR PROCESSING OCCUPANCIES COVERAGE

In order to be covered by the standard business owners' policy, a **mercantile service or processing occupancy** must be no more than 25,000 square feet. Such a building may include a separate storage building, though only business personal property will be covered. Finally, in order to be eligible for the standard business owners' policy, the mercantile service or processing occupancy may not have gross sales of more than $3 million at any one insured location. The following risks are **ineligible** for coverage under the standard business owners' policy: auto repair stations; bars and restaurants; contractors; businesses that include more than one manufacturing, processing, or servicing operation; household property (with the exception of the landlord's personal property); one- and two-family residences; amusement parks; financial institutions; gas stations; and wholesalers.

COMMON CONDITIONS FOR THE STANDARD BUSINESS OWNERS' POLICY

The standard business owners' policy has a set of **conditions** similar to those of the commercial package policy. One difference is that many of the coverages of the standard business owners' policy are **automatic**, whereas those of the commercial package policy may be optional. Business income and peak season coverage, for instance, are automatic for the business owners' policy. The business owner property coverage form is identical to the building property coverage form. The covered buildings include any named on the declarations page, as well as any completed additions, fixtures, or outdoor fixtures. Coverage also extends to personal property in apartments which the insured owns as well as any equipment that is required to maintain or service the property. **Business personal property**, meanwhile, includes all of the business property owned by the named insured, or all of the property in the care of the named insured. Improvements made by tenants and leased personal property are also covered by the standard business owners' policy.

BUSINESS PERSONAL PROPERTY COVERAGE

The standard business owners' policy covers **business personal property**, which includes the property owned by the named insured, property in the custody or control of the named insured, improvements made by tenants, and leased personal property. The standard coverage of business personal property only covers **loss and damage** caused by the named perils. Specifically, the standard business personal property coverage insures against loss or damage caused by fire and lightning, vandalism and malicious mischief, sprinkler leakage, sinkholes, building collapse, volcanic action, and damage that occurs while property is in transit. There is also special coverage available

104

for business personal property policy. Unless specifically indicated, this policy will not cover the loss of **income**. However, policies that do cover loss of income will only do so for a maximum of one year.

CONDITIONS, LIMITS, DEDUCTIBLE, AND ADDITIONAL COVERAGE

The business personal property coverage form of the standard business owners' policy does not require **coinsurance**. It is typical for losses to be settled at **actual cash value**, except in cases when the property was insured to at least 80 percent of its value, in which case losses will be settled on a replacement cost basis. In the standard policy, the **maximum coverage** for business personal property that is away from the insured location, either temporarily or because it is in transit, is $1000. The **standard deductible** for business personal property coverage is $250, though policyholders may obtain deductibles of $500, $1000, and $2500 for loss of business income and extra expenses. Fire department service charges are not included in the calculation of the deductible. This policy does offer some **additional coverages**, including up to 25 percent of the loss plus the deductible for the expense of removing debris after a covered event. The policy will also offer additional coverage for the expense of removing property in order to preserve it from a named peril, so long as this occurs within 30 days of the peril. Policyholders who obtain the special form of business owners' policy may receive coverage for damage caused by the collapse of the building due to the weight of people or animals, or by water damage.

COVERAGE EXTENSIONS, LIMITED PERILS, AND EXCLUSIONS

The business personal property coverage offered by the standard business owners' policy provides some **coverage extensions**. Personal property at newly acquired premises may receive extended coverage up to $10,000. Personal property located off of the named premises may receive extended coverage up to $1000. Outdoor property may receive extended coverage up to $1000, and trees, plants, and shrubs, may receive extended coverage up to $500. However, some losses and damages are subject to **coverage limitations**. Signs, important papers, and records are only eligible for coverage up to $1000. The business personal property coverage offered by the standard business owners' policy does **not cover** loss or damage caused by ordinance or governmental action; nuclear hazard; war and military action; water and flood; power surge; damage to steam apparatus; delay due to strike; earth movement; or poor design, workmanship, or materials. This policy will not cover any losses suffered by the policyholder because of the suspension of a license or the cancellation of a lease or contract.

LIMITS OF INSURANCE AND PROPERTY LOSS CONDITIONS

The business personal property coverage will be subject to whatever **limit** is indicated on the declarations page. This limit may be increased by $10,000 for the cleanup and removal of **pollution**. For the purposes of this insurance policy, the **property value** of the building will be increased by whatever percentage is indicated on the declarations page. If the average annual level of inventory is 100 percent, the policy will increase the **business personal property stock coverage** by 25 percent during the peak season. There are certain limits on special loss due to **theft**. Specifically, there is a limit of $2500 for the theft of jewelry, precious metals, patterns, dies, and molds, and there is a limit of $250 for the theft of stamps and tickets.

PROPERTY LOSS CONDITIONS AND PROPERTY GENERAL CONDITIONS

The typical property loss conditions apply to the business personal property coverage offered by the standard business owners' policy. **Abandoned property** is not covered by the policy. If there is a dispute about the value of property, the **appraisal protocol** used for other insurance policies will be applied. In the event of loss or damage, the insured party is responsible for immediately **notifying** the insurance company and, if necessary, the law enforcement authorities. The insured

105

party is responsible for providing total **access** to records, property, and relevant documents. The loss payment will typically be made within 30 days after the insurance company receives proof of loss. The insured party may elect to have recovered property **restored**, or to grant ownership of the recovered property to the insurance company and instead retain the **monetary benefit**. A property will be considered **vacant** if it has been empty for 60 consecutive days. As for the general conditions of the business personal property coverage, the **policy period** is indicated on the declarations page, and the **coverage territory** is the United States, Puerto Rico, and Canada. **Optional coverage** is available for outdoor signs, employee dishonesty, mechanical breakdown, and exterior grade floor glass.

COVERAGE, LIMITS OF INSURANCE, AND ENDORSEMENTS

The **business owner liability coverage** offered by the standard business owners' policy will apply to loss and damage that occurs on the insured party's premises, as well as loss and damage that are the result of the insured party's operations. The policy will cover loss or damage caused by the products of the policyholder, as well as any advertising and personal injury for which the business owner is found liable. The definition of **liability** for the business owners' policy is the same as for the commercial general liability policy. The insurance company will typically cover medical expenses up to $5000 per person, no matter which party is at fault. The **basic occurrence limit** for the business owner liability policy is $300,000, though the payment of an additional premium may raise the basic occurrence limit to $1 million. For the standard policy, the **general aggregate limit** is twice the occurrence limit. However, the aggregate limit for loss or damage caused by products completed operations is the same as the occurrence limit. The amount of liability for damage caused by fire is typically $50,000. Certain business owners may elect to obtain specific **endorsements**, as for instance for non-owned or rented automobiles. Also, some professionals may obtain specific liability endorsements, as for instance barbers, druggists, and veterinarians.

Workers Compensation Insurance

OBLIGATIONS OF AN EMPLOYER TO EMPLOYEES

Workers' compensation laws establish that employers have certain **responsibilities** with regard to their employees. If an employer fails to satisfy any of these conditions, an employee can bring legal action against the employer for **negligence**. The burden of proof is still largely on the employee. To begin with, the employer is obliged to provide a **safe place** to work. The employer must also provide **safe tools and equipment**. The employer must ensure that other employees are reasonably competent, and that managers are diligent about enforcing **safety rules**. Finally, employers must provide **reasonable warnings** about any dangers that are likely to exist on the job. An employer can escape legal liability for negligence if the employer can prove that the injury was caused by the negligence of a fellow employee rather than the employer. Another defense is contributory negligence, in which the employer proves that the injured employee was partly at fault. Finally, an employer may be able to escape liability if he or she can prove that the employee assumed some risk at the beginning of the job.

STANDARD WORKERS' COMPENSATION POLICY

The standard workers' compensation policy begins with an **information page**, followed by a **general introduction**. There are **six separate parts** within the standard policy: workers' compensation, employers' liability, other states insurance, duties if injury occurs, premium, and conditions. In each section of the policy, the insurance applies to any accidental injury, disease, or death occurring during the specified period and either caused or exacerbated by the conditions of employment. One unique aspect of workers' compensation and employers' liability coverage is that it contributes equal shares even when other insurance applies. In the **standard agreement**, the insurance company agrees to provide a basic legal defense and to investigate and settle any claims or suits caused by the insurance.

WORKERS' COMPENSATION AND EMPLOYERS' LIABILITY INSURANCE POLICY

The general section of a workers' compensation and employers' liability insurance policy will begin with a **general agreement**, indicating that payment of the premium will guarantee the provision of insurance in accordance with all the terms of the policy. The general section continues by introducing the **information page**, which in most other insurance policies is called a declarations page. The information page will list the **name and address** of the employer, as well as the **type of business** (e.g., sole proprietorship, partnership, corporation). The information page will also indicate the **policy term**, which begins at 12:01 AM standard time at the policy address. The information page will also include a list of the **states** in which workers' compensation coverage will apply. This list should include all of the states in which the employer has operations.

The information page in the general section of a workers' compensation and employers' liability insurance policy will also indicate the employers' liability coverage limits. It is typical for the limits to be $100,000 per accident for injuries and $100,000 per employee for disease, with a $500,000 annual aggregate limit for disease. It is possible, however, to purchase higher limits. The information page will also include a space where the employer can list additional states in which it might have **future exposure**. Coverage for these states is described in part three of the standard worker's compensation and employers' liability insurance policy. Finally, the information page will detail job classifications and codes, estimated payrolls, estimated premiums, and rates. Depending on the policy, premiums may be paid monthly, quarterly, semiannually, or annually.

Following the information page, the general section of a workers' compensation and employers' liability insurance policy will designate **who is insured** by the policy. Typically, it will indicate that a person is insured if he or she is named on the information page. If the employer is a partnership, **partners** are only insured in their capacity as employers of the partnership's employees. The general section goes on to indicate that workers' compensation law as designated in the policy refers to the **workers or workmen's compensation law and occupational disease law** within each jurisdiction named on the information page. Moreover, any amendments to this legislation that are in effect during the policy period are applicable. The standard policy does not include any federal workers or workmen's compensation law, any federal occupational disease law, or any law that provides non-occupational disability benefits.

PART ONE (WORKERS COMPENSATION' INSURANCE)

Part one of the standard workers' compensation and employers' liability insurance policy describes the **application of the policy**. It begins by stating that the **workers' compensation insurance** applies to bodily injury, including death, caused by accident or disease. There are a couple of **conditions**. For one, any bodily injury by accident must occur during the policy period. Bodily injury by disease, on the other hand, may qualify if it is caused or exacerbated by the conditions of employment. In order for the workers' compensation to apply, however, the last day of the last exposure to the conditions that caused or exacerbated the disease must occur during the policy interval. Part one goes on to assert that the insurance company will promptly pay the benefits required by the applicable workers' compensation law. Insurance companies generally pay medical benefits, income benefits, death benefits, and rehabilitation benefits

Part one of the standard workers' compensation and employers' liability insurance policy offers a very brief description of when the insurance company will pay **benefits**, and then offers a somewhat longer explanation of the circumstances under which the company will **contest** the claim. The insurance company will typically assert the right and duty to defend, at its own expense, any claim or proceeding for benefits. The insurance company states that it has no duty to defend any claim or proceeding unrelated to workers' compensation or employers' liability insurance. The policy goes on to state that the insurance company will also pay reasonable expenses incurred by the policyholder at the request of the company during such an investigation. However, the insurance company is not obliged to compensate the policyholder for loss of earnings incurred during an investigation. Typically, the insurance company will also guarantee payment for premiums for bonds to release attachments and for appeal bonds in bond amounts equal to or less than the amount payable under the insurance. The insurance company may guarantee reimbursement for litigation costs, as well as interest on judgments required by law.

Part one of the standard workers' compensation and employers' liability insurance policy indicates that the insurance company will not pay more than its **share** of the benefits and costs covered by this insurance and other insurance, including self-insurance. The employer is typically responsible for making the payments in **excess** of the benefits regularly provided by workers' compensation law when these excess payments are required because of serious and willful misconduct, conscious employment of an individual in violation of law, failure to comply with a health or safety law or regulation, or discrimination against any employee in violation of the workers' compensation law. If the insurance company makes any payments in excess of the regularly provided benefits, the employer must reimburse the insurance company promptly.

Part one of the standard workers' compensation and employers' liability insurance policy continues by indicating the insurance company's **rights to recovery** from others. The insurance company will typically declare that it has the right, as well as the right of anyone entitled to benefits from the insurance policy, to recover payments made by the insurance company from anyone liable for injury. The employer is responsible for assisting the insurance company in protecting those rights and enforcing them. This is generally known as the **subrogation clause**. Essentially, it gives the insurance company the right to recover any payments it has made if a third party is found to be responsible for the worker's injury. This prevents the injured employee from making collections from both the insurance company and the negligent party.

The final section of part one of the standard workers' compensation and employers' liability insurance policy outlines some **statutory provisions**. All of these provisions are considered to apply automatically when they are the law of the relevant jurisdiction. First, the insurance company declares that it is considered to have **notice of an injury** when the employer has notice. In other words, the notice of an injury given to the employer by the worker has the same legal effect as notice given to the insurer. The second statutory provision is that the insurance company will not be relieved of its duties under the policy should the employer or the employer's estate **default, go bankrupt, or become insolvent**. In other words, the insurance company still has to pay benefits even if the employer becomes bankrupt.

The third statutory provision outlined in the last section of part one of the standard workers' compensation and employers' liability insurance policy is that the insurance company agrees to be **directly and primarily liable** to anyone entitled to benefits payable by the insurance policy. This obligation may be enforced by the rightful recipient of benefits, as well as by any agency authorized by law. This enforcement may be leveled against the insurance company alone, or against the insurance company and the employer. The next provision establishes that any workers' compensation law establishing **jurisdiction** over the employer in effect establishes jurisdiction over the insurance company. In other words, the insurance company agrees to be bound by any decisions made against the employer under workers' compensation law.

The fifth statutory provision outlined in part one of the standard workers' compensation and employers' liability insurance policy describes the aspects of workers' compensation law that apply to the policy. Specifically, the policy will abide by **workers' compensation law** with respect to benefits payable by the insurance, as well as with respect to special taxes, payments into security or other special funds, and assessments payable under workers' compensation law. The insurance covers any statutory benefits, special taxes, assessments, and payments required by the workers' compensation law. Finally, the last statutory provision in part one assures the policyholder that any terms of the insurance policy that conflict with workers' compensation law will be changed automatically to **conform** to that law.

PART TWO (EMPLOYERS' LIABILITY INSURANCE)
APPLICATION OF THE INSURANCE

The **second part** of the standard workers' compensation and employers' liability insurance policy begins by indicating how employers' liability insurance applies. Typically, the section will begin by indicating that employers' liability insurance applies to any **bodily injury**, including death, caused by accident or disease. In order to be covered by the insurance, the bodily injury must arise out of and in the course of the injured party's **employment** by the employer. This employment must be either necessary or incidental to the employer's business in one of the states named on the information page. Any bodily injury by accident must occur during the policy period, and bodily injury by disease must be either caused or aggravated by the conditions of employment. In order for the insurance policy to apply, the employee's last day of **exposure** to the conditions causing or aggravating the disease must occur during the policy period. Finally, the policy typically states that any suit or legal action against the employer must be brought in the **United States, its territories or possessions, or Canada**.

DAMAGES TO BE PAID

The **second part** of the standard workers' compensation and employers' liability insurance policy details the **damages** that will be paid by the insurance company under the employers' liability insurance. Typically, the policy indicates that the insurance company will pay all sums **legally owed by the employer** as damages because of bodily injury to employees. This includes damages for which the employer is liable to a third party because of a claim or suit against the employer by that third party to recover damages claimed by the third party caused by injury to an employee. The insurance company will also pay for **care and loss of services**, as well as for any **consequential bodily injury** to a spouse, child, parent, brother, or sister of the employee who is injured, assuming that this injury can be proved to be a direct consequence of the injured employee's employment. The insurance company also promises to pay for any bodily injury suffered by employees during the course of employment, but which are claimed against the policyholder in a capacity **other than as employer**.

EXCLUSIONS

Part two of the standard workers' compensation and employers' liability insurance policy also describes what is **not covered** by the employers' liability insurance. To begin with, the typical policy will declare that it does not cover any liability assumed under a **contract**. The employers' liability insurance will not cover any punitive or exemplary damages resulting from an employee who is working in **violation of law**. Neither will the employers' liability insurance cover any bodily injury to an employee who is employed in violation of law with the **actual knowledge** of the employer or any of the executive officers of the employer. The insurance policy also does not cover the obligations imposed by **workers' compensation, occupational disease, unemployment compensation, or disability benefits law**. Of course, this coverage is provided in a different part of the policy.

Part two of the standard workers' compensation and employers' liability insurance policy asserts that the employers' liability insurance does not cover any bodily injury **intentionally caused or exacerbated** by the employer. This portion of the policy also does not cover any bodily injury that occurs **outside the United States, its possessions or territories, or Canada**. However, this exclusion does not necessarily apply to citizens or residents of the United States or Canada who are temporarily elsewhere. Employers' liability insurance does not apply to any **damages** arising out of coercion; criticism; demotion; evaluation; reassignment; discipline; defamation; harassment; humiliation; discrimination against or firing of any employee; or any damages related to personnel practices, policies, acts or omissions.

Part two of the standard workers' compensation and employers' liability insurance policy concludes the discussion of exclusions by indicating that the employers' liability policy will not cover injury to any person whose employment is subject to the Longshore and Harbor Workers Compensation Act, the Non-appropriated Fund Instrumentalities Act, the Outer Continental Shelf Lands Act, the Defense Base Act, the Federal Coal Mine Health and Safety Act of 1969, or any other **federal workers' compensation or occupational disease law**. The employers' liability insurance policy will not cover injury to any employee whose work is subject to the **Federal Employers Liability Act**. This policy will not cover bodily injury to a master or crew member of any vessel. Employers' liability insurance will not cover any fines or penalties that result from violations of federal or state law, nor will it cover any damages payable under the Migrant and Seasonal Agricultural Worker Protection Act.

DEFENSE INTENTIONS AND ADDITIONAL PAYMENTS

Part two of the standard workers' compensation and employers' liability insurance policy indicates that the insurance company retains the right and duty to **defend**, at its own expense, any claim or proceeding against the employer for damages payable by the insurance. However, the insurance company has no duty to defend or continue defending after the applicable limit of liability under the policy has been paid. Besides the amounts typically payable under the employers' liability policy, the insurance company will also pay any **reasonable expenses** incurred by the employer at the request of the insurance company. However, the insurance company will not compensate the employer for a loss of earnings incurred because of investigation or defense of the claim. The insurance company will also pay any **litigation costs** that are taxed against the employer, as well as the premiums for bonds to release attachments up to the limited liability indicated by the policy. The policy also asserts that the insurance company will pay any **interest** on a judgment as required by law, so long as it is within the limits established by the policy.

OTHER INSURANCE AND LIABILITY LIMITS

Part two of the standard workers' compensation and employers' liability insurance policy typically declares that the employers' liability policy will not pay more than its share of the damages and costs covered by it and **other insurance or self-insurance**. Moreover, within the limits of applicable liability, the shares paid by each policy should be **equal** until the loss is fully paid. Part two also describes some **limitations on the liability** of the employers' liability policy. These limits have been indicated on the information page. Diseases are not considered to be bodily injuries by accident unless they result directly from the accident. Similarly, the limitations for bodily injury by disease do not apply to diseases that result directly from an accident.

RECOVERY FROM OTHERS AND ACTIONS AGAINST THE INSURANCE COMPANY

Part two of the standard workers' compensation and employers' liability insurance policy declares that the insurance company retains the rights of the employer to **recover payments** made by the insurance company from any party liable for an injury covered by the policy. The insurance company notes that the employer is responsible for taking whatever steps are necessary to protect those rights and to help the insurance company enforce them. Part two goes on to state that the employer will not have the right to **take action against the insurance company** unless the employer has complied with all the terms of the policy and the amount owed is determined with the consent of the insurance company or by actual trial and final judgment. The insurance company may not be named as a defendant in an action to determine the liability of the employer. At the same time, the insurance company will not be relieved of its obligations by the bankruptcy or insolvency of the employer or the employer's estate

PART THREE (OTHER STATES INSURANCE)

Part three of the standard workers' compensation and employers' liability insurance policy outlines the **other states** workers' compensation insurance, which only takes effect if an employee is injured in one of the other states listed on the information page. Basically, this provision indicates that the workers' compensation insurance will apply to any work that begins in one of the named states after the effective date of the policy and for which the employer is not insured. The insurance company declares that it will reimburse the employer for any benefits required by the workers' compensation law of the state in situations where the insurance company is not allowed to pay the benefits directly to the injured party. If the employer is operating in any of the other states on the effective date of the workers' compensation policy, coverage will not be provided for that state unless the insurance company is notified within 30 days. Essentially, the employer is responsible for **reporting** the initiation of work in any of the other states listed on the information page as soon as possible.

PART FOUR (EMPLOYER'S DUTIES IF INJURY OCCURS)

Part four of the standard workers' compensation and employers' liability insurance policy outlines the **duties of the employer** when an injury occurs. To begin with, the employer is responsible for **notifying** the insurance company immediately whenever an injury that may be covered by this policy occurs. The employer should also provide for whatever **immediate medical or other services** are mandated by the workers' compensation law. The employer should provide the agent of the insurance company with the **names and addresses** of the injured persons as well as of any witnesses. The employer should also provide any **notices, demands, or documents** related to the injury, claim, suit, or proceeding. The employer should assist the insurance company in the **investigation or defense** of any claim or suit. The employer should refrain from any actions that may **interfere** with the insurance company's right to recover from others. Finally, the employer should not voluntarily make payments, incur expenses, or assume obligations with the expectation of **reimbursement** from the insurance company.

PART FIVE (PREMIUM)
MANUALS AND CLASSIFICATIONS

Part five of the standard workers' compensation and employers' liability insurance policy describes the **premium**. To begin with, it will typically state that the **pricing structure** for the policy is to be based on the insurance company's manuals of rules, rates, rating plans, and classifications. The insurance company will usually reserve the right to **change** these manuals when authorized or required by law. Part five goes on to note that the rate and premium basis for various business or work classifications are detailed on the **information page**. The policy will typically state that the **classifications** are based on an estimate of the employer's likely exposures during the period of the policy. If the actual exposures are not reflected in the given classifications, the insurance company agrees to adjust them by endorsement.

REMUNERATION

The **third section** of part five of the standard workers' compensation and employers' liability insurance policy discusses the most common premium basis, **remuneration**. The remuneration basis for premiums includes the **payroll** and all other amounts that are paid or payable during the period of the policy for the services of two groups. The first group produces all of the **officers and employees** engaged in work covered by this particular policy. The second group is any other persons engaged in work that has the potential to create **liability** for the insurance company under the workers' compensation insurance section of this policy. When there are not payroll records related to these employees, the premium basis can be calculated from the **contract price** for their services and materials. The second group of employees will not be covered by this insurance policy if the employer can prove that these employees have lawfully received their workers' compensation obligations from a different employer.

PREMIUM PAYMENTS AND FINAL PREMIUM

The **fifth part** of the standard workers' compensation and employers' liability insurance policy declares that the employer must pay the **entirety of the premium** when it is due. This premium is to be paid even when part or all of a workers' compensation law is rendered invalid. It should be noted that the premium amounts indicated on the information page, endorsements, and schedules are only estimates. The actual premium basis and the appropriate classifications and rates for the business will determine the **final premium**. The difference between the estimated premium and the actual premium must be paid by the filing party, whether it is the employer or the insurance company. In any case, the final premium will at least be the highest minimum premium for the classifications covered by this policy.

DETERMINATION OF FINAL PREMIUM

The **fifth part** of the standard workers' compensation and employers' liability insurance policy describes the protocol for determining the final premium in the event of **policy cancellation**. If the policy is canceled by the insurance company, the **final premium** will be prorated according to the length of time the policy was in force. Under no circumstances will the final premium be less than the prorated portion of the minimum premium. If the policy is canceled by the employer, on the other hand, the final premium will be greater than the prorated amount for the time the policy is in force. The final premium will at least be equal to the minimum premium, and will be based on the amount of time the policy was in force and the value taken from the short rate cancellation table.

RECORD-KEEPING AND AUDIT

The fifth part of the standard workers' compensation and employers' liability insurance policy declares that the employer should maintain **records** of all the information that will be used in the calculation of the premium. The employer should be able to provide copies of these records upon request from the insurance company. The insurance company also reserves the right to **examine and audit** any records related to this insurance policy. These records may include ledgers, journals, vouchers, contracts, registers, payroll and disbursement records, and tax reports. The insurance company reserves the rights to conduct this audit at any time during the period of the policy, as well as within three years after the termination of the policy. Any of the information obtained from the audit may be used to calculate the **final premium**. All of the auditing power granted to the insurance company is likewise granted to insurance rate service organizations.

PART SIX (CONDITIONS)
INSPECTIONS

In the **sixth part** of the standard workers' compensation and employers' liability insurance policy, the insurance company outlines the rules regarding **inspection of the employer**. Specifically, the insurance company declares that it has the right but not the obligation to inspect the employer's place of business at any time. These are not safety inspections per se, but rather are investigations into the **insurability** of the workplace and the appropriate **premium** to be charged. The insurance company may provide a report related to this inspection, and may recommend alterations in the workplace. These inspections are not intended to replace the responsibility of the employer to create a safe and healthy work environment. Inspections do not indicate that the workplace is safe or healthful, or that it conforms to codes, laws, regulations, or standards. As with the power of auditing, the insurance company grants identical powers of inspection to insurance rate service organizations.

LONG-TERM POLICY, THE TRANSFER OF RIGHTS AND DUTIES, AND CANCELLATION

After outlining the inspection protocol, the standard workers' compensation and employers' liability insurance policy asserts that if the period of the policy is longer than one year and 16 days, the provisions of the policy will be applied as if a **new policy** were being issued on each yearly anniversary during which the policy is in effect. The insurance company will typically assert that the employer's rights or duties under the policy **may not be transferred** without the written consent of the insurance company. If the employer dies and the insurance company is given notice within 30 days, the legal representative of the employer will be covered under the insurance policy. In order to **cancel** the policy, the employer must mail or deliver advanced written notice indicating when the cancellation will take effect. If the insurance company elects to cancel the policy, it must give at least 10 days of notice to the employer.

Longshore and Harbor Workers' Compensation Act, the Federal Employers Liability Act, and the Jones Act

The United States Longshore and Harbor Workers' Compensation Act, otherwise known as the **Longshore Act**, provides workers' compensation coverage for dock workers and other maritime workers. The coverage provided by this act typically grants two-thirds of the average weekly wage to workers undergoing medical treatment or unable to work because of injury. The **Federal Employers Liability Act** was established in 1908 to provide basic workers' compensation protection to railroad employees. This legislation was remarkable because it only required the employee to demonstrate that negligence on the part of the employer contributed to the injury. (Before, the employee also had to prove that he or she did not contribute to the negligence or risk.) The **Jones Act of 1920** declared that any seaman injured during the course of his or her employment may sue for damages against his or her employer. According to the Jones Act, employees may sue because the employer was negligent or because the vessel in question was not seaworthy.

Surety Bonds and Fidelity Coverages

SURETY BONDS

A surety bond asserts that either a certain action will be performed or a third party will make payment to the party injured by the failure to perform that action. The party that is promising to perform the described action is known as the **principal**. The principal will purchase the surety bond. The party that will be paid by the insurance company should the described action not be performed is called the **obligee**. The insurance company that makes this payment is called the **obligor**. Surety bonds are considered a standard part of many common business agreements. An insurance claims adjuster should be capable of handling all aspects of the surety bond process.

BID, PERFORMANCE, PAYMENT (LABOR AND MATERIAL), SUPPLIES, JUDICIAL, AND LICENSE AND PERMIT

There are a few specialized types of surety bond. A **bid bond** provides assurance that the purchasing contractor will obtain a necessary performance bond and do the required work if he or she is awarded a contract. The **performance bond** guarantees that the contractor will perform the work according to the required specifications. A **labor and material payment bond** guarantees that the contractor will pay for labor and material costs as they are incurred. A **supply bond** guarantees that the contractor will provide all of the required supplies, products, and equipment. A supply bond may require the contractor to install certain equipment. A **judicial bond**, otherwise known as a court bond, may be of either the fiduciary or litigation variety. *Fiduciary bonds* are obtained by the guardians, administrators, or trustees of an estate to manage the property of some other party. *Litigation bonds* assert that the principal in a trial will pay any appeal or court costs. Finally, **license and permit bonds** have to do with the licenses issued by government agencies.

Aviation Insurance

BASIC AVIATION INSURANCE POLICY

Aviation insurance is a package policy that provides coverage against physical damage and legal liability for complete aircraft. **Aviation insurance** does not cover personal property. However, it does cover the aircraft's frame, engine, controls, electronics, and communications equipment. Aviation insurance is required for certification by the **Federal Aviation Administration**. Airlines may also provide coverage for liability that derives from the ownership or the operation of aircraft. Some policies include coverage for all damage, medical payments, bodily injury, and property damage. Some aviation insurance policies cover passengers, and all policies extend to aircraft when it is stationary on the ground, in motion, and in flight. In some cases, an aviation insurance policy will cover property damage to an aircraft while it is in the care, custody, or control of a non-owner. Flying a plane without basic aviation insurance can result in the **loss of a pilot's license**.

Other Coverages and Options

NATIONAL FLOOD INSURANCE PROGRAM

The standards for the National Flood Insurance Program (**NFIP**) were established by the Federal Emergency Management Agency. However, rate, eligibility, and coverage parameters are established by the Federal Insurance Administration. The National Flood Insurance Program offers a **write-your-own policy option**, whereby companies can retain a specific portion of the premium for commission and service expense. If the business suffers any losses above the premium, these will be reimbursed by the National Flood Insurance Program. All profits for the NFIP are returned to the **United States Treasury**, and the United States government underwrites the risk of loss. The NFIP essentially aims to increase participation in flood insurance.

ELIGIBILITY AND THE COVERED PERILS FOR THE NATIONAL FLOOD INSURANCE PROGRAM

In order to be **eligible** for flood insurance, one must live in a **participating community**. Any community that agrees with the requirements established by the Federal Emergency Management Agency may be eligible. Qualifying communities will receive a **flood insurance rate map**. The general flood insurance policy includes a dwelling and a general property form. The special form will be used to cover condominiums and building associations. The following perils are covered by a National Flood Insurance Policy: flood, overflow of inland or tidal wave, rapid accumulation or runoff of surface water, mudslide and mudflows, and the collapse of land along a shore. There is no coverage for property that extends over water.

LIMITS AND THE DEDUCTIBLE FOR THE NATIONAL FLOOD INSURANCE PROGRAM

The National Flood Insurance Program offers different **limits** for various situations. The maximum limits for buildings under the emergency program are $35,000 for single-family homes and $100,000 for other residential and nonresidential buildings. With regard to the contents of a building, the maximum limits for the emergency program are $10,000 for residential buildings and $100,000 for nonresidential buildings. For the regular program, the combined maximum limits for buildings are $250,000 for residential buildings and $500,000 for nonresidential buildings. As for contents, the maximum limits in the regular program are $100,000 for residential buildings and $500,000 for nonresidential buildings. The deductible for the National Flood Insurance Program is $750 for emergency coverage and $500 for other coverage. This deductible applies both to the building and the contents.

UMBRELLA POLICIES AND BASIC EXCLUSIONS

Umbrella policies are designed to provide extremely broad coverage in excess of underlying liability policies. In order for an **umbrella policy** to be issued, the insurance company must know the limit of the **underlying policy**. If the underlying policy is allowed to lapse, this will require the insured to make payment equal to the policy limits of the lapsed policy before the payment of excess liability. An umbrella policy may include coverage for some risks not covered by the underlying policy, however, and there may be a self-insurance retention limit for these policies. Typically, the exclusions for an umbrella policy are for intentional acts, events covered by workers' compensation, and events that occur while at work or in pursuit of business objectives.

PROFESSIONAL LIABILITY POLICIES

Professional liability policies are specialty liability insurance policies that are popular in certain occupations. Professional liability policies cover loss due to negligence, error, or omission during the **performance of professional services**. There is no standardized form for the professional liability policy. Some of the most common professional liability policies are for accountants, insurance agents, dentists, doctors, lawyers, pharmacists, and real estate agents. The standard exclusions to a professional liability policy are for **fraudulent, intentional, dishonest, or criminal acts**. There are some specialized versions of the professional liability policy, as for instance for directors and officers. There is also a policy for the **fiduciary liabilities** that may be incurred during compliance with the Employment Retirement Income Security Act. It is standard for this fiduciary liability policy to have a $1000 deductible and a $1 million basic limit. There are also specialty liability policies for businesses that distribute or sell **alcohol**. Finally, there is specialized employment liability insurance for defense against charges of **discriminatory employment practices**.

FEDERAL CRIME INSURANCE

The federal government offers insurance against **crimes** like burglary and robbery for geographic areas in which private insurance companies refuse to offer coverage. This policy is administered by the **Federal Insurance Administrator** and the **Office of Housing and Urban Development**. In approved states, both businesses and homes may receive federal crime insurance. It is typical for buildings to require protective devices or security guards in order to be eligible for federal crime insurance. The typical federal crime insurance policy has two coverage forms: one for **discovery** and one for **sustained losses**. It is also possible to obtain federal crime insurance for employee theft, both on a per loss and a per employee basis.

Claims Adjuster Practice Test

1. Which type of coverage relates to damage to or destruction of detached structures in a typical homeowner's policy?

    a. Coverage A
    b. Coverage B
    c. Coverage C
    d. Coverage D

2. The unfair trade practice of offering inducements for the purchase of insurance is called:

    a. misrepresentation.
    b. controlled business.
    c. rebating.
    d. false advertising.

3. In which type of group life insurance policy may the holder allocate the net premiums to one or more of several investment accounts?

    a. Comprehensive long-term care insurance
    b. Group universal life insurance
    c. Yearly renewable term insurance
    d. Group variable universal life insurance

4. Which of the following distinguishes the conditions of the standard business owners' policy from those of the standard commercial package policy?

    a. Many of the coverages that are automatic for the standard commercial package policy are optional for the standard business owners' policy.
    b. Many of the coverages that are automatic for the standard business owners' policy are optional for the standard commercial package policy.
    c. The standard commercial package policy extends automatic business income and peak season coverage.
    d. The standard business owners' property coverage form is different than the building property coverage form.

5. How much of a property must be unoccupied for it to be defined as vacant by the standard commercial property policy?

    a. 25 percent
    b. 30 percent
    c. 40 percent
    d. 50 percent

6. With regard to homeowner's insurance, business is defined as any activity that has:

    a. revenue.
    b. continuity.
    c. Both A and B.
    d. Neither A nor B.

7. An expense plan that indicates an employer will reduce benefits for persons over the age of 65 to the extent that they are payable under Medicare for the same expense is known as a:
 a. Medicare secondary rule.
 b. maturity value benefit.
 c. Medicare carve-out.
 d. Medicare supplement.

8. Which of the following vehicles would NOT be defined as mobile equipment by the standard business auto policy?
 a. Snowplow
 b. Bulldozer
 c. Forklift
 d. Farm machinery

9. Which of the following events would NOT be covered by the standard dwelling policy?
 a. Losses caused by spacecraft
 b. Smoke damage from fireplaces
 c. Losses caused by volcanic eruption
 d. Smoke damage from furnaces

10. Which of the following injuries would be covered by the standard farm liability policy?
 a. Those suffered by residence employees while performing duties associated with their employment
 b. Those that occur on locations owned by the insured but not named on the declarations page
 c. Those suffered by people who are on the insured location for the purpose of providing professional services
 d. Those that occur on locations rented by the insured but not named on the declarations page

11. Which of the following is NOT an advantage of an umbrella policy?
 a. Higher defense costs
 b. Coverage for injuries that occur while at work
 c. Gap coverage
 d. Higher coverage limits for injuries and property damage caused by the policyholder

12. Which type of claims adjuster handles property and liability claims?
 a. Multiline
 b. All-lines
 c. Both A and B
 d. Neither A nor B

13. Which of the following people would NOT be covered by the standard business auto policy?
 a. A person who is liable for the conduct of the insured party
 b. An employee who is moving property from a covered automobile
 c. A person who is using a covered automobile with the permission of the named party
 d. A person from whom the named insured borrows a covered auto

14. **Which of the following structures would be covered by Coverage B of the standard farm property policy?**
   a. Grain silo
   b. Cabins rented by non-employees
   c. Barn
   d. Private garage

15. **Which of the following must be true in order for towing charges to be covered under the physical damage section of the standard business auto policy?**
   a. The towing must be performed by an approved service.
   b. The towing charges must exceed the limit published in the declarations.
   c. The labor must be performed within twenty-four hours.
   d. All of the labor must be performed at the site of the breakdown.

16. **A driver is involved in an accident for which he is not responsible. He elects to have the damages paid for by his Collision coverage rather than by the driver at fault. The transfer of rights from the responsible driver to the insurance company is known as:**
   a. liberalization.
   b. subrogation.
   c. underwriting.
   d. waiver.

17. **In which of the following situations could a minor be forced to adhere to a contract?**
   a. If he or she has been emancipated
   b. If the contract is not for necessaries
   c. If the minor is out of his or her home state
   d. If the contract is written

18. **A change in an insurance policy that increases coverage without raising premiums is called a:**
   a. liberalization.
   b. subrogation.
   c. subscription.
   d. premium-delay arrangement.

19. **In the standard farm property policy, which of the following will be considered in the determination of replacement cost?**
   a. Foundations
   b. Attached sheds
   c. Underground drains
   d. Excavations

20. **Which piece of legislation enabled seamen to sue for damages against their employers?**
   a. Longshore and Harbor Workers Compensation Act
   b. Federal Employer's Liability Act
   c. Jones Act
   d. Open America's Waters Act

Mometrix

21. Which of the following events terminates COBRA continuation coverage?
- a. The covered person reaches the age of 50.
- b. Premiums remain unpaid sixty days after the due date.
- c. The covered person reports income greater than $100,000 for the previous tax year.
- d. The covered person receives Medicare coverage.

22. Damage to which of these buildings would be covered by Part A of the standard personal auto policy?
- a. Residence
- b. Public parking deck
- c. Office
- d. Government building

23. In which of the following situations would loss caused by earth movement be covered by the standard dwelling policy?
- a. When the earth movement is an earthquake
- b. When the earth movement causes an explosion
- c. When the earth movement is caused by humans
- d. When the earth movement is a mudslide

24. Which of the following would be covered by the standard commercial property policy?
- a. Domestic pets
- b. Livestock owned by the insured
- c. Currency
- d. Land on which property is situated

25. Which domestic employees would be covered for bodily injury by Part A of the standard personal auto policy?
- a. Domestic employees who are not eligible for workers compensation benefits
- b. Domestic employees who cause property damage on purpose
- c. Domestic employees who are injured during the course of their employment
- d. Domestic employees who are operating a vehicle as a public conveyance

26. Which of the following statements about Medicare is false?
- a. Medicare offers no prescription drug coverage.
- b. Medicare will never pay for unapproved expenses.
- c. The maximum allowed room and board is between 90 and 150 days.
- d. Covered individuals may receive care anywhere in the world.

27. How are losses typically settled under the standard business owners' policy?
- a. Actual cash value less depreciation
- b. Replacement cost less depreciation
- c. Replacement cost
- d. Actual cash value

122

28. When part of a building is damaged, and the value of the insurance policy at the time of loss is less than 80 percent of the full replacement cost of the building prior to the loss, how much coverage will the standard homeowners' policy provide?

    a. The actual cash value of the damaged building part
    b. The proportion of the cost to fix the damaged building part
    c. The larger of A or B
    d. The smaller of A or B

29. What is required for the standard homeowners' policy to be assigned?

    a. The written consent of the policyholder
    b. The oral consent of the policyholder
    c. The written consent of the insurance company
    d. The oral consent of the insurance company

30. In the standard commercial property policy, how is a value assigned to stock that has been sold but not yet delivered?

    a. Selling price less any foreseeable discounts or expenses
    b. Actual cash value at the time of loss or damage
    c. Purchase price
    d. Purchase price less any foreseeable discounts or expenses

31. Which form of permanent life insurance offers a fixed cash value yield?

    a. Whole life
    b. Universal life
    c. Variable life
    d. All of the above

32. Which of the following statements about federal crime insurance is true?

    a. Federal crime insurance is administered solely by the Office of Housing and Urban Development.
    b. Federal crime insurance policies typically include discovery and sustained loss coverages.
    c. Federal crime insurance policies are only available to businesses.
    d. Federal crime insurance obviates the need for security guards.

33. Why does the standard business auto policy exclude bodily injury that occurs during the course of employment?

    a. To prevent the business auto policy from covering injuries that occur during the normal course of employment
    b. To prevent the business auto policy from covering injuries related to the operation of mechanical devices
    c. To prevent the business auto policy from covering losses that should be covered by a worker's compensation policy
    d. To prevent the business auto policy from covering losses for which the insured party has already assumed liability through a contract

34. What is the maximum limit of emergency coverage for single-family homes under the National Flood Insurance Program?

    a. $35,000
    b. $50,000
    c. $60,000
    d. $100,000

35. Which of these expenses will not be paid for a claim under Coverages H and I of the standard farm liability policy?

    a. The expense of prejudgment interest charged to the insured after a decision rendered against the insurance company
    b. The full expense of bail bonds required because of the use of a covered vehicle
    c. The expense incurred during the investigation of a claim
    d. The expense of any taxes charged against the insured as part of a suit

36. What happens to the rights and duties of the named insured in a standard commercial crime policy should he or she die?

    a. All rights and duties are terminated after an interval of ten days.
    b. All rights and duties are immediately terminated.
    c. All rights and duties are immediately transferred to the next of kin.
    d. All rights and duties are immediately transferred to the legal representative of the named insured.

37. Which of the following events would be covered by the standard commercial inland marine policy?

    a. The named insured destroys property while committing a crime.
    b. The named insured accidentally discharges pollutants, causing damage to the covered property.
    c. Covered property is spoiled because of the failure of refrigeration equipment.
    d. An employee of the insured business destroys property while performing his job.

38. In which of these situations would the standard homeowners' policy provide coverage?

    a. Damage from water driven by wind
    b. Water damage leads to direct loss by fire
    c. Loss caused by the failure of electricity services
    d. Loss caused by water leaking through a building foundation

39. Which of the following types of business is eligible for coverage under the standard business owners' policy?

    a. Restaurant
    b. Gas station
    c. Amusement park
    d. Retailer

40. Which insurance producers are not required to meet the continuing education requirements in order to maintain their licensure?

   a. Producers who are older than 65
   b. Producers with at least 15 years of experience
   c. Both A and B
   d. All insurance producers are required to meet the continuing education requirements.

41. Which of the following events would NOT be covered by Coverage I of the standard farm liability policy?

   a. Advertising injuries related to written publication of slander
   b. Advertising injuries related to a breach of contract
   c. Advertising injuries related to the oral dissemination of private information
   d. Advertising injuries related to infringement upon copyright

42. Which of the following statements regarding workplace inspections under the standard workers compensation policy is false?

   a. After a workplace inspection, the insurance company may recommend alterations in the workplace.
   b. The insurance company reserves the right to inspect the employer's place of business at any time.
   c. The insurance company delegates identical powers of inspection to insurance rate service organizations.
   d. Workplace inspections by an insurance company take the place of inspections by the employer.

43. In the standard equipment breakdown policy, when is a newly built property considered to have been acquired by the policyholder?

   a. When the coverage for previously owned buildings terminates
   b. When the finished product has been accepted by the new owner
   c. When the newly acquired property is eligible for coverage
   d. When the policyholder pays for the property

44. How long must an insurance producer wait to reapply for his or her license after it is suspended for misconduct?

   a. One year
   b. Two years
   c. Five years
   d. An insurance producer whose license is suspended for misconduct may never reapply.

45. Which of the following is required for a resident's insurance producer license?

   a. Pre-licensing education program
   b. Examination
   c. Battery of forms
   d. All of the above

46. Which type of surety bond guarantees that a contractor will provide any necessary equipment?

    a. Labor and material payment bond
    b. Supply bond
    c. Bid bond
    d. Fiduciary bond

47. In which of the following situations would a piece of property not be considered complete for the purposes of the standard business auto policy?

    a. All of the work at the relevant job site has been completed.
    b. All of the tasks listed on the contract have been completed.
    c. A contractor has put the relevant part of the work to its intended use.
    d. The relevant part of the work at a job site has been put to its intended use by the owner.

48. What is the maximum payment for losses related to credit cards under the standard homeowners' policy?

    a. $50
    b. $100
    c. $500
    d. $1000

49. Which of the following would conform to the definition of a products-completed operations hazard under the standard commercial general liability policy?

    a. Property damage that is caused by the insured party but occurs away from premises owned by the insured
    b. Property damage to work that has been abandoned
    c. Property damage to work that has not yet been finished
    d. Property damage to work that is still in the physical possession of the insured party

50. Which form of permanent life insurance does not include the option to vary or suspend premiums?

    a. Whole life
    b. Universal life
    c. Variable life
    d. All of the above

Answer Key and Explanations

1. B: Coverage B relates to damage to or destruction of detached structures in a typical homeowner's policy. Specifically, this coverage applies to any structures located on the residence premises but separated from the dwelling by a clear space. Any structures that are connected to the dwelling by a fence or utility line are included under Coverage B. In the standard homeowner's policy, Coverage A applies to dwellings, Coverage C applies to personal property, and Coverage B applies to loss of use.

2. C: The unfair trade practice of offering inducements for the purchase of insurance is called rebating. This practice is usually illegal, although insurance companies are allowed to pay dividends to policyholders. Misrepresentation, in the context of insurance sales, is an intentionally inaccurate or incomplete communication to a policyholder or potential policyholder. Controlled business is defined as a situation in which an insurance provider's personal income is greater than 25 percent of his or her gross commission from insurance. False advertising is considered an unfair trade practice with respect to all forms of communication.

3. D: In group variable universal life insurance, the holder may allocate the net premiums to one or more of several investment accounts. In this arrangement, the investment risk is borne by the holders of the certificates. A comprehensive long-term care insurance policy includes benefits for home health care and facility care in a single contract. A group universal life insurance policy has flexible premiums and separates the pure protection and cash value accumulations. These policies have variable interest rates credited to cash value accumulations, though it is standard for there to be a minimum guaranteed interest rate.

4. B: Many of the coverages that are automatic for the standard business owners' policy are optional for the standard commercial package policy. This is the only major distinction between the conditions of the standard business owners' policy and the standard commercial package policy. Business income and peak season coverage are automatic for the business owner's policy, but are only optional for the commercial package policy. The business owners' property coverage form is exactly the same as the building property coverage form.

5. B: In order for a property to be defined as vacant by the standard commercial property policy, 30 percent of it must be unoccupied. In addition, the building must be suitable for habitation. The definition of a building as vacant is important in the standard commercial property policy because vacant buildings are subject to special provisions. Buildings that have been vacant for more than sixty days previous to loss or damage will not receive payments for vandalism, sprinkler leakage, glass breakage, water damage, or theft. Any losses or damages caused by a covered cause of loss will be subject to a payment reduction of 15 percent.

6. C: With regard to homeowners' insurance, business is defined as any activity that has revenue and continuity. In other words, it is any activity that the homeowner earns money from and pursues repeatedly or consecutively through time.

7. C: An expense plan that indicates an employer will reduce benefits for persons over the age of sixty-five to the extent that they are payable under Medicare for the same expense is known as a Medicare carve-out. The Medicare secondary rules are a set of regulations that indicate when Medicare will be considered secondary to the employer's medical expense plan for disabled employees, as well as active employees older than sixty-four. A maturity value benefit is a provision in a group term life insurance plan, in which the face value of a fully disabled employee's life

127

insurance benefit will be paid to the employee in monthly installments or a lump sum. Finally, a Medicare supplement is a medical expense plan provided by an employer to employees age sixty-five or older, in which benefits are provided for certain specific expenses not covered by Medicare. The expenses may not be paid by Medicare because of deductibles, copayments, coinsurance, or other expenses (for instance, prescription drugs) that are excluded by Medicare.

8. A: The standard business auto policy would not define a snowplow as mobile equipment. Any equipment designed primarily for snow removal, street cleaning, or road maintenance will be classified as an auto. Bulldozers, forklifts, and farm machinery are all classified as mobile equipment. In addition, mobile equipment includes any vehicles designed to be used off public roads; any vehicles propelled by crawler treads; any vehicles that are used solely on the premises owned or rented by the insured party; and any vehicles maintained primarily for purposes other than the transport of cargo or people. Construction and resurfacing vehicles may be classified as mobile equipment.

9. B: Smoke damage from fireplaces would not be covered by the standard dwelling policy. This policy will cover losses caused by spacecraft, as well as losses caused by aircraft and self-propelled missiles. Any losses caused by volcanic eruptions will be covered, though losses caused by tremors or earthquakes will not. The smoke damage from furnaces and boilers will be covered, but not the smoke damage caused by fireplaces or agricultural or industrial operations.

10. A: Injuries suffered by residence employees while performing duties associated with their employment would be covered by the standard farm liability policy. However, in general, injuries that occur on locations owned, rented, or controlled by the insured are not covered by the standard farm liability policy. Also, injuries suffered by people who are on the insured location for the purpose of providing professional services or engaging in business are not covered by the standard farm liability policy.

11. B: Coverage for injuries that occur at work is not an advantage of an umbrella policy. Umbrella policies are meant to provide very broad liability coverage in excess of other underlying policies. In some cases, an umbrella policy will cover the risks that are not covered by the underlying policy. However, an umbrella policy typically excludes intentional acts, events covered by workers compensation, and events that occur while at work or in pursuit of business objectives.

12. C: Both multiline and all-lines claims adjusters handle property and liability claims. A multiline claims adjuster handles both property and liability claims, while an all-lines claims adjuster handles these claims as well as professional liability, excess liability, bond loss, boiler and machinery damage, and other claims.

13. D: A person from whom the named insured borrows a covered auto would not be covered by the standard business auto policy. Similarly, the employees of the insured party are not covered if the covered automobile is owned by that employee or a member of his or her household. However, any person liable for the conduct of the insured party is covered, though only up to the limit of his or her liability. Employees, partners, lessees, and borrowers are covered when moving property to or from a covered automobile, but all other people are not. Finally, in most cases any person who is using a covered automobile with the permission of the named insured is covered by the standard business auto policy.

14. D: A private garage would be covered by Coverage B of the standard farm property policy. Coverage B applies to private structures appurtenant to dwellings. However, this policy does have some common exclusions, such as any structures that are rented or held by individuals who are not tenants of the covered dwelling. Similarly, Coverage B does not apply to any structures that are primarily used by the policyholder for farming. The only exception to this rule, as a matter of fact, is for private garages.

15. D: In order for towing charges to be covered under the physical damage section of the standard business auto policy, all labor must be performed at the site of the breakdown. If this condition is met, the insurance company will pay up to the limit published in the declarations for any towing and labor costs incurred when a covered auto is disabled. There is no list of approved service providers, and it is not necessary for the towing charges to exceed the limit published in the declarations. Finally, it is not necessary for the labor to be performed within twenty-four hours of the accident.

16. B: The transfer of rights from the responsible driver to the insurance company is known as a subrogation. A subrogation clause permits the insurance company to recover from a third party who is responsible through negligence or other wrongdoing for the injury to a covered party for which a claim is paid by the insurance company. A liberalization is an expansion of coverage that is not accompanied by an increase in premium. Underwriting is the process of evaluating applicants for an insurance policy. A waiver is a voluntary renunciation of a right.

17. A: A minor could be forced to adhere to a contract if he or she has been emancipated. However, in most other situations the contracts entered into by a minor may be avoided if they are found to be unfair. One exception is when the contract is for necessaries, a general category including things required for day-to-day life.

18. A: A change in an insurance policy that increases coverage without raising premiums is called a liberalization. A subrogation, meanwhile, is a transfer of rights of recovery to the insurance company when a third party has been responsible for an injury to a covered insured for which a claim has been paid by the insurance company. Subscription is the process of signing up for an insurance policy. A premium-delay arrangement is an alternative method of funding that allows the employer to defer the payment of monthly premiums.

19. B: In the standard farm property policy, attached sheds will be considered in the determination of replacement cost. These structures are included under Coverage A (dwellings). However, the standard farm property policy will not include excavations, footings, foundations, piers, or other support structures. Moreover, it will not include underground drains, pipes, flues, or wiring. The total amount of loss settlement is equal to the ratio of the limit of insurance for the affected covered property to the full replacement cost.

20. C: The Jones Act enabled seamen to sue for damages against their employers. This act, which was enacted in 1920, allowed workers who were injured during the course of their employment to sue for damages because of employer negligence or because the vessel in question was not seaworthy. This was considered a landmark piece of legislation for workers compensation. The Longshore and Harbor Worker's Compensation Act, more commonly known as the Longshore Act, grants workers compensation coverage to dock and other maritime workers. Typically, the Longshore Act grants two-thirds of the average weekly wage to any workers who are undergoing medical treatment or cannot work because of injury. The Federal Employers Liability Act, passed in 1908, provided basic workers compensation protection to railroad employees. At the time it was passed, this act was considered to be groundbreaking because it only required the injured employee to demonstrate that employer negligence contributed to the injury. Before the passage of the Federal Employers Liability Act, the employee was also required to indicate that he or she had not contributed to the negligence or risk that precipitated the injury. The Open America's Waters

Act was a 2010 effort to repeal the workers compensation rights afforded to seamen under the Jones Act. The Open America's Waters Act was not passed.

21. D: If a covered person receives Medicare coverage, this terminates COBRA continuation coverage. However, reaching the age of fifty or reporting income greater than $100,000 in the previous tax year would not terminate COBRA continuation coverage. Furthermore, COBRA continuation coverage is not terminated when premiums remain unpaid sixty days after they are due.

22. A: Damage to a residence would be covered by Part A of the standard personal auto policy. Part A of the standard personal auto policy has to do with liability coverage. The general rule is that the insurance company will not provide liability coverage for any property that is used by, rented to, or in the care of the insured party. The only exceptions to this rule are for residences and private garages.

23. B: If earth movement causes an explosion, any resulting loss will be covered by the standard dwelling policy. Similarly, when the earth movement causes a fire, any loss that directly results is covered by the standard dwelling policy. However, the standard dwelling policy does not cover losses caused by earthquake, landslide, mudslide, sinkholes, or other subsidences. For the purposes of the standard dwelling policy, it does not matter whether the earth movement is caused by human, animal, or natural forces.

24. B: Livestock owned by the insured would be covered by the standard commercial property policy. However, the standard commercial property policy does not cover most animals. The only exceptions are for animals boarded by the named insured but owned by other people, and animals owned as livestock by the insured. The standard commercial property policy also does not cover the loss of currency, accounts, bills, or food stamps. This policy does not cover any land, including the land on which covered property is situated. Moreover, it does not cover water, crops, or lawns.

25. A: Domestic employees who are not eligible for workers compensation benefits would be covered for bodily injury by Part A of the standard personal auto policy. Domestic employees who are eligible for workers compensation benefits would not receive coverage from Part A of the standard personal auto policy. Similarly, the insurance company will not provide liability coverage for those who cause bodily injury or property damage on purpose. The policy will not cover any domestic employees who are injured during the course of their employment, or any person, domestic employee or not, who is operating a vehicle as a public conveyance.

26. D: It is not true that individuals who are covered by Medicare may receive care anywhere in the world. Medicare recipients may only receive care in the United States and its territories and possessions. The other answer choices are true statements. Medicare does not offer any prescription drug coverage, and Medicare will never pay for unapproved expenses. Finally, the maximum allowed room and board is between 90 and 150 days.

27. D: Under the standard business owners' policy, losses are typically settled at actual cash value. The only exception to this procedure occurs when the property was insured to at least 80% of its value. When this is the case, losses are settled on the replacement cost basis.

28. C: When part of a building is damaged, and the value of the insurance policy at the time of loss is less than 80 percent of the full replacement cost of the building prior to the loss, the standard homeowners policy will provide coverage equal to the larger of the actual cash value of the damaged building part and the proportion of the cost to fix the damaged building part. In order to determine whether the value of the insurance policy at the time of loss is less than 80 percent of the

130

full replacement cost of the building prior to the loss, excavations, foundations, piers, or underground pipes, wiring, or drains should be excluded from the calculation. The cost of fixing the damaged building part includes the deductible but not depreciation.

29. C: In order for the standard homeowners' policy to be assigned, the insurance company must provide written consent. Otherwise, the assignment is invalid. In general, any waiver or change of provisions to the standard homeowners' policy must be put in writing by the insurance company to be considered valid. A request for an appraisal or examination does not waive any of the rights of the insurance company. The insurance company is allowed to decline renewal of the policy, but must notify the policyholder of this intention at least thirty days before the expiration of the policy.

30. A: In the standard commercial property policy, stock that has been sold but not yet delivered is valued at the selling price less any foreseeable discounts or expenses. All other types of property will be valued at actual cash value at the time of loss or damage.

31. A: Whole life insurance offers a fixed cash value yield. The cash value yield for universal and variable life insurance policies, however, fluctuates depending on when the policy was initiated and when benefits begin to be paid.

32. B: Federal crime insurance policies typically include discovery and sustained loss coverages. It is also possible to obtain federal crime insurance for employee theft, both on a per-loss and a per-employee basis. The federal crime insurance program is administered by the Office of Housing and Urban Development in cooperation with the Federal Insurance Administrator. Within approved states, businesses and homes are eligible for federal crime insurance. However, buildings may need to have security guards or protective devices to be eligible for these policies.

33. C: The standard business auto policy excludes bodily injuries that occur during the course of employment to prevent the policy from covering losses that should be covered by a worker's compensation policy. The standard business auto policy will not cover any obligations of the insured that derive from a worker's compensation, disability benefit, or unemployment compensation law. This includes all bodily injuries suffered by employees during the normal course of employment. Moreover, the insurance company will not cover any bodily injuries to fellow employees that occur during the course of the fellow employee's work.

34. A: The maximum limit of emergency coverage for single-family homes under the National Flood Insurance Program is $35,000. For other residential buildings and nonresidential buildings, the maximum limit of emergency coverage is $100,000. The contents of a residential building will receive a maximum of $10,000 of emergency coverage, while the contents of a nonresidential building may receive up to $100,000 of coverage from the emergency program. In the regular program, the combined maximum limits for residential buildings are $250,000 and for nonresidential buildings, $500,000. The regular program provides $100,000 of coverage for the contents of a residential building, and $500,000 for the contents of a nonresidential building. The standard deductible is $750 for emergency coverage and $500 for regular coverage. The deductible applies to both the building and the contents.

35. B: The full expense of bail bonds required because of the use of a covered vehicle will not be paid under Coverages H and I of the standard farm liability policy. Instead, the insurance company will promise to pay only up to $250 towards this cost. However, the insurance company will pay any expenses incurred during the investigation or settlement of a claim. The insurance company will also pay for all of the costs taxed against the insured as part of a suit. Any prejudgment interest charged to the insured after a decision rendered against the insurance company will be covered by the standard farm liability policy. Finally, the expense of any taxes charged against the insured as part of a suit will be covered by the standard farm liability policy.

36. D: If the named insured in a standard commercial crime policy dies, his or her rights and duties are immediately transferred to his or her legal representative. The legal representative maintains these rights so long as he or she is acting on behalf of the deceased. If the property of a deceased named insured is in the temporary custody of some other party, the party has the rights and duties of the named insured with respect to the property.

37. D: If an employee of the insured business destroys property while performing his job, this would be covered by the standard commercial inland marine policy. However, the standard commercial inland marine policy will not cover any loss or damage that is the result of dishonest or criminal behavior by the named insured or any other party with an interest in the property. Indeed, the only exception to this exclusion is for destructive acts committed by employees during the course of their employment. The standard commercial inland marine policy does not cover loss or damage related to the discharge, release, or escape of pollutants, with the exception of situations in which these problems are the result of a covered cause of loss. The standard commercial inland marine policy does not cover loss related to spoilage caused by the failure of refrigeration equipment.

38. B: Water damage leading directly to a loss by fire would be covered by the standard homeowners' policy. Similarly, when water damage leads to a direct loss by theft or explosion, the standard homeowners' policy will provide coverage. However, the standard homeowners' policy will not cover losses directly or indirectly caused by most forms of water damage, including flood, overflow of a nearby water body, waves, or tidal water. Any water damage related to water backed up in sewers or drains, or overflowing from a sump, will not be covered by the standard homeowners' policy. The insurance company will decline to pay for losses caused by the failure of electricity or other utility services, unless the failure of the services is limited to the residence premises. Finally, the standard homeowners' policy will not pay for damage caused by the leaking of water through a building foundation.

39. D: Retailers are eligible for coverage under the standard business owners' policy. However, restaurants, gas stations, and amusement parks are all ineligible for this coverage. Moreover, auto repair stations, bars, contractors, financial institutions, and wholesalers may not receive coverage from the standard business owners' policy. Mercantile service or processing occupancies may not receive coverage if they occupy more than 25,000 ft. Moreover, mercantile service and processing occupancies may not have gross sales of more than $3 million at any one insured location and remain eligible for coverage by the standard business owners' policy.

40. C: Producers who are older than sixty-five or have at least fifteen years of experience are not required to meet the continuing education requirements in order to maintain their licensure. Otherwise, producers with only a property and casualty license must take twenty-four hours of courses. Producers with property and casualty and life and health licenses must complete twenty hours of continuing education to retain the property and casualty license, but those who merely want to retain their life and health license only have to take sixteen hours. Finally, licensed insurance producers with both life and health and property and casualty insurance are required to complete twelve hours of continuing education courses annually. Half of the continuing education requirements must be completed in a classroom, and licensees may carry over up to ten extra hours from one year to the next.

41. B: Advertising injuries related to a breach of contract would not be covered by Coverage I of the standard farm liability policy. The only exception to this exclusion is when the insured party had an implied contract to use the advertising idea of another party in his or her promotional materials. Coverage I of the standard farm liability policy relates to personal and advertising injury liability. Advertising injury derives from one or more of the following offenses: oral or written publication of slander or libel; oral or written publication of private information; unauthorized use of another party's advertising idea in an advertisement; or infringement upon copyright or slogan in an advertisement. Coverage I of the standard farm liability policy will only apply to the obligations that occur as a result of personal activities or operations typical of farming.

42. D: It is not true that workplace inspections by an insurance company take the place of inspections by the employer. The employer is still responsible for creating a safe and healthy work environment. Moreover, inspections do not guarantee that a workplace is safe or healthful, or that it conforms to codes, laws, regulations, or standards. It is typical for the insurance company to issue a report and a set of recommendations after an inspection. The right to inspect the place of business may be exercised at any time, and the insurance company grants identical powers of inspection to insurance rate service organizations.

43. B: In the standard equipment breakdown policy, a newly built property is considered to have been acquired by the policyholder when the finished project has been accepted by the new owner or lessor. Any coverage that applies to newly acquired locations will terminate at the same time as coverage for previously insured locations. If the policy has a limit or deductible that varies by location, newly acquired locations will be assigned the highest limits and deductibles. Insured parties may be charged an additional premium for newly acquired property.

44. A: An insurance producer whose license is suspended for misconduct must wait one year before reapplying. After a second offense, the license holder will have to wait five years. An insurance producer may have his or her license suspended or revoked, or denied renewal, for intentional misrepresentations, fraud, and a failure to provide appropriate information to policyholders.

45. D: In order to obtain a resident's insurance producer license, an applicant must complete a pre-licensing education program, pass an examination, and complete a battery of forms, and must either reside in the state or have his or her principal place of business there. A producer's license indicates that the holder is allowed to transact business and enter into contracts on behalf of an insurer in that state.

46. B: A supply bond guarantees that a contractor will provide any necessary equipment for a project. This is one of the specialized types of surety bond. A surety bond asserts that either a certain action will be performed or a third party will make payment to the party injured by the failure to perform that action. A labor and material payment bond guarantees that the contractor will pay labor and material costs as they are incurred. A bid bond guarantees that the contractor will obtain any necessary performance bond and do the work required if he or she is awarded a contract. A fiduciary bond guarantees that the estate or property of another party will be managed in good faith.

47. C: A piece of property would not be considered complete just because the relevant part of the work at the job site has been put to its intended use by a contractor. For the purposes of the standard business auto policy, work is only considered to be complete when the relevant piece has been put to its intended use by someone besides a contractor or subcontractor. Work is also considered complete when all of the tasks indicated in the contract have been finished, or when all of the work at a particular job site has been finished. A piece of work may be considered complete even when it requires continuing service, correction, maintenance, repair, or replacement.

48. C: The maximum payment for losses related to credit cards under the standard homeowner's policy is $500. Similarly, the standard homeowner's policy offers $500 worth of coverage for losses related to funds transfer cards, forgery, and counterfeit money. However, this additional coverage does not include situations in which the insured has failed to comply with all the terms and conditions of the card issuer, or the card was used by a resident of the insured's household or another person who was entrusted with the card.

49. A: Property damage that is caused by the insured party but occurs away from premises owned by the insured conforms to the definition of a product-completed operations hazard under the standard commercial general liability policy. The other three answer choices are exceptions to the general treatment of products-completed operations hazard. Products that are still in the physical possession of the insured party, or that have not yet been finished, or that have been abandoned, will not be part of a products-completed operations hazard.

50. A: Whole life insurance does not include the option to vary or suspend premiums. However, in both universal and variable life insurance policies, the policyholder retains the right to adjust or suspend premiums. Of course, diminishing or suspending premiums will result in a smaller benefit

How to Overcome Test Anxiety

Just the thought of taking a test is enough to make most people a little nervous. A test is an important event that can have a long-term impact on your future, so it's important to take it seriously and it's natural to feel anxious about performing well. But just because anxiety is normal, that doesn't mean that it's helpful in test taking, or that you should simply accept it as part of your life. Anxiety can have a variety of effects. These effects can be mild, like making you feel slightly nervous, or severe, like blocking your ability to focus or remember even a simple detail.

If you experience test anxiety—whether severe or mild—it's important to know how to beat it. To discover this, first you need to understand what causes test anxiety.

Causes of Test Anxiety

While we often think of anxiety as an uncontrollable emotional state, it can actually be caused by simple, practical things. One of the most common causes of test anxiety is that a person does not feel adequately prepared for their test. This feeling can be the result of many different issues such as poor study habits or lack of organization, but the most common culprit is time management. Starting to study too late, failing to organize your study time to cover all of the material, or being distracted while you study will mean that you're not well prepared for the test. This may lead to cramming the night before, which will cause you to be physically and mentally exhausted for the test. Poor time management also contributes to feelings of stress, fear, and hopelessness as you realize you are not well prepared but don't know what to do about it.

Other times, test anxiety is not related to your preparation for the test but comes from unresolved fear. This may be a past failure on a test, or poor performance on tests in general. It may come from comparing yourself to others who seem to be performing better or from the stress of living up to expectations. Anxiety may be driven by fears of the future—how failure on this test would affect your educational and career goals. These fears are often completely irrational, but they can still negatively impact your test performance.

Review Video: <u>3 Reasons You Have Test Anxiety</u>
Visit mometrix.com/academy and enter code: 428468

135

Elements of Test Anxiety

As mentioned earlier, test anxiety is considered to be an emotional state, but it has physical and mental components as well. Sometimes you may not even realize that you are suffering from test anxiety until you notice the physical symptoms. These can include trembling hands, rapid heartbeat, sweating, nausea, and tense muscles. Extreme anxiety may lead to fainting or vomiting. Obviously, any of these symptoms can have a negative impact on testing. It is important to recognize them as soon as they begin to occur so that you can address the problem before it damages your performance.

Review Video: 3 Ways to Tell You Have Test Anxiety
Visit mometrix.com/academy and enter code: 927847

The mental components of test anxiety include trouble focusing and inability to remember learned information. During a test, your mind is on high alert, which can help you recall information and stay focused for an extended period of time. However, anxiety interferes with your mind's natural processes, causing you to blank out, even on the questions you know well. The strain of testing during anxiety makes it difficult to stay focused, especially on a test that may take several hours. Extreme anxiety can take a huge mental toll, making it difficult not only to recall test information but even to understand the test questions or pull your thoughts together.

Review Video: How Test Anxiety Affects Memory
Visit mometrix.com/academy and enter code: 609003

Effects of Test Anxiety

Test anxiety is like a disease—if left untreated, it will get progressively worse. Anxiety leads to poor performance, and this reinforces the feelings of fear and failure, which in turn lead to poor performances on subsequent tests. It can grow from a mild nervousness to a crippling condition. If allowed to progress, test anxiety can have a big impact on your schooling, and consequently on your future.

Test anxiety can spread to other parts of your life. Anxiety on tests can become anxiety in any stressful situation, and blanking on a test can turn into panicking in a job situation. But fortunately, you don't have to let anxiety rule your testing and determine your grades. There are a number of relatively simple steps you can take to move past anxiety and function normally on a test and in the rest of life.

Review Video: How Test Anxiety Impacts Your Grades
Visit mometrix.com/academy and enter code: 939819

Physical Steps for Beating Test Anxiety

While test anxiety is a serious problem, the good news is that it can be overcome. It doesn't have to control your ability to think and remember information. While it may take time, you can begin taking steps today to beat anxiety.

Just as your first hint that you may be struggling with anxiety comes from the physical symptoms, the first step to treating it is also physical. Rest is crucial for having a clear, strong mind. If you are tired, it is much easier to give in to anxiety. But if you establish good sleep habits, your body and mind will be ready to perform optimally, without the strain of exhaustion. Additionally, sleeping well helps you to retain information better, so you're more likely to recall the answers when you see the test questions.

Getting good sleep means more than going to bed on time. It's important to allow your brain time to relax. Take study breaks from time to time so it doesn't get overworked, and don't study right before bed. Take time to rest your mind before trying to rest your body, or you may find it difficult to fall asleep.

Review Video: The Importance of Sleep for Your Brain
Visit mometrix.com/academy and enter code: 319338

Along with sleep, other aspects of physical health are important in preparing for a test. Good nutrition is vital for good brain function. Sugary foods and drinks may give a burst of energy but this burst is followed by a crash, both physically and emotionally. Instead, fuel your body with protein and vitamin-rich foods.

Also, drink plenty of water. Dehydration can lead to headaches and exhaustion, especially if your brain is already under stress from the rigors of the test. Particularly if your test is a long one, drink water during the breaks. And if possible, take an energy-boosting snack to eat between sections.

Review Video: How Diet Can Affect your Mood
Visit mometrix.com/academy and enter code: 624317

Along with sleep and diet, a third important part of physical health is exercise. Maintaining a steady workout schedule is helpful, but even taking 5-minute study breaks to walk can help get your blood pumping faster and clear your head. Exercise also releases endorphins, which contribute to a positive feeling and can help combat test anxiety.

When you nurture your physical health, you are also contributing to your mental health. If your body is healthy, your mind is much more likely to be healthy as well. So take time to rest, nourish your body with healthy food and water, and get moving as much as possible. Taking these physical steps will make you stronger and more able to take the mental steps necessary to overcome test anxiety.

Review Video: How to Stay Healthy and Prevent Test Anxiety
Visit mometrix.com/academy and enter code: 877894

Mental Steps for Beating Test Anxiety

Working on the mental side of test anxiety can be more challenging, but as with the physical side, there are clear steps you can take to overcome it. As mentioned earlier, test anxiety often stems from lack of preparation, so the obvious solution is to prepare for the test. Effective studying may be the most important weapon you have for beating test anxiety, but you can and should employ several other mental tools to combat fear.

First, boost your confidence by reminding yourself of past success—tests or projects that you aced. If you're putting as much effort into preparing for this test as you did for those, there's no reason you should expect to fail here. Work hard to prepare; then trust your preparation.

Second, surround yourself with encouraging people. It can be helpful to find a study group, but be sure that the people you're around will encourage a positive attitude. If you spend time with others who are anxious or cynical, this will only contribute to your own anxiety. Look for others who are motivated to study hard from a desire to succeed, not from a fear of failure.

Third, reward yourself. A test is physically and mentally tiring, even without anxiety, and it can be helpful to have something to look forward to. Plan an activity following the test, regardless of the outcome, such as going to a movie or getting ice cream.

When you are taking the test, if you find yourself beginning to feel anxious, remind yourself that you know the material. Visualize successfully completing the test. Then take a few deep, relaxing breaths and return to it. Work through the questions carefully but with confidence, knowing that you are capable of succeeding.

Developing a healthy mental approach to test taking will also aid in other areas of life. Test anxiety affects more than just the actual test—it can be damaging to your mental health and even contribute to depression. It's important to beat test anxiety before it becomes a problem for more than testing.

Review Video: <u>Test Anxiety and Depression</u>
Visit mometrix.com/academy and enter code: 904704

Study Strategy

Being prepared for the test is necessary to combat anxiety, but what does being prepared look like? You may study for hours on end and still not feel prepared. What you need is a strategy for test prep. The next few pages outline our recommended steps to help you plan out and conquer the challenge of preparation.

STEP 1: SCOPE OUT THE TEST

Learn everything you can about the format (multiple choice, essay, etc.) and what will be on the test. Gather any study materials, course outlines, or sample exams that may be available. Not only will this help you to prepare, but knowing what to expect can help to alleviate test anxiety.

STEP 2: MAP OUT THE MATERIAL

Look through the textbook or study guide and make note of how many chapters or sections it has. Then divide these over the time you have. For example, if a book has 15 chapters and you have five days to study, you need to cover three chapters each day. Even better, if you have the time, leave an extra day at the end for overall review after you have gone through the material in depth.

If time is limited, you may need to prioritize the material. Look through it and make note of which sections you think you already have a good grasp on, and which need review. While you are studying, skim quickly through the familiar sections and take more time on the challenging parts. Write out your plan so you don't get lost as you go. Having a written plan also helps you feel more in control of the study, so anxiety is less likely to arise from feeling overwhelmed at the amount to cover.

STEP 3: GATHER YOUR TOOLS

Decide what study method works best for you. Do you prefer to highlight in the book as you study and then go back over the highlighted portions? Or do you type out notes of the important information? Or is it helpful to make flashcards that you can carry with you? Assemble the pens, index cards, highlighters, post-it notes, and any other materials you may need so you won't be distracted by getting up to find things while you study.

If you're having a hard time retaining the information or organizing your notes, experiment with different methods. For example, try color-coding by subject with colored pens, highlighters, or post-it notes. If you learn better by hearing, try recording yourself reading your notes so you can listen while in the car, working out, or simply sitting at your desk. Ask a friend to quiz you from your flashcards, or try teaching someone the material to solidify it in your mind.

STEP 4: CREATE YOUR ENVIRONMENT

It's important to avoid distractions while you study. This includes both the obvious distractions like visitors and the subtle distractions like an uncomfortable chair (or a too-comfortable couch that makes you want to fall asleep). Set up the best study environment possible: good lighting and a comfortable work area. If background music helps you focus, you may want to turn it on, but otherwise keep the room quiet. If you are using a computer to take notes, be sure you don't have any other windows open, especially applications like social media, games, or anything else that could distract you. Silence your phone and turn off notifications. Be sure to keep water close by so you stay hydrated while you study (but avoid unhealthy drinks and snacks).

Also, take into account the best time of day to study. Are you freshest first thing in the morning? Try to set aside some time then to work through the material. Is your mind clearer in the afternoon or evening? Schedule your study session then. Another method is to study at the same time of day that you will take the test, so that your brain gets used to working on the material at that time and will be ready to focus at test time.

STEP 5: STUDY!

Once you have done all the study preparation, it's time to settle into the actual studying. Sit down, take a few moments to settle your mind so you can focus, and begin to follow your study plan. Don't give in to distractions or let yourself procrastinate. This is your time to prepare so you'll be ready to fearlessly approach the test. Make the most of the time and stay focused.

Of course, you don't want to burn out. If you study too long you may find that you're not retaining the information very well. Take regular study breaks. For example, taking five minutes out of every hour to walk briskly, breathing deeply and swinging your arms, can help your mind stay fresh.

As you get to the end of each chapter or section, it's a good idea to do a quick review. Remind yourself of what you learned and work on any difficult parts. When you feel that you've mastered the material, move on to the next part. At the end of your study session, briefly skim through your notes again.

But while review is helpful, cramming last minute is NOT. If at all possible, work ahead so that you won't need to fit all your study into the last day. Cramming overloads your brain with more information than it can process and retain, and your tired mind may struggle to recall even previously learned information when it is overwhelmed with last-minute study. Also, the urgent nature of cramming and the stress placed on your brain contribute to anxiety. You'll be more likely to go to the test feeling unprepared and having trouble thinking clearly.

So don't cram, and don't stay up late before the test, even just to review your notes at a leisurely pace. Your brain needs rest more than it needs to go over the information again. In fact, plan to finish your studies by noon or early afternoon the day before the test. Give your brain the rest of the day to relax or focus on other things, and get a good night's sleep. Then you will be fresh for the test and better able to recall what you've studied.

STEP 6: TAKE A PRACTICE TEST

Many courses offer sample tests, either online or in the study materials. This is an excellent resource to check whether you have mastered the material, as well as to prepare for the test format and environment.

Check the test format ahead of time: the number of questions, the type (multiple choice, free response, etc.), and the time limit. Then create a plan for working through them. For example, if you have 30 minutes to take a 60-question test, your limit is 30 seconds per question. Spend less time on the questions you know well so that you can take more time on the difficult ones.

If you have time to take several practice tests, take the first one open book, with no time limit. Work through the questions at your own pace and make sure you fully understand them. Gradually work up to taking a test under test conditions: sit at a desk with all study materials put away and set a timer. Pace yourself to make sure you finish the test with time to spare and go back to check your answers if you have time.

After each test, check your answers. On the questions you missed, be sure you understand why you missed them. Did you misread the question (tests can use tricky wording)? Did you forget the information? Or was it something you hadn't learned? Go back and study any shaky areas that the practice tests reveal.

Taking these tests not only helps with your grade, but also aids in combating test anxiety. If you're already used to the test conditions, you're less likely to worry about it, and working through tests until you're scoring well gives you a confidence boost. Go through the practice tests until you feel comfortable, and then you can go into the test knowing that you're ready for it.

Test Tips

On test day, you should be confident, knowing that you've prepared well and are ready to answer the questions. But aside from preparation, there are several test day strategies you can employ to maximize your performance.

First, as stated before, get a good night's sleep the night before the test (and for several nights before that, if possible). Go into the test with a fresh, alert mind rather than staying up late to study.

Try not to change too much about your normal routine on the day of the test. It's important to eat a nutritious breakfast, but if you normally don't eat breakfast at all, consider eating just a protein bar. If you're a coffee drinker, go ahead and have your normal coffee. Just make sure you time it so that the caffeine doesn't wear off right in the middle of your test. Avoid sugary beverages, and drink enough water to stay hydrated but not so much that you need a restroom break 10 minutes into the test. If your test isn't first thing in the morning, consider going for a walk or doing a light workout before the test to get your blood flowing.

Allow yourself enough time to get ready, and leave for the test with plenty of time to spare so you won't have the anxiety of scrambling to arrive in time. Another reason to be early is to select a good seat. It's helpful to sit away from doors and windows, which can be distracting. Find a good seat, get out your supplies, and settle your mind before the test begins.

When the test begins, start by going over the instructions carefully, even if you already know what to expect. Make sure you avoid any careless mistakes by following the directions.

Then begin working through the questions, pacing yourself as you've practiced. If you're not sure on an answer, don't spend too much time on it, and don't let it shake your confidence. Either skip it and come back later, or eliminate as many wrong answers as possible and guess among the remaining ones. Don't dwell on these questions as you continue—put them out of your mind and focus on what lies ahead.

Be sure to read all of the answer choices, even if you're sure the first one is the right answer. Sometimes you'll find a better one if you keep reading. But don't second-guess yourself if you do immediately know the answer. Your gut instinct is usually right. Don't let test anxiety rob you of the information you know.

If you have time at the end of the test (and if the test format allows), go back and review your answers. Be cautious about changing any, since your first instinct tends to be correct, but make sure you didn't misread any of the questions or accidentally mark the wrong answer choice. Look over any you skipped and make an educated guess.

At the end, leave the test feeling confident. You've done your best, so don't waste time worrying about your performance or wishing you could change anything. Instead, celebrate the successful

completion of this test. And finally, use this test to learn how to deal with anxiety even better next time.

Review Video: 5 Tips to Beat Test Anxiety
Visit mometrix.com/academy and enter code: 570656

Important Qualification

Not all anxiety is created equal. If your test anxiety is causing major issues in your life beyond the classroom or testing center, or if you are experiencing troubling physical symptoms related to your anxiety, it may be a sign of a serious physiological or psychological condition. If this sounds like your situation, we strongly encourage you to seek professional help.

Thank You

We at Mometrix would like to extend our heartfelt thanks to you, our friend and patron, for allowing us to play a part in your journey. It is a privilege to serve people from all walks of life who are unified in their commitment to building the best future they can for themselves.

The preparation you devote to these important testing milestones may be the most valuable educational opportunity you have for making a real difference in your life. We encourage you to put your heart into it—that feeling of succeeding, overcoming, and yes, conquering will be well worth the hours you've invested.

We want to hear your story, your struggles and your successes, and if you see any opportunities for us to improve our materials so we can help others even more effectively in the future, please share that with us as well. **The team at Mometrix would be absolutely thrilled to hear from you!** So please, send us an email (support@mometrix.com) and let's stay in touch.

> **If you'd like some additional help, check out these other resources we offer for your exam:**
>
> **http://MometrixFlashcards.com/ClaimsAdjuster**

Additional Bonus Material

Due to our efforts to try to keep this book to a manageable length, we've created a link that will give you access to all of your additional bonus material.

Please visit
https://www.mometrix.com/bonus948/claimsadjuster to
access the information.

144